A History of the
Vandals

A History of the
Vandals

Torsten Cumberland Jacobsen

WESTHOLME
Yardley

Frontispiece: A 21 nummi coin of the Vandal king Gelimer, with a reverse showing a horse's head which refers both to the Vandals as well as the Punic past of North Africa. (*Author*)

Westholme Publishing, LLC
904 Edgewood Road
Yardley, Pennsylvania 19067
Visit our Web site at www.westholmepublishing.com

First Printing June 2012
10 9 8 7 6 5 4 3 2 1

ISBN: 978-1-59416-159-9

Also available as an eBook.

Printed in the United States of America.

For Jana and Vaclav

Contents

List of Maps

Preface

The fifth century AD was a period of great political changes in the Mediterranean world. At the start of the century, the Roman Empire ruled from the lowlands of Scotland to the Upper Nile, and from Portugal to the Caucasus. It was almost at its widest extent, and though presided over by two rulers—one in the West and one in the East—it was still a single empire. One hundred years later, the whole of Western Europe and Western North Africa had been lost, and there was no longer an emperor of the West. Instead, a number of Germanic kingdoms had been established in these regions. Hundreds of thousands of Germanic and other barbarians had settled permanently inside the former borders of the empire. Though North Africa, Italy, and parts of Spain were temporarily retaken in the sixth century, the lost parts of the Western Empire were already slowly moving culturally away from the remaining Eastern part.

The migration period of late antiquity, or the Dark Ages, as some have termed it in the past, is a period of great importance to European and world history. The migrations took place over great space and time, and spanned the period of late antiquity to the Early Middle Ages. For the Romans, it was the fall of Eternal Rome, but for the Germanic tribes, who settled in Western and Central Europe, and the Slavonic tribes who came after them, it was the birth of Medieval Europe. As has often been pointed out, there had always been migrations, but in this period all of Europe saw particularly great movements and upheavals. The migrating tribes numbered but a fraction of the Roman population, which remained settled in its ancestral regions, but the migrations nevertheless caused great changes in Roman culture and society. Throughout history, it has been speculated how a number of small Germanic tribes, who had little technology and were considered primitive, were able to end the greatest empire Europe has ever seen. The Western Empire did not fall because of the migrations alone, but from a number of deciding factors, though the migrations must be said to have been one of the major factors in the revolution of existing society.

The great migrations came in three waves, from the end of the fourth century to the end of the sixth century. The first and most important of these was caused by the migration of the Huns from the East, and affected the whole of Europe and even beyond to North Africa, and pushed several Germanic tribes before them from one end of Europe to the other. In the case of the Iranian Alans, they moved from the region around the Caspian Sea to the region of modern-day France, Spain, and North Africa. The following two waves were weaker and happened over a smaller geographical extent. Later ones, like the migration of the Bavarians, were quite localized affairs. The Germanic kingdoms of the first wave did not last beyond the fall of the Visigothic kingdom in 711, but part of the second wave created the modern state of France, which owes its origins more or less directly to the migration of the Franks.

One of the most fascinating tribes of the migration period is the Vandals, who traveled from the woodland regions of the Baltic Sea across Europe and ended in the deserts of North Africa. In the middle of the fifth century, they created the first permanent Germanic successor state in the West and were one of the deciding factors in the downfall of the Western Roman Empire. Their sack of Rome in 455 and their vehement persecutions of the Catholics in their kingdom gave birth to the term "vandalism," which is used in many countries around the world.

A hundred years later, they were the first target of Emperor Justinian's (527–565) reconquest of the Roman lands. In less than four months, what had been considered one of the strongest Germanic kingdoms was defeated by an army of fifteen thousand soldiers, of which only five thousand saw action. Despite later rebellions, this was the end of the long-haired, blond Germanic peoples of North Africa, and in many ways the end of the Arian heresy of Christianity, as the Vandals were its most aggressive proponents. For the Romans, it was the incredibly successful start of the retaking of the lost lands of the Western Empire.

Despite the significance of the Vandal tribes to history, only one monograph has been published in English that examines parts of the history of the Vandals, and that only in 2010. The aim of this book is therefore to provide a general overview of the Vandal history, from their first appearance to the end of the tribe. The text is meant to be easily approachable for the general reader as well as students of the subject, and to be readable while still being thoroughly researched. The bibliography and appendix on the sources provide possibilities for further and more-detailed studies. I do not pretend to reveal any startling new interpretations of the history of the Vandals—although I hope that I present a number of new views—but rather focus on giving an overview of Vandal history in English, which is in itself new. I must disappoint any specialists who might read this book: they will not find any detailed textual evaluations of the sources and their statements, which would create an unwieldy narrative for the benefit of few. I have decided to use a traditional chronological perspective, combined with a focus on various central subjects such as religion, the administration, the economy, and the military.

Since my early years at Copenhagen University, I have studied the migration period and the fascinating history of the various tribes. In my book *The Gothic War* (2009), I had to examine the Vandal kingdom of North Africa in detail because of its impact on the war. Who were the Vandals, how

did a Germanic tribe come to rule North Africa, how was the
kingdom organized—these were some of the questions that
came up while I was writing *The Gothic War*. I was greatly surprised by the lack of even a simple overview in English on
their history. Available were only—if "only" is the right word,
as they are studies of great quality—the works of Christian
Courtois (1955) in French, and Ludwig Schmidt (first published in 1901 and republished in 1942) and Hans-Joachim
Diesner (1968) in German, with Diesner basing his work
strongly on Courtois. These works are all of a highly academ-
ic nature, and are not for the general reader. Neither do they
take into account the great archaeological work made since
the printing of Diesner in 1968. In recent years, the Vandals
have begun to receive much greater attention and interest,
mainly in the German literature, but monographs and articles
on various Vandal-related subjects have also begun to appear
in English. As a sign of this growing interest in the Vandals,
the German scholar Helmut Castritius published a monograph in German in 2007, and in 2010, Andy Merrills and
Richard Miles published a history of the Vandal kingdom of
Africa in English.

After my book on the Gothic War was published, and as I
had recently moved to Danish North Jutland—the traditional "original" homeland of the Vandals—it felt natural to
explore this subject more and bring the fascinating Vandals
before a general audience, and hopefully to spark further
interest in the subject.

ONE

Early Vandal History

"Their [the Germanic tribes'] ancient hymns . . . celebrate a god Tuist . . . and his son Mannus [Man], as the original founders of their race. To Mannus they assign three sons, after who are named three tribes. . . . Some authorities . . . pronounce for more sons to the god and a larger number of tribes, i.e. the Marsi, Gambrivii, Sueves and Vandilii."
—Roman historian Tacitus in his work Germania on the Germanic tribes, finished in AD 98

To attempt to trace the origin of the Vandals, we must combine archaeological and historical sources, which are shaky and contradictory at best. The difficult and scanty sources mean that each statement about the early history of the Vandals should be preceded with, "We believe that possibly . . .," and end with, ". . . but we have little or no real evidence of it." What follows is, therefore, still debated among historians and archaeologists.

THE HOMELAND OF THE VANDALS

The Vandal tribes are believed to have originated in southern Scandinavia, based on archaeological evidence, particularly pottery, and a similarity of names. In their later history, two Vandal tribal groups are found—the Hasdings and the Silings. "Hasding" is a Germanic word, probably meaning "long-haired." It is believed that the tribe of Hasding Vandals is connected to the ancient Norwegian noble family of Hadding, which lived in the Hallingdal area of southern Norway and were called Heardingas in Anglo-Saxon. The name of the Vandals also appears in central Sweden in the parish of Vendel, in old Swedish Vaendil, and in northern Denmark, which is named Vendill or Vandill in old Nordic and is still today named Vendsyssel (a *syssel* being a medieval administrative unit similar to the English shire). The Skagen Peninsula in the Danish region of North Jutland was in Old Norse named Vandilsskagi, so it had this name before the term Vandals was used more often in medieval times.

The Siling Vandals are believed to have been settled in the island of Zealand in Denmark, mainly based on the similarity of names (Danish: Sjælland).

First migration of the Vandals

The first migration of the two Vandal tribes took place sometime in the second century BC. Archaeology has proven that the region of Danish North Jutland was thickly settled at that time, with a great number of burial grounds and villages, which were situated in what is now barren heather land or forests. Most of these settlements were abandoned in the second century BC. The first archaeological evidence of the Vandals as part of the so-called Przeworsk culture emerges in the more-or-less empty region between the Elbe, Oder, and Vistula rivers also during this century. Accordingly, the disappearance of a great people and the appearance of one in another place have been connected. We may assume that the Vandals initially settled for a while in the region close to the shores of the Baltic Sea, where they had landed.

According to the Gothic historian Jordanes and the Langobard historian Paul the Deacon, who wrote in the sixth and seventh centuries, respectively, after the arrival of the Langobards, who migrated after the Vandals from Scandinavia, battles soon followed between the Vandals, Goths, and Langobards, as well as with other tribes in the area. After several defeats, the Vandals were forced into the historical regions of Galicia and Silesia in modern-day Poland and western Ukraine. Particularly for the Langobards—or Winnili, as they were termed then—the victorious battle against the Vandals under their two chieftains, Ambri and Assi, was important in establishing their identity as a tribe. They even believed that their tribal name—the Langobards ("Longbeards")—was given to them by the gods because of a stratagem by which they won the battle.

In Silesia and Galicia, the Vandals occupied the former lands of the Sciri and Bastarnae tribes, who had left these regions, and so the occupation went almost without skirmishes, apart from minor ones with a Celtic tribe, the Boii, who had been settled in parts of the regions since the fourth century BC. While large parts of the tribe had left for other lands, there was still a remnant left. The skirmishes ended in the defeat of the Boii and their removal from the area of the Vandals. As with other migrations, the Vandal migrations most likely did not mean a total replacement of the existing populations but the absorption of these, who adopted the name of their conquerors. In this way, the Vandals took over elements of the Celtic culture in the making of weapons and jewelry. It is also believed that some of the Vandals began to bury the bodies of their dead, as the Celts had done, instead of burning the bodies and burying the ashes in urns, as had been the Vandals' custom. Furthermore, they partly took over the Celtic concept of towns.

THE PRZEWORSK CULTURE

When the Vandals got to the region of Poland and eastern Germany in the second century BC, they became part of the Przeworsk culture. The culture is named from the village near the town Przeworsk in southeast Poland where the first artifacts were found, and describes an Iron Age archaeological complex that dates from the late third century BC to the fifth century AD. It initially covered central and southern modern Poland but later spread to parts of eastern Slovakia and

Carpathian Ruthenia, ranging between the Oder and the middle and upper Vistula rivers into the headwaters of the Dniester and Tisza rivers.

The Przeworsk culture had elements of continuity with the preceding Pomeranian culture, albeit modified by significant influences from the La Tene and Jastorf cultures. In the early and mid-twentieth century, these cultures were believed to be connected with individual tribes or peoples, but modern scholars now understand them more as systems incorporating many separate population groups and political units. So the borders of the cultures were not political borders, but more the geographical limits within which population groups interacted with sufficient intensity to make some or all of the remains of their physical culture—such as burial customs and goods, pottery, metalwork, and so on—look very similar.

The great area covered by the Przeworsk culture included Germanic, Celtic, and proto-Slavonic tribes, but it appears to have been dominated by Germanic tribes, particularly the Vandals. The tribes had different cultures, but also many similarities, which made up the common features of the Przeworsk culture. The main feature was their burials, which were mostly cremations and occasional inhumations. A number of warrior burials have been excavated, and they often contain burial gifts in the form of horse gear and spurs. Some of these burials are very rich, surpassing graves of Germanic tribes farther west in wealth, particularly after the fourth century AD.

The Wielbark and Chernyakhov cultures
The other dominating material cultural system in the region was the Wielbark culture, which appeared during the first half of the first century AD around modern-day eastern Pomerania and the lower Vistula River. It is believed that the main tribes of the culture were the Goths. In the first half of the third century, the Wielbark tribes left their settlements by the Baltic Sea and expanded into the regions east of the

Vistula and all the way to Ukraine, probably forming the powerful Chernyakhov culture. It is much debated, however, whether the Wielbark culture actually created the Chernyakhov culture, or formed a part of it, or whether they were entirely separate cultures. One hundred years later, the Chernyakhov culture had spread through what is now Wallachia, Moldavia, and southern Ukraine, and from the Carpathians to the river Don.

The Wielbark and Chernyakhov cultures were dominated by the Goths but included other Germanic tribes in the northern Black Sea region, as well as indigenous Dacians of the Carpathian region and Iranian-speaking Sarmatians. The geographical area of the culture included a number of smaller kingdoms. Many aspects of the Przeworsk, Wielbark, and Chernyakhov cultures are similar, such as their glass vessels, but their main difference is that the Wielbark and Chernyakhov groups rarely buried weapons and tools with their dead, while the Przeworsk did so regularly.

As an interesting point, archaeology shows that since the beginning of Roman imperial times, the area of the Przeworsk culture was surrounded by a belt of about thirty to sixty miles of no-man's-land where no tribes were settled. This supports the belief that the Przeworsk culture was so distinct as to be connected to a certain common population group.

Vandals and Lugi

Whereas the name "Vandals" in later historical times was limited to two tribal confederations, the Hasding and the Siling Vandals, in prehistory it covered a greater number of tribes under the name "Vandili." The first time the Vandals appear in the historical sources are in the geographical part of the Roman statesman Pliny the Elder's *Natural History*, which was finished in the year 77 AD, making them one of the longest known Germanic tribes. Pliny names in his list of the five greatest Germanic tribes the Vandili, which consisted of the Burgundiones (Burgundians), Varines, Charines, and

Gutones (Goths). There can be little doubt that the Vandili
are the same people as the historic Vandals, who are called
Bandili or Bandeli by Greek historians.

The Roman historian Tacitus, who wrote his *Germania* at
the end of the first century, explains the Germanic foundation
myth:

> Their ancient hymns—the only style of record or his-
> tory which they [the Germanic tribes] possess—cele-
> brate a god Tuist, an earth-born deity, and his son
> Mannus [Man], as the original founders of their race.
> To Mannus they assign three sons, after who are
> named three tribes, the Ingaevones, who live nearest
> to the ocean, the Herminones in the middle of the
> country, and the Istaevones, who occupy the remain-
> der. Some authorities, using the licence, which per-
> tains to antiquity, pronounce for more sons to the god
> and a larger number of tribes, i.e. the Marsi,
> Gambrivii, Sueves and Vandilii. These, they say, are
> the real and ancient names, that of the Germani is a
> modern one, first given in fear by the vanquished
> Gauls to the warriors who crossed the Rhine to
> invade them and afterwards proudly assumed by the
> conquerors.

So the term "Vandilii" was used for a group of East
Germanic tribes, and later in his work, Tacitus also uses the
name Lugi for the same tribes.

And here complications arise. It is difficult now to fully
understand the ethnic groups that were settled in the regions
around the Oder and Vistula rivers because some tribal
names were used as umbrella terms for larger groups comprising several other tribes with independent names. As mentioned, Pliny the Elder counts among the Vandili most of the
important tribes of eastern Germania. While Tacitus refers to
the "genuine and ancient name" of the Vandilii, it doesn't
appear in his list of tribes at all. Instead he calls the Lugi the
main ethnic group in the region, with the Harii and the

Naharnavali as part of the tribal confederation. The Gutones are classed as an independent group, together with the Rugi and Lemovii, while the Burgundiones mentioned by Pliny the Elder are missing completely.

Many scholars accept that "Vandals" and "Lugi" are more or less synonymous. Whether this means that Lugi was another name for the Vandals or that the Vandals were the dominant tribe in the Lugi tribal confederation cannot be made clear, and we have no clear evidence for either suggestion.

The Lugi have been known longer than the Vandals. The "great people" of the Lugi are mentioned by the Greek historian and geographer Strabo at the end of the first century BC as in alliance with the Marcomannic tribes of Maroboduus, which were settled in the region of modern Bohemia.

The Greek geographer Ptolemy, who wrote in the first half of the second century, mentions different names for the tribes of the Lugi confederation, possibly because of errors introduced during the copying of his text over the centuries. He does not mention the Vandals at all, but includes the Burgundiones. Ptolemy also speaks of the Silings who were settled west of the middle Oder River in the region of Silesia, and who were later in the migration period considered one of the two main tribes in the Vandal confederation. Since most of these groups were to be found in southern and western regions of modern-day Poland and parts of the Czech Republic, it has been assumed that the name "Lugi," which only disappeared in the third century AD, might be a pre-Germanic foreign term used for those peoples who termed themselves Vandilii. However, to Ptolemy, the Silings were not counted among the Lugi at all. The result is that instead of the fixed classifications observed in the older literature, we must take the description of the larger tribal confederations with considerable elasticity. This does not limit itself to the Vandals only, but also to the other tribal confederations, such as the Sueves, which changed character dramatically in the period between Julius Caesar (100–44 BC) and Tacitus.

The Lugi as a religious confederation?

Tacitus mentions in his *Germania* a subgroup of the Lugi, the Naharnavali, who were administering the cult of the twin gods, the Alci (the so-called Elk brothers), which appears to have been important to the Lugi. The Naharnavali are believed to have lived in Lower Silesia, and in their territory was the holy place of the Lugi on Mount Ślęża (Ger.: Zobten), south of Wrocław. Here there was an ancient cult site that archaeology shows already existed during the time of the Celtic Boii. But the attempt to localize the Naharnavali in Silesia is based on the purely hypothetical localization of the cult site of the twin gods on the mountain due to a similarity of names from the Middle Ages, and no other evidence proves the connection. The Lugi have therefore often been regarded as a cultic or religious confederation, connected by the common worship of the Alci. But again, this builds upon meager evidence. In fact, we do not know for certain if this cult was important to the Lugi, or even if the Lugi was a religious confederation.

To sum up, it is believed that when the historical sources first speak of the Vandals, they were located in the central and eastern part of modern-day Poland. As with all other tribal confederations, the borders of their territory are difficult to define precisely, but they appear to have been the dominant element of the Przeworsk culture. Furthermore, there appears to be a close connection between the Vandals and the Lugi, and the terms might even be interchangeable.

The tribes

Unfortunately, the Vandals had no "national" historians writing their tribal history, in the manner of Jordanes and Cassiodorus of the Ostrogoths, Gregory of Tours of the Franks, or Paul the Deacon of the Langobards. So we are forced to use the Roman and Greek sources, which had great difficulty distinguishing between individual tribes, in which barbarian (as the Germanic and other foreigners were called) groupings probably changed rapidly.

We now use the term "ethnicity" to describe group cohesion based on belief in shared ancestry and shared past with consequent common cultural traits and political goals. However, ethnicity in a tribe was fluent. To be a Vandal or to be part of the Vandal confederation was more a question of attitude than a question of race and ethnicity. In this way, the Vandal confederation consisted of changing tribes that either left the alliance or slowly lost their ethnic identity, such as the Alans, who later joined the Vandals. Accordingly, a Goth or a Sarmatian could call himself a

The so-called Osterby Man with a Suevian knot hairstyle. Found in 1948 in the Köhlmoor near Osterby in Schleswig, Germany. It is now on display at the Archäologisches Landesmuseum in Gottorp Castle in Schleswig. (*Author*)

Vandal even if he would be considered otherwise with modern eyes. Sometimes, appearance defined the affiliation to a tribal group, such as the painting of the body with woad by the Picts, or the use of the Suevian knot hairstyle, or even status, such as the long hair of the Frankish Merovingian kings. We also have the testimony of the fourth century Roman historian Ammianus Marcellinus, who speaks of the Alan tribes: "the tribes are called Alans because of the similarity in their customs, their savage way of life and their weapons. . . . Almost all of the Alans are tall and good looking, and their hair is generally blond." It was the existence of one or more special customs or appearance that created an identity for the Alans and their observers.

When speaking of Germanic tribes, we must also be aware that the term "Germanic" refers to a language family and not a specific culture, ethnic group, or race. The Vandals, for example, are counted among the eastern Germanic tribes because of their language, which was similar to Gothic. However, we have no contemporary evidence that indicates that speakers of different Germanic languages or dialects were aware that their language gave them anything else in common. Neither do we see distinct proof of a pan-Germanic identity.

THE VANDALS IN THE FIRST AND SECOND CENTURIES

In the first century, we begin to hear more of the Lugi. In AD 50, Lugi tribes supported the Germanic Marcomanni by taking part in an assault on the tribal confederation of Vannius, which was settled in the region of modern-day Slovakia and Moravia. Most likely they were fighting over control of the Amber Trail—a great trade route running from the shores of the Baltic, through the area of the Przeworsk culture, ending around the city of Carnuntum in the Roman Empire (Petronell in modern-day Austria). We also learn that around the year 92, during the reign of Emperor Domitian (81–96), there was a conflict between the Lugi and the Suebi or Marcomanni in which the Romans sided with the Lugi and sent troops to help them.

Part of the Vandals migrated slowly south just before the Marcomannic War (166–180) into the area of northern Bohemia and Moravia, where they gave their name—the Vandal Mountains, as they were known to the Romans—to the Riesengebirge (Krkonoše Mountains in modern-day Czech Republic). Other tribes followed, and this pressure of the east Germanic tribes brought on the Marcomannic War, in which the tribes on the middle Danube sought to enter the Roman Empire between the provinces of Pannonia and Dacia. Emperor Marcus Aurelius (161–180) succeeded only with difficulty in defeating the Marcomanni tribes. This migration also brought the Vandal tribes closer to the Roman sphere.

The *History* of Peter the Patrician states that the Astiggoi—believed to be the Hasding Vandals—and the Lacringi were among Marcus Aurelius's allies in this period, but the late fourth-century historian Eutropius names the Vandals among those peoples Marcus Aurelius defeated in his Germanic wars.

We also learn from the historian Cassius Dio that in 171, a barbarian group called the Astingi—generally identified with the Hasding Vandals—came to the northern borders of the province of Dacia. They were led by two kings, Raus and Raptus, whose aim was not to raid the empire but to settle in Dacia and receive money and land as Roman federates.

From the account of Cassius Dio, it appears that the Roman governor Sextus Cornelius Clemens faced the problem of controlling several barbarian peoples: the Lacringi, the Costoboci, and now the Astingi. Clemens encouraged the Astingi to attack the Costoboci, whom they soon defeated, but did not interfere when the Astingi were in turn attacked by the Lacringi. Defeated, the Astingi submitted to Marcus Aurelius and proved themselves to be useful allies. After the war, the Hasding Vandals were settled in the region of the upper Tisza River (northeast Hungary and parts of Slovakia). This settlement, which was to last more than two hundred years, is also proved by many archaeological finds in the region.

When Emperor Commodus (180–192) made peace with the Marcomanni after his father died, the Vandals were put under Roman protection. The Marcomanni were forbidden to make war against the Iazyges, Buri, and Vandals. Furthermore, the Vandals were to keep their settlements at least forty stadies (about four and a half miles) from the border of Dacia.

The Tabula Peutingeriana, a copy of a Roman map believed originally to have been made in the time of Emperor Septimius Severus (193–211), shows just on the other side of the Danube the name of the tribe Vanduli, and just beyond them the Marcomanni, in the region of modern-day Bohemia. It must be supposed that these Vandals were Hasdings. The Siling Vandals stayed in their abodes north of the Carpathian Mountains in what later became Silesia (the regional name can be traced back to them through Slavic forms).

Cassius Dio later mentions that around 212 or 213, Emperor Caracalla (211–217) sent a letter to the Senate declaring that he had succeeded in turning the friendship between the Marcomanni and the Vandals into hostility. The Vandals mentioned here were probably the Siling Vandals, who were the northern neighbors of the Marcomanni.

At the beginning of the third century, the territory of the Przeworsk culture appears to shrink to about half its size, due to loss on the eastern side toward the Wielbark culture. Why this is, we do not know, as no sources tell us of any great wars between the Vandals and their associated tribes and the tribes to the east. However, the shrinkage does not necesarily signify political changes, as it could also be explained by a change in the use of ceramics or similar objects that identify the culture.

The Vandals are next mentioned in 248, when some Hasding groups joined the Gothic warlords Argaith and Guntheric, who raided Lower Moesia. However, the Vandals did not participate in the great Gothic invasions of the Roman Empire (ca. 249–270) and generally appear to have been quiet in this period.

War with the Romans 270–271

In autumn 270, the Sarmatians, together with two unknown Vandal kings, crossed the Danube to assault Roman Pannonia. For these events, we follow the remnants of a history composed by the Athenian dignitary Publius Herennius Dexippus. In 271, Emperor Aurelian (270–275) won a great battle over the Vandals—or Vandeloi, as Dexippus calls them in Greek. We don't know anything about the battle and the reasons for it, only of the negotiations afterward.

After their defeat, the Vandal kings and nobles asked for peace. Aurelian gathered his victorious army and asked it whether or not to accept the surrender of the Vandals. The Roman army accepted it, and the two Vandal kings and chief nobles gave their sons as hostages. The emperor gave the Vandal army enough provisions for the journey home to its Dacian lands, but a band of five hundred warriors straggled from the main army and began to pillage the province of

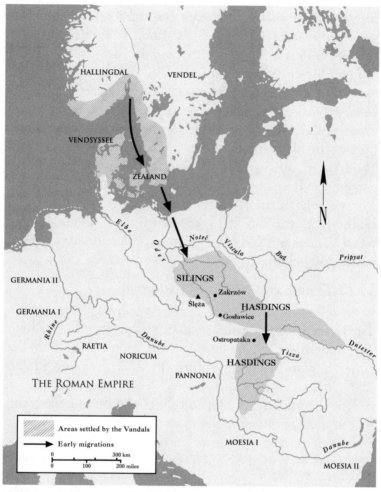

Vandal movements from Scandinavia to Central Europe.

Moesia. Here they were soon defeated by the Romans, and to honor the treaty, the Vandal kings put to death all the warriors they could find of this unruly band. Aurelian took the title Sarmaticus after the victorious battle, and so we may also surmise that the Sarmatians were the greater part of the invasion, or perhaps that the cavalry of the Vandals were seen as Sarmatians, as they looked similar. When Aurelian held the triumph for the victorious campaign in Rome in 274, Vandal prisoners were also led in the procession. As was common in peace settlements of the time, the Vandal tribes had to supply federate troops for the Roman army, in this case two thousand horsemen. Militarily, this showed that by the end of the third century, they already could muster great numbers of cavalry. This condition of the peace treaty seems to have been observed, as an army list of the Roman Empire at the beginning of the fifth century shows a military unit, the Ala VIII Vandilorum, serving in Egypt. In this fashion, some Vandals entered the Roman army and society. The father of Stilicho, who was one of the foremost Roman statesmen of the fifth century and would play a great part in later Vandal history, was a Vandal and served as a cavalry officer under Emperor Valens (364–378).

Vandals defeated by Emperor Probus

In the following years, a small part of the Siling Vandals wandered together with a Burgundian group toward the Rhine. This movement appears not to have been a migration, but rather a plundering expedition. In 277, Emperor Probus (276–282) defeated a part of these Siling Vandals. Again in 278, he defeated the combined Silings and Burgundians, this time at the Lech River in the western Bavarian Alps. The two forces were facing each other on opposite sides of the river, but by a stratagem, the emperor lured the Germanic warriors, who were more numerous than the Romans, across the river and defeated them. They were offered peace on condition that they handed over their plunder and prisoners. Probus claimed that this had not been done fully and struck at the retreating barbarians, defeating them again. Many were killed, but some were taken prisoner, including their chieftain, Igila. The prisoners were enrolled in the Roman army and sent to Britain, where they later served the emperor faithfully during some minor insurrection. It is believed that the Vandals were settled somewhere in modern Cambridgeshire, based on the statement of Gervasius of Tilbury, who notes in the thirteenth century that near Cambridge there was an ancient fortress named Wandlebiria that the Vandals had built. However, this story appears much too late to be considered reliable.

The late fifth century Roman historian Zosimus, when describing the events of 277, writes that Probus defeated a group of Logionen. This is the last mention of the name of the Lugi in known history. For the events of 278, Zosimus relates that Probus fought Burgundians and Wandils.

Wars with the Goths

Most of the wars the Vandals fought were against their neighbors. In the second half of the third century, the Hasdings had at their settlement at the upper Tisza River the following neighbors. The Sarmatian Iazyges were to the west between the Danube and the Tisza; to the northwest, in what is modern western Slovakia, at the Waag and Nitra rivers, lived the Suevian Quadi; south of the Hasdings were the Lacringi, and farther south, at the Danube, were the Sarmatian Roxolani. North of the Carpathian Mountains at the Sereth and Dniester rivers were the Gepids. The eastern regions of modern Romania were settled by the Gothic Tervingi—later known as Visigoths—who were encroaching on the Vandal lands. In the later years of the third century, the Hasdings tried to expand their lands and fought with the Sarmatians and the Tervingi. We know this from a panegyric delivered in 291 for Emperor Maximian (285–305) that speaks of the Tervingi and Taifali who fought the Gepids and Vandals. The Tervingi and the Taifali were victorious in a battle near the town of Galtis. The site of Galtis is not known, but it is believed to have been situated in the region of the upper or middle Pruth River in the border region between Romania and Moldavia, where there were probably many clashes between the tribes.

By the time of Emperor Constantine the Great (306–337), the Siling and Hasding Vandals were still settled in modern-day Moravia and the northwest of Hungary, with the Marcomanni in Bohemia as their western neighbors. On their south were the Danube and the Romans, and on their east were the Tervingi under their king, Geberich. Around 331–337, Geberich challenged the Hasding King Visimar to battle, and the two armies met at the river Marisus (modern-day Maros River in Hungary) and fought a whole day. At the end the Goths were victorious, and Visimar and a large part of his army lay dead on the field. According to Jordanes, with their military strength destroyed, the Vandals asked Constantine to permit them to enter the empire and settle as his subjects in the province of Pannonia. The request was granted, and Jordanes relates that for almost seventy years, the Vandals lived peacefully in Pannonia. However, no other sources mention a settlement of the defeated tribes on Roman soil, and Jordanes's statement is not supported by archaeology. His perspective was that of a sixth century Gothic historian with the clear aim to celebrate the ancient glories of the Goths, so the story must be seen as quite unlikely. Jordanes later mentions a Gothic king of the late fourth and early fifth century named Vandalarius, that is, Conqueror of Vandals. If we believe that Jordanes is correct, this shows that the wars between the Vandals and Goths were significant to the tribes. However, we must treat his statement with caution, as his main aim was to present the Goths as victorious over all their enemies.

According to Jordanes, the Vandals also invaded Gaul around 380 and fought Emperor Gratian (375–383), but again the statement is not supported by other sources and must be considered doubtful.

VANDAL SOCIETY

It is difficult for scholars to see the differences between the Vandals and the other tribes of eastern Germania, such as the Goths and Langobards, because we base our knowledge on the Roman sources. To Roman eyes, most of the Germanic barbarians looked much the same and had similar customs, and this lack of differentiating between the tribes is clearly seen in the sources.

The sixth century historian Procopius, who observed the last years of the Vandal kingdom, tells us that the Vandals were closely related to the Goths and the Gepids. They were tall with fair skin and light blond hair, and were considered good looking. They all had the same laws, they shared the same Gothic language—an east Germanic dialect—and when they converted to Christianity, they became Arians, like most other Germanic tribes. Procopius even believed that the Vandal, Goth, and Gepid tribes were all originally parts of the same nation, and only afterward were distinguished from each other by the names of their chieftains. The priest Salvian wrote the treatise *On the Government of God* (*De Gubernatione Dei*) between 439 and 451, criticizing the wicked ways of the Roman West and praising the morality of its barbarian adversaries. He describes the Vandals as the weakest of the barbarian tribes who had invaded Gaul in the early fifth century, but on the other hand he considered them more chaste in their lives than the other Germanic tribes, and their moral standard in Spain and North Africa was considered to be of a high caliber. The Vandals were a horse nation, and known for their strong cavalry. Already by 270, the Athenian Dexippus described the Vandals as horsemen, and many spurs have been found in excavations of Vandal graves. In this they differed greatly from the other Germanic tribes, who did not use horses extensively. No doubt they had learned these skills from their Sarmatian neighbors.

Although the Hasdings lived closer to the Danube and the Roman Empire, they do not appear to have developed their civilization further than the Silings, who were settled farther north. Most likely, the two tribal confederations had much contact during this period, including through the trade along the Amber Trail, although they considered themselves separate groups.

Farming
The Vandals were settled in farms and villages, which were often situated in river valleys. Many have been excavated, so

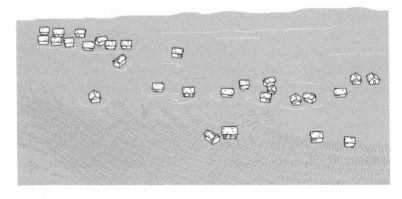

Top: Reconstruction of a Przeworsk village based on excavations in Tarnowiec, Poland. (*After T. Krajewski*) Bottom: Reconstruction of a Przeworsk house based on an excavation at Drążgów. (*After R. Czerniak*)

we have quite a clear picture of their settlements. The farms, while somewhat isolated, were held together in a group, as the large number of graves found in excavations of connected cemeteries has shown. The houses were one or two rooms, with walls of wood, or wicker covered by clay. A number of smaller buildings have been found that were used for smithing and other crafts. Baking ovens of stone and clay have also been found. Deep wells made of oak planks supplied the water.

Many farm implements have been excavated, such as plow-shares and sickles. Farming among the barbarian tribes was a subsistence economy, and most people would have to spend almost all of their time producing food to cover their need. Hunger was a constant threat to the tribes. The most common crops were cereals, pulses, and vegetables. Meat was provided by cattle and pigs, both of which could be grazed in woodland, and by sheep, which also provided wool. The farming products were supplemented by hunting and fishing. An important role was that of tending horses for warfare.

CRAFTS

The Vandals were also craftsmen. Among the crafts, weapon smithing was highly respected and was still important as late as their African kingdom of the fifth century. The Vandal smiths also produced bronze fibulas (brooches used as safety pins to fasten clothes), which were made in various styles. Much Vandal pottery has also been found; sometimes it was made with meanders and other decorations. By the fourth century, the Vandals had learned to use the pottery wheel from the Romans, and new shapes appeared. Fabrics of wool and flax were also made, some of high quality. These and other examples can be seen in the splendid quality of items found in an excavation at Zakrzów in modern-day Poland.

TRADE

Trade was economically important for the Vandals and a way to gain access to luxury items from the Roman Empire. Through their settled regions went the great trading route the Amber Trail, from Carnuntum by the Danube toward modern Wroclaw and to the lower Vistula River. Here, amber from the Baltic Sea went to the Roman markets as well as furs, honey, and human hair. The Vandals probably gained much wealth from having control of the Amber Trail, and we may assume that several of the wars fought in the region were over control of the lucrative trade route. The Roman civilization and objects reached the Vandals initially through the great Marcomannic tribal confederation, which also introduced, among other things, the Roman short sword to the Vandals.

Burial customs

Many Vandal graves have been found, and these give us an insight into their burial customs. In the first century AD, they mainly burned their dead, and the ashes were put in an urn and buried. In the fourth century, their customs changed and they began to bury the dead, apart from one group in northern Silesia, which continued the custom of urn burial. Usually the dead were buried with gifts—the men with weapons and tools, the women with jewelry, needles, spinning whorls, keys, and similar items. Imported wares are found almost only in wealthy graves, such as the two prince burials in Goslawice and Zakrzów in modern-day Poland (Goslawitz and Sacrau in the old German excavation reports). The one in Goslawice is dated to the first century and contains Roman wares, including a drinking bowl, a bronze bucket, and local Vandal products, such as drinking horns and pottery. Three graves from the fourth century found at Zakrzów contained great numbers of luxury items. The grave rooms were fully furnished with table service and luxury items for the afterlife. The graves also contained many types of glass vessels, silver table service, and many items of gold and silver, amber, carnelian, and mountain crystal. The items were highly decorated in various techniques.

Warfare

War was a characteristic part of early Vandal history, as with the other Germanic tribes, but it rarely turned into major warfare that involved all the tribes. The few sources we have on their early history make it clear that big wars were rare and short and often resolved in a single major battle. Cattle raids, plundering expeditions, and military competition between war bands were, on the other hand, commonplace.

The main weapons were lances, which could be used for stabbing and throwing, and mostly two-edged swords, mainly

Top left: Przeworsk grave from Lugi, Poland, containing a warrior and his horse. (*Drawing after G. Beuthner*) Top right: The treasure of a Vandal prince from a grave at Ostropataka (Ostrovany), Slovakia. (*Photograph from the collection of the Hungarian National Museum. Copyright the Hungarian National Museum*) Bottom: Silver vessel from the princely burial at Opole-Goslawice, Poland. (from *Die Vandalen*, 2003)

longswords, for use on horseback. War axes have also been found. Some of the weapons had artful decorations. The Vandals do not appear to have used armor, apart from shields with iron buckles. Bow and arrow were almost unknown in early Vandal history and never came into fashion for anything but hunting. Unfortunately, we know nothing of their tactics or warfare, apart from the fact that they used mainly cavalry from around the third century and possibly earlier. However, as with the other barbarian tribes, their tactics probably did not develop remarkably between the third and fifth centuries. Emperor Maurice (582–602) sums up the main deficiencies of the Germanic tribes in his handbook on military strategy and tactics: they lacked a cohesive military command and control, as well as such technological elements as efficient siege techniques, and they did not have the patience needed to use tactical reserves. Probably the Vandals, being mainly cavalry-orientated tribes, would use tactics similar to the Sarmatians, that is, outflanking maneuvers and riding their horses hard and fast to reach a battle conclusion before the horses tired out. They probably also used fast operational strikes to surprise the enemy.

KINGSHIP

The Germanic king was not an absolute ruler, but first among equals. In many cases with other tribes, such as the Tervingi, only the severe threat to the existence of the tribes in the fourth century created more than temporary kings. Otherwise, local chieftains held the power in their subtribes. When Dexippus describes the events of the Scythian War in 270, he mentions that the Vandal kings and the nobles conducted the negotiations with Emperor Aurelian. The kings could not decide for the Vandals on their own, but had to have the support of the nobles. The decisions to leave the Danube region and later Spain were also made among the king and the nobles.

During peace time, the authority of the leaders in the tribes depended entirely on their social influence and on the number of their loyal followers. The kings had an undefined form of religious prestige, but the nobles and the local assemblies of free men had the power. These assemblies were held periodically, possibly in connection with religious festivals. In war, one or more kings were elected or chosen from among the hereditary chieftains. They were then given power to coordinate the attack or defense of the tribe, and act as spokesmen for the tribe, provided that they followed a number of traditional rules, such as the common warrior's right to a fixed amount of plunder.

Tribal confederations could have many kings. At the battle of Argentoratum (Strasbourg in modern-day France) in 357, Emperor Julian (355–363) faced an Alamanni army led by no less than seven kings and ten princes, who ruled separate kingdoms. At other times an overking might be elected to coordinate the efforts of several tribes, although this was often temporary, for the duration of a campaign or a crisis, such as the Tervingian Athanaric, who was elected *iudex*—a form of overking over the Tervingi tribes—when faced by the massive invasion of Emperor Valens (364–378) in the 360s. Vandal King Godegisel, who led the Vandal tribal confederacy during the migration to Gaul, was probably a kind of overking.

THE TWIN KINGS

An interesting point about Vandal kingship is the long existence of double kings, which we first hear of from Paul the Deacon, who describes the earliest Langobard history. At the time, possibly in the second century BC, the Langobards fought the Vandals under their leaders Ambri and Assi on the shores of the Baltic Sea. This double kingship appears to have lasted centuries, possibly until Visimar in the mid-fourth century, who is the first sole king we hear of. Attempts at seeing the later Gunderic and Geiseric as double kings are not convincing. The end of the double kingship can possibly be traced to the Christianization of the Vandals, which probably ended the pagan sacral duties of the kings. Modern research connects the double kingship with the Lugian worship of the Alci, the Elk brothers. Tacitus describes the cult of the Alci as similar to that of the Roman divinities Castor and Pollux, the Dioscuri, who were worshipped as twin brothers and so have been connected to the twin kingship. However, we have no proof of this connection.

Double kingship is generally connected to the worship of a sacred pair of brothers, who are seen as the representatives of the gods on Earth. The cultic significance is strengthened by their curious names, such as the Vandal Kings Raus and Raptus, probably meaning "pole" and "beam," and so might be connected to the curious wooden idols of the Germanic tribes. But in the history of the early Vandal tribes we find no explanation of the significance of the double kingship. Another suggestion could be that they were the kings of the Hasdings and Silings since their first migrations, but this is pure speculation.

Interestingly, the concept of double kings is seen in many other Germanic tribes—for example Ebor and Agio of the Langobards, Sido and Vangio of the Quadi, Hengest and Horsa of the Anglo-Saxons, Cimberius and Nasua of the Sueves, as well as Mallorix and Verritus of the Frisians. Double kings are also found outside the Germanic world, such as Bellovesus and Segovesus of the Celts, Bleda and Attila of the Huns, and in Greek Sparta.

Religion

As mentioned earlier, the Vandals are believed to have been connected to the tribal confederation of the Lugi, who, according to Tacitus, worshipped the Elk brothers. To the worship were connected priests, who performed the rituals. It appears that before their conversion to Christianity, the Vandals also worshipped a number of traditional Germanic deities, including Nerthus and Freia, the gods of agriculture and fertility; Wodan/Wotan, the god of war and magic; Tyr/Ziu, the god of laws and assemblies; and Donar, the god of thunder. The Hasdings also worshipped Wodan as god of the wind and of the dead, and appealed to him in their battle against the Langobards. According to Tacitus, several of the Germanic tribes who worshipped Wodan entered battle during the night with blackened shields and blackened skin to frighten with their appearance as an army of the dead. Some scholars believe that this was not only a tactical consideration, but also to worship their god. The Vandals are also believed to have worshipped the spirits of their forefathers, as many other tribes did.

When Tacitus described Germanic society in the early second century, he wrote that only priests—not warlords or even kings—were allowed to punish warriors. It appears that the nobility and the kings were the keystones in the actual cult practice, but we do not know for sure if the Vandals had holy sites as such or how they worshipped their gods, unless we accept the connection to the Lugi and the worship on the holy mountain of Ślęza.

Many mystical signs have been found on objects exacavated in the early Vandal regions, such as symbols of the sun and the moon on weapons. The swastika, symbolizing the movement of the sun, has also been found on pottery and other objects. Runic inscriptions exist on such items as urns and weapons, and were possibly used as magical inscriptions. A spearhead found in Rozwadow in eastern Galicia, dated to around the third century, has an inscription that spells "Ik Eruls." Its meaning has not been determined, but it is the earliest instance of Vandal writing.

Ulfilas and the conversion of the Germanic tribes

The barbarian raids on the Roman lands in the third century brought many Christian captives to the Gothic lands north of the Danube. They continued to worship during their slavery and would also inspire Goths to change their religion. Around 311, a Goth named Ulfilas (Little Wolf) was born from a family whose ancestors had been captured in the raids of the Goths, possibly in Cappadocia in Asia Minor. While the sources on the life of Ulfilas are difficult to interpret because of their different opinions on Arianism, it can be reconstructed that the young Ulfilas made his first trip to Constantinople between 332 and 337, as a member of a delegation to the Romans. The Romans found in Ulfilas a strong Christian belief and a person who was able to bring Christianity to the tribes north of the Danube. During a later visit, in 341, Ulfilas was consecrated bishop by Eusebius of Nicomedia at the great Council of Antioch and was sent back north of the Danube. He stayed there for seven years but was driven out during a Gothic persecution of Christians and moved to the Roman province Moesia, where he settled with other Christian Goths. There he translated the Bible into the Gothic language using an alphabet he invented, using Greek, Latin, and Germanic runic script.

The Goths did not immediately take to Christianity. The first persecution of Christians in the Gothic lands took place in 348, possibly after a war against the Romans, and a second one started in 369, lasting four years. It might be that in the Christians, the Goths saw Romans and adherents of the Roman way of life. Several martyrs were made because they resisted worshipping the pagan gods, but otherwise the persecutions do not seem to have been severe.

The missionary work by Ulfilas and his followers had great impact on the Vandals and the other Germanic tribes, who were living close to the Goths. The Vandal conversion to Christianity probably happened around the second half of the fourth century, and most likely the followers of Ulfilas helped this conversion. Ulfilas died in Constantinople in 383 and was carried to his grave by many people. While his impact on the conversion of the Goths is undoubted, particularly because of his translation of the Bible, it can be speculated that it mainly focused on the nobility, who could read and write and had the leisure to speculate over religion. The conversion of the common farmers most likely took much longer and happened more gradually. Some parts of the Vandal tribal confederation, such as the Alans, resisted and might never have converted to Christianity.

The priest Orosius writes in the fifth century that the Vandals were heathens when they crossed the Rhine in 406–407. However, this is highly unlikely. We know for sure through the priest Salvian that the Vandals were Arian Christians when they came to Spain, and it is not likely that a conversion would have happened during their few years in

Gaul. Possibly Orosius confused the Vandals with some of the many other barbarian tribes that invaded Gaul at the same time.

ARIANISM

Being an Orthodox Christian in the fourth century meant walking a narrow path. There were a host of heresies, such as Donatists and Pelagians—some of them localized in extent. According to the writings of St. Augustine in the early fifth century, there were at least eighty-seven different heresies.

Arianism was the teaching of the priest Arius (250–336), who lived in Alexandria, Egypt, in the early fourth century. His main belief was that the Son, Jesus, had been created by his father, God. God was therefore unbegotten and had always existed, and so was superior to the Son. The Holy Spirit had been created by Jesus under the auspices of the Father, and so was subservient to them both. The Nicene or Orthodox belief was that God existed as three persons—the Father, the Son, and the Holy Spirit—but as one being. The teachings of Arius were first condemned as heretical in 325 at the First Council of Nicaea, but later were accepted. Only at the Second Ecumenical Council, in Constantinople in 381, was Arianism finally decreed a heresy.

Ulfilas became an adherent to the Arian creed when it was well accepted, and this was the form of Christianity he taught the Goths. His strong beliefs stayed with him until his death, before which he repeated his adherence to the creed of Arius. Arianism spread from the Goths to many other Germanic tribes, such as the Vandals, Burgundians, Heruli, and Langobards. So while Arianism had never been particularly popular within the Roman Empire, it became dominant among the Germanic tribes. The Franks were the only major tribe who were Catholic Christians. The Vandals kept to Arianism until the destruction of their kingdom.

So why did the Vandals and the other Germanic tribes stay Arian throughout their later history inside the Roman Empire? It is doubtful that they really understood or appreciated the subtle religious differences between Arianism and the Orthodox creed. Some modern historians believe it was a means of differentiating themselves from the other peoples in the empire and from the Romans. Being Arian was simply being Germanic. However, it cannot be said that the tribes were uninterested in Christianity. After all, it must have been somewhat important to them, as there was never any discussion of returning to paganism. On the other hand, the farther away from the royal court they were, the more the Germanic tribes became Christian in name rather than in deed. When Radagaisus the Goth invaded Italy in 405–406, he made human sacrifices. The Catholic Franks did the same later in the first half of the sixth century, but they were still regarded as Christians. During the time of the Vandal kingdom of Africa, the Vandals held strongly to their form of Christianity and fervently tried to convert the local Catholics.

THE CHANGES IN THE GERMANIC WORLD

But the Vandals would not stay much longer in their homes north of the Danube. The Germanic world was changing around them, and outside forces would soon threaten their settlements. The third and fourth centuries changed Germania radically. The tribal confederations that Pliny and Tacitus mention, which were based more on community of worship than on political convenience, split up, and new confederations of a more military nature appeared from the end of the second century on.

In the first half of the third century, the tribes in the regions of modern-day central Germany combined into the powerful Alamannic confederation, and the tribes close to the Roman border on the lower Rhine changed into the confederation known as the Franks. The Chauci of the North Sea coastal region changed into the Saxons. The Hermunduri were gone by the fourth century, and the Thuringians emerged. Later in the fifth century, the Bavarians formed as the last of the greater tribal groupings.

In the same period, southern Scandinavia changed: the former tribes of Jutland—the Cimbri, Teutones, and

Charudes—disappeared, the Heruli of the Danish islands emigrated south, and in their place the Jutes and the Danes appeared. Furthermore, from around 285, the north Germanic tribes along the coast began to move to the seas and raid the coasts of Gaul, Britain, and even northern Spain. Overall, the changes appear to have been a consolidation of the numerous smaller tribes into greater and more powerful confederations in response to internal developments as well as the Roman threat, and later the threat of the great migrating tribes of the East.

The Tervingi and Greuthungi—later known as Visigoths and Ostrogoths—and other powerful Germanic tribes began to dominate the territory north of the Danube and all the way to the Don River, as seen archaeologically in the Chernyakhov civilization. They even began to challenge the power of the Roman Empire in the second half of the third century. These eastern confederations were created by a migration of Germanic tribes mainly from the regions of what is now central and northern Poland. These migrations were not on a grand scale, but more a steady series of small migrations of families and lesser tribes from 180 to 320. Great as they appear, for the Germanic world these convulsions were only the beginning of the changes that the great migrations of the fourth, fifth, and sixth centuries would bring.

TWO

The Sack of Gaul and the Road to Spain

"The Huns threw themselves upon the Alans, the Alans upon the Goths, and the Goths upon the Taifali and Sarmatians; the Goths, exiled from their own country, made us exiles in Illyricum, and the end is not yet."
—*Bishop Ambrose of Milan, written c. 378*

In the later part of the fourth century, the Vandals increasingly became embroiled in the great migrations caused by the coming of the Huns from the plains of what is now Ukraine. The movement of the Huns caused a domino effect, pushing one tribe to pressure another, which in turn pushed a third, and so on. To the east of the Vandal territories, great wars had blossomed between the two Gothic groups—the Tervingi and the Greuthungi—and the Romans. In the 360s, Emperor Valens made war on the Goths, who were soundly defeated. The severe Roman threat to the existence of the Goths caused strong leaders to emerge in both tribal confederations, which were experiencing a new unity.

When the Huns began their attacks on the Greuthungi around 375, the Goths once again faced extinction. Their king, Ermanaric, committed suicide rather than submit to the Huns. A new king, Vithimir, was elected, but fell in battle shortly after. Vithimir's son, Videric, a minor, then became king under the guidance of two nobles, Alatheus and Saphrax, and was left with a people in chaos and under attack. With a choice between the Romans and the Huns, the Greuthungi were caught between the hammer and the anvil, and had to choose whom to submit to. Most of them surrendered to the Huns; the rest, under Videric, fled to the borders of the Roman Empire. But the remnants of the Greuthungi confederation reached the Danube too late: the Tervingi were already crossing into the Roman Empire, also fleeing the Huns.

In summer 376, the Tervingian king, Athanaric, had led a strong army all the way to the west bank of the River Dniester to confirm the rumors of the coming of the Huns. The Tervingi were surprised by the Huns in a night attack and retreated. Shortly after, they were again defeated in the region of modern-day Moldavia. At the same time, other Hun war bands ravaged the regions of modern-day Moldavia and Bessarabia, destroying the food supply for the Tervingi confederation, which was still suffering from the destruction of its villages and crops during the war with Emperor Valens. With its army defeated repeatedly and facing starvation, the Tervingi confederation began to dissolve. A large Tervingi group under the nobles Alavivus and Fritigern broke off from the confederation and sought refuge in the Roman Empire. It was this group that was crossing the Danube when the Greuthungi appeared.

The Roman Empire was used to smaller migrations, but the migration of entire tribes was unusual. When the Roman administration understood the dimensions of the migration, the Danube fleet was sent to block the river. No one was allowed to cross, and those who tried were turned back with force. The local Roman administration sent urgent messages explaining the situation to Emperor Valens, who was at Antioch in the East. The situation was much debated at the imperial court, but it was decided that the advantages outweighed the disadvantages and that the Tervingi should be allowed into the empire. In autumn 376, the local Roman officials received permission to accept the Tervingi, disarm them, and settle them in the devastated Thracian provinces. Alavivus, Fritigern, and their Tervingi were allowed to cross over. There were several advantages for the Romans in allowing the tribes to enter the empire: they gained cheap manpower for the army and settled the empty Thracian provinces, and it provided an important buffer at the frontier against future barbarian invasions.

The Tervingi leader, Athanaric, knew of the Roman reluctance to let such large tribes enter the empire and so did not believe that the Romans would accept the remaining Tervingi. Instead he led the starved remains into a region known as Caucalanda in the Carpathians to get out of the way of the Huns. There they drove out the local Sarmatian tribes from their villages to get enough food to survive the winter. In so doing, the domino effect caused by the Hun migration was furthered in the region, as the Sarmatians were forced to find food farther west.

The late-arriving Greuthungi envoys also asked the Roman emperor to allow their people to be received into the empire, but without success. The Roman commanders in Thrace tried to stem the growing migration and control it as much as possible. It was no longer barbarian war bands of a few hundred or a thousand, but entire tribal confederations asking to be received into the empire. The immigrants who had already crossed the river were checked for weapons and dispersed to several camps in the area. The pressure on the local food supplies was growing daily. While waiting for the emperor's decision, Gothic groups had for several months plundered the areas north of the Danube. Famine among the Tervingi who had already crossed was so great that some parents even sold their children to the Roman slave traders rather than see them starve to death. Dishonest Roman officials increased the tensions, and the Romans were forced to take away troops from the navy patrolling the Danube to use as escort for the Tervingi. When the navy stopped patrolling, three tribes, including the Greuthungi under Alatheus and Saphrax, crossed the Danube along with their allied Alans, who were also fleeing from the Huns.

VISIGOTHS AND OSTROGOTHS

Around this time, the sources begin to distinguish between the two Gothic tribes with the name Visigoths for the Tervingi and Ostrogoths for the Greuthungi. It is not clear why this change of names happens, but the use of the names Tervingi and Greuthungi soon disappears from the sources.

The massive buildup of desperate Goths was creating a situation that was getting out of hand. A group of Visigoth warriors marched to the local Roman commander's headquarters at the city of Marcianopolis (Devnya in modern-day Bulgaria) and demanded food for their starving families. The Roman commander sought to defuse the situation by murdering the Gothic leaders and thereby deprive the barbarians of organized leadership, but the result was quite the opposite. Many Gothic leaders, including the head of the Visigoth confederation, Alavivus, were killed, but a number of others, such as Fritigern, escaped and rallied the Gothic warriors. The Visigoths struck back at the Roman soldiers, and fights erupted in several places. The Goths then started to plunder the province in search of food.

In early 377, Roman General Lupicinus gathered a large number of troops to stop the revolt, but he suffered a terrible defeat some nine miles outside of Marcianopolis. The battle destroyed almost the entire Roman army in Thrace, which caused other Gothic war bands to rise up, supported by Thracian miners, the overtaxed Roman rural population, and the lower classes in the cities, who all saw a chance for gain. A Roman military unit stationed near Adrianopolis composed of Visigoths even switched sides and revolted. The desperate Visigoths also attacked the other groups of Goths to get food. Several Roman weapons factories were captured, and the

Goths were now able to rearm themselves to some extent using Roman equipment and weapons. The situation was growing more critical each day.

BATTLE OF AD SALICES

Emperor Valens was not fully aware of the seriousness of the escalating situation and reacted slowly. He had been preparing a war against Persia and did not see the uprising of some unarmed and starving barbarian tribes as a great problem. Some Armenian elite troops were dispatched, and Valens asked his nephew and co-emperor in the West, Gratian, for support to quell the uprising. Gratian sent the experienced General Frigeridus with some troops, but he was himself troubled by the Alamanni tribes, who had heard of the chaos in the Danube region and, like some of the other tribes on the border, were mustering to take advantage of it.

However, initially Valens seemed to have judged the situation correctly. The Armenian units succeeded in pushing the Goths into the mountain region of the Dodrudja, where the lack of food was expected to cause them to soon surrender from starvation. Gratian sent more troops from Gaul under General Richomeres, but the Romans were still outnumbered, and the commanders could not agree on how to fight the Goths.

Late in summer 377, the Goths were encamped at a place called Ad Salices (At the Willows). The Romans planned to wait for the Goths to starve and so be forced to move on. They would then attack them while they were marching and vulnerable with women and children. However, Fritigern did not appear to move, and the impatient Romans decided to attack anyway.

The Roman army opened the battle, and both sides suffered heavy casualties, but there was no real victor. The Goths retreated to their camp, and the Romans retreated to Marcianopolis. The Romans then blocked the Balkan passes and concentrated the food reserves in the cities, which were impregnable to the Goths, who knew little of siegecraft. The situation now seemed to be in hand, so Frigeridus went to Illyricum to await new orders, and Richomeres went to Gaul for reinforcements. Valens saw no point in going in person to the region and instead sent Saturninus, a general of cavalry, to support Generals Traianus and Profuturus, who were already there.

It appeared that the Romans had succeeded in their starvation tactics, but Fritigern was not so easy to defeat and entered into negotiations with the Ostrogoths and their Alan allies. The result of the negotiations was that Alatheus and Saphrax promised to help Fritigern, and so they attacked the Roman forces blocking the passes of the Balkan Mountains and forced Saturninus to withdraw. All of Thrace was now open to the tribes, who plundered everything in sight and even attempted unsuccessfully to take several cities. A Roman elite unit was even surprised and defeated at Dibaltum (Burgas in modern-day Bulgaria).

In response, Frigeridus was ordered to move to Beroea to establish a new defensive line, thus continuing the sound Roman strategy of starving the Goths. If the Goths were to survive the winter of 377–378, they had to drive Frigeridus from the region of central Thrace. Accordingly, they moved toward Beroea from several sides and forced Frigeridus to retreat to the west. On his way across the mountains, Frigeridus encountered a large group of Ostrogoths and Taifali, who also had crossed the Danube when the Roman fleet withdrew its patrols, and defeated it. Frigeridus then fortified the Succi pass between Serdica (Sofia) and Philippopolis (Plovdiv) to stop the Goths from moving west.

Meanwhile, Gratian was gathering his armies to help his uncle, Valens. But the Alamanni had invaded the province of Raetia, so Gratian had to stop and eventually counterattack the troublesome tribes. Valens had moved to Constantinople in May 378 with his main army—some thirty thousand to forty thousand troops—and appointed Sebastianus commander of the infantry in Thrace instead of Traianus, who had proven himself incompetent.

In early June 378, while Valens was troubled with a religious revolt in Constantinople, Sebastianus moved against the scattered Gothic war bands. It was a general weakness of all barbarian tribes of the period that they could stay concentrated for only a short time, and they soon had to disperse to get supplies, particularly as the regions were already plundered and whatever food there was had been collected in the impregnable cities. Thus Sebastianus was able to attack a Gothic war band that was returning from a plundering expedition and destroy it with only two thousand men. With news of the approaching Roman armies, Fritigern was desperately trying to reconcentrate his troops at the city of Cabyle (Yambol in modern-day Bulgaria). In mid-July, Valens reached Adrianopolis and was informed of the victory of Sebastianus. He also learned that Gratian had won a great victory over the Alamanni; Gratian was now marching to his aid, and had already reached Castra Martis (Kula) in northwestern Bulgaria. Furthermore, scouts reported that the Goths under Fritigern were marching toward the nearby village of Nike, some fourteen miles north of Adrianopolis, with only ten thousand warriors.

Suddenly it was a question of haste to destroy the annoying Goths before Gratian would arrive and share the victory. With his junior colleague coming straight from his great victory over the Alamanni, Valens needed a victory to boost his prestige. Around August 7, 378, General Richomeres arrived at Valens's headquarters with news from Gratian. Ostrogoth and Alan cavalry had attacked Gratian's troops at Castra Martis and caused some casualties. These elements were still at large and might join Fritigern before the battle. Gratian therefore urged caution and to wait for the Western army and fight the Goths with united forces. Valens was undecided and called a war council to decide what course of action to pursue. Sebastianus pointed to his recent victory and urged separate action while Fritigern was weak. As this was probably consistent with Valens's own views, he decided upon battle.

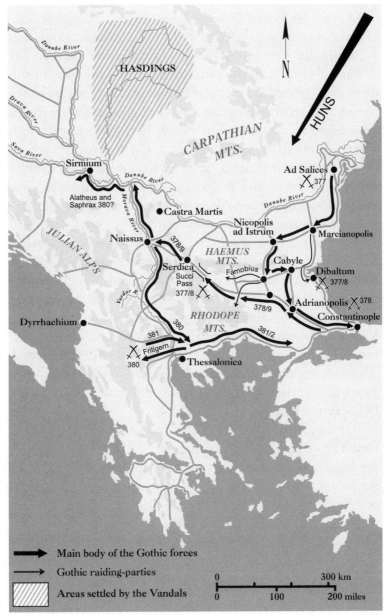

Battles in Southeastern Europe, 376–382.

Battle of Adrianopolis

On the morning of August 9, 378, Valens's army left Adrianopolis. The Goths were waiting in their camp. The eleven-mile march in the summer heat tired the Roman soldiers, who started to suffer from hunger and lack of water. Scouts then returned to report that Fritigern had more troops than expected. Fritigern sent envoys to negotiate peace with Valens—probably just to gain time for more troops to arrive—and some time was spent in the details of arranging a negotiation with the emperor. Two Roman units then attacked without orders, dragging the rest of the army, more or less disorganized, into the battle.

The battle had just started when the Ostrogothic cavalry returned from foraging. Its charge broke the back of the Roman army, and the Roman cavalry fled along with the infantry reserves, leaving the main body with the emperor surrounded. The Roman army was cut down along with Valens and most of his generals and other high-ranking officers. Two-thirds of the imperial army had been destroyed. The contemporary historian Ammianus Marcellinus compared the disaster with the Roman defeat at Cannae in 216 BC against Hannibal.

But the Goths were not able to follow up on the great victory. They tried to take Adrianopolis with the imperial treasure but failed. In the storm on the city August 10–12, they suffered heavy casualties, just as they had in their first attack on Adrianopolis in 377, when Fritigern is said to have reminded his troops that he "kept peace with stone walls." The Goths then tried to take Philippopolis and Perinthus (Eregli in modern-day Turkey) to relieve their serious food problems, but again they were repulsed by the local garrisons. Only at Nikopolis (Stari Nikub in modern-day Bulgaria) did they win a victory, when the local garrison did not fight.

To force the Roman authorities to give them food, they finally marched on Constantinople, which was almost devoid of troops. The city's fortifications were daunting, however, and the Goths were soon routed by Saracen cavalry stationed in the city. Although they had won a great victory at Adrianopolis, the Goths of Fritigern were still starving and fragmented into war bands in their desperate search for food. Despite the military disaster, the Roman authorities reacted to the Gothic threat calmly and in an organized manner. Their main aim was again to starve the Goths to prevent the revolt from spreading further.

THEODOSIUS

On January 19, 379, Gratian made one of his experienced generals, Theodosius, co-emperor and emperor of the East in Sirmium (Sremska Mitrovica in modern-day Serbia). Theodosius had a daunting task in front of him: to re-establish the court army. He did this by enlisting just about anybody, even large numbers of Goths. With the dispersal of the army of Fritigern, it was reasonably easy to once again close up the Goths between the Danube and the Balkan Mountains, where they would slowly be starved into submission. The numerous Gothic war bands were either defeated or shut up north of the Balkan Mountains, and on November 17, 379, victories over the Goths, Alans, and Huns were proclaimed in Constantinople.

The Ostrogoths were now ready for peace, and Gratian settled them in the province of Pannonia Secunda. Their Alan allies were settled in the province of Valeria.

In 380, Fritigern and his Visigoths were plundering Macedonia, and after this they went south and plundered all the way to Thessaly. To contain Fritigern, Gratian sent an army, which united with the troops of Theodosius and drove Fritigern north into the province of Moesia, where he was once again shut up and starving. Finally, on October 3, 382, the Visigoths of Fritigern also surrendered, and a treaty was made.

While the peace with the Ostrogoths was important, it was completely overshadowed by the peace with the much more numerous Visigoths and their capable leader, Fritigern. The Visigoths received much better terms than originally planned in 376, when they might have been eliminated as a nation or tribe by being distributed all over the empire. Now they would be settled together and under their own leaders.

But this was not the end. In the coming years, several Gothic groups from north of the Danube would try to escape the reoccurring Hun incursions and enter the empire, with varying success. In 386, thousands of Ostrogoths under Odotheus attempted to cross the Danube but were decisively defeated by the Danube flotilla.

In 395, Theodosius I died, leaving two sons. Arcadius received the Eastern Empire and Honorius the Western. The Roman Empire was now in practice divided administratively into halves, which were to move in different directions during the crisis of the fifth century caused by the massive barbarian migrations. The death of Theodosius in 395 can therefore be regarded as one of the major turning points in Roman history.

END OF THE PRZEWORSK AND CHERNYAKHOV CULTURES

It was this chaotic situation that the Vandals faced at the end of the fourth century. They were pressed by their neighbors, who were starving and fleeing from the Huns, and behind them, the fearsome Huns were slowly moving on. The Roman Danube border had been breached and was no longer strongly held by Roman forces. The field army of the Eastern Empire had been destroyed and was only slowly being rebuilt, and the Western army was tied up in defending against the many tribes that had entered the empire, as well as fighting various pretenders to the throne. Driven by hunger and pressure from other tribes as well as the coming of the Huns, the Vandal kings and nobles decided to seek a new future inside the Roman Empire.

We can also follow archaeologically the migrations of the Vandals and the Goths. The two dominant cultures—the Przeworsk and the Chernyakhov—disappeared in the late Roman period. The Przeworsk culture in southern Poland had disappeared by about 420, and the Chernyakhov culture was gone by about 450. Archaeological evidence—or rather the sudden lack of it—shows a massive depopulation of the area of the Przeworsk culture in the early fifth century. These remnants were swallowed up by the Huns in the first half of the fifth century and probably submitted to them. In the second half of the fifth century, only small remnants of the Przeworsk culture can be traced, mainly in central Poland and the Carpathian Mountains. After the fall of the Huns in the mid-fifth century, they were absorbed by other Germanic tribes such as the Gepids, and finally by the Slavonic invasions of the sixth century.

The period of decline for both cultures began around 375. Many archaeologists have seen their disappearance as reflecting the migration period, whose massive relocations dissolved the tribal groups. The main idea behind this reasoning is that the Vandals and Goths, traditionally the main bearers of the two cultures, began their migrations in this period, so the cultures disappeared with the tribes generating them. However, we must remember that the cultures are mainly identified on the basis of particular items, such as pottery, weapons, personal ornaments, and metalwork. So when the archaeological evidence no longer shows these items, we say that the culture has disappeared. Recently, it has been argued that many of the culture-bearing items were expensive, and so only produced for a small, elite nobility. In that case, the archaeological evidence shows that these moved on, but that does not imply that the entire population disappeared as well—or at least it is debatable. Migration therefore didn't necessarily mean the total disappearance of the existing population.

THE VANDALS LEAVE THEIR HOMELANDS

In the year 400, the Siling and Hasding Vandals, or at least a great part of the Vandal tribal confederacy, left their homelands together with the Germanic Sueves or Quadi, as some of the sources term them, which were settled in the southern part of modern-day Slovakia. Presumably the Hasdings, who were settled more easternly, started the migrations led by their king, Godegisel. They crossed the Danube, broke through the Pannonian fortified border, and marched to the west along the Danube, intending to find new settlements inside the Roman Empire, safe from the Huns and the pressure of other tribes threatened by the Huns. Food for the starving people was also a main goal—food that could be obtained in the fruitful and well-farmed Roman Empire. In the account of sixth-century historian Procopius, the migration was made because of famine among the Vandals. This seems very likely, as their regions had been devastated many times by barbarian invasions. The prospect of plunder was no doubt of only small importance compared to their other aims, even though they knew of the possibilities of gaining such in the now-less-well-defended empire. After all, this was a migration with women and children, and was not well suited for raiding and pillaging.

On their way through Pannonia, semibarbarian peasants, who had been settled there earlier by the Romans, and some Alan tribes joined them. Other tribes such as the Alans and Sueves also decided to migrate at the same time, probably sharing the motives of the Vandals. No doubt their route was the great road along the Danube by Aquincum (near Budapest in modern-day Hungary), Brigetio (Komarno in modern-day Slovakia), and Carnuntum toward the west, where food and safety were believed to exist. Their initial goal might have been the rich and fruitful lands of Italy, inspired perhaps by the Visigoths under Alaric, who had already entered Italy with his tribes. However, we must not expect that the Vandals had any carefully thought-out plan or any great geographical knowledge—other than moving to the West to gain security and food—but made up the plan as they went along.

The Vandals, Sueves, and Alans were to stay together for more than a decade. The tribes were quite different from each other and surprising allies. In 411, when they were no longer threatened by Roman armies, they split up and soon began to fight each other.

The Alans

The history of the Iranian nomadic tribe of the Alans is quite complicated. In 375, the Huns destroyed the kingdoms of the Alans in the area of the Caspian Sea. Some Alans submitted, and other tribes fled to the West. After the great defeat, they never managed to form a cohesive group of all Alans again, but instead a number of tribal splinters existed that seem to have had no common interests. By 377, the Alans were working together with the Goths south of the Danube, and their cavalry played an important role in the Battle of Adrianople in 378. After the initial defeat of the Goths, they were settled in the province of Valeria. Despite very different ethnic origins, they attached themselves to the Vandals. No doubt since their settlement in Valeria they would have found some common ground with the Hasding Vandals, for example in their shared love of horses.

The Alans were nomads and lived in wooden wagons covered with bark canopies and drawn by cattle. They were polygamous and pagan, but according to Ammianus Marcellinus, they did not practice slavery, which was quite unusual for the period. The wagons were the center of family life and used for all activities. Being nomadic, the Alans drove herds of horses and cattle as well as flocks of sheep along with them, as they traveled from place to place. Some of the nomadic tribes of the East, such as the Huns and the Alans, bound the heads of babies, which provoked a distinctive, elongated skull. These have been found at a number of sites settled by Alans that have been excavated in modern-day France.

A part of the Alans would follow the Vandals until the end of their kingdom of Africa, but already during the migrations, Alan tribes were splitting up from the main group. We see this in Italy in 401, and after the Rhine crossing of 406–407, where soon afterward one group under King Goar took service with the Romans, first in the Rhineland and then in central Gaul. Another group, under King Respendial, stayed with the Vandals and, following in their wake, settled in Spain and later again joined the Vandals. Other Alans besieged Vasatica (Bazas in modern-day France) around 414. Another separate Alan group is mentioned thirty years later as settled in the Rhône district, near Valence in modern-day France, and ruled by a King Sambida. The Alans were the only non-Germanic people of the migration period who made long-lasting settlements in Western Europe.

Artificially shaped skull found in France and associated with the 5th century Alan culture. (*Author*)

The Sueves

The third major component of the migrations from the middle Danube was the Germanic Sueves. The Sueves are well known to history. At first the term "Sueves" was used to describe a great subgroup of the Herminones, and at the same time was also used as a term for a tribal group that appeared about 72 BC, led by their chieftain Ariovistus. At that time, the Sueves lived in the region of the middle Rhine. Later they were to be found in modern-day Moravia, either bearing the same name or occasionally being called Quadi. At the end of the first century, Tacitus terms the Baltic Sea Suebicum Mare—the Suevian Sea—and mentions the Suevian Nicretes living on the Neckar River in Germany, making it appear that there were Sueves in several places in Germania. At the time of the great migrations in the late fourth and fifth centuries, the Sueves were to be found more or less everywhere—in the modern-day region of Schwaben (to which they gave their name), in Venetia, in Flanders, in Britain, and later in Spain. Quite possibly, as with the Alans, the Sueves split up into several different tribes that settled in a number of places and without any common interests.

A PEOPLE ON THE MOVE

Sometimes the sources make the mistake of describing the migrating tribes as a cohesive group moving from point A to point B. However, we now understand that the tribes did not move in an organized fashion. The great numbers of people meant that they could not stay in one place for a long time, as supplies would soon run out. Furthermore, they could not move in a closed group for very long because of the same reason. Neither were the tribes strictly organized. We must therefore imagine a core of tribes with women and children moving slowly toward their goal, which was probably determined on the way by, among other things, simply following the Roman road system. Around this core would move a swarm of foragers and perhaps advance war bands, eager to get to the plunder first, with stragglers moving behind the core, and perhaps minor tribes or war bands on occasion departing or joining the main group. The migrating tribes would therefore move over a large territory, which would also explain the many sightings of Vandals on their way to Gaul and after their invasion. If one war band was defeated, the Romans might claim victory over "the Vandals," while other parts of the tribes were already on their way somewhere else. In other cases, as with the Alans, a tribal confederation could lose cohesion and permanently create a number of splinter tribes.

THE STATE OF THE WESTERN ROMAN EMPIRE

During this period, the powerful Stilicho was the man behind the throne in the Western Empire. He had risen through the ranks of the army of Emperor Theodosius, had been promoted to the rank of *magister militum*, or master of the soldiers (the senior commanding general in a praetorian prefecture, or, if without additional titles, a general assigned the rank with duties under the emperor), and had even married the emperor's adopted niece, Serena. After the death of the Western Emperor Valentinian II in 392, he fought as one of the leaders in the army of Theodosius at the Battle of the Frigidus

River against the Western Roman usurper Eugenius. Shortly before Theodosius died in 395, he appointed Stilicho guardian of his son Honorius. Neither Honorius (Western emperor from 395–423) nor Arcadius (Eastern emperor from 395–408) proved to be strong, and Stilicho became the de facto ruler in the West.

In 397, Stilicho defeated the Visigoths, now ruled by the able King Alaric, although Alaric managed to escape the battlefield into the mountains with his remaining troops. In the same year, Stilicho also defeated the rebellion of Gildo, the Count of Africa. For his efforts, Stilicho was appointed consul in 400.

At this time, the Roman Empire was in a state of dissolution, with strong barbarian tribes entering its lands with almost no resistance. In 401, Stilicho withdrew the Roman troops along the Rhine to support the struggle against Alaric and his Visigoths, who were again threatening Italy. To protect the Rhine border, Stilicho made treaties with the neighboring Germanic tribes, among which the Franks were the strongest. In 401, Stilicho, himself of Vandal origins, managed to stop the Vandals' plundering migration through the province of Raetia and engaged them as federates to settle in the provinces of Vindelica and Noricum. The contemporary poet Claudian also mentions that Vandals were used to break up the Visigothic siege of Mediolanum (Milan in modern-day Italy) in 401. Whether these Vandals were the tribes of King Godegisel or just a small part of them is not known. However, the tribes broke the treaty almost immediately and plundered Noricum and parts of Raetia at will, as Claudian relates.

The Vandal migration was no doubt helped by the migration of Alaric's Visigoths, who were considered a much more dangerous enemy for the Roman forces in Italy. In 401, the Visigoths again invaded Italy, fighting inconclusive battles against Stilicho at Pollentia (Pollenzo in modern-day Italy) and Verona in 402, and then retreating to the Balkans. Alaric then began negotiations for an alliance with Stilicho, but these were upset by the arrival of another great Gothic force in Italy under Radagaisus in 405. These tribes came from outside the empire and crossed the Danube into Raetia to reach Italy. The movement of the Goths of Radagaisus and Alaric probably made the Vandals, Sueves, and Alans feel unsafe again, and at the same time the regions where they were settled were too poor and plundered to furnish them with supplies. Possibly the Vandals and Alans also objected to the regions in which they were settled, which were not optimal for the use of cavalry. So the tribes began to move again in late 405, using the cover of the Gothic invasions of Italy, which held Stilicho's attention.

Consular diptych of Stilicho, his wife Serena, and their son Eucherius, carved in ivory around 395. Now in the cathedral of Monza, Italy. (*Author*).

THE ROAD TO THE RHINE

In summer 406, Stilicho was busy fighting Radagaisus's invasion of Italy. He blockaded this Gothic group at Florentia (Florence in modern-day Italy), with some allied Huns and Alans, and finally defeated them in battle. Then Stilicho turned to deal with the Visigoths in northern Italy. The fighting was indecisive, but through diplomacy, Stilicho managed to make Alaric leave the peninsula and guard Illyricum for the Western Empire.

While the Romans were busy fighting for their lives, and with the border gaping open and the road to the rich provinces of Gaul luring them, the Vandals, Alans, and Sueves moved toward Gaul. Some sources say that Stilicho himself, being half Vandal, called the Vandals to Gaul to ensure so much confusion that he could put his own son on the throne. However, this story is not to be believed, as the Vandals were only a small part of the great number of tribes invading Gaul, and we see no other evidence of an alliance between Stilicho and the Vandals.

It is important to regard the movement of the Vandals and their associated tribes in the larger perspective of the chaotic migrations of the late fourth and early fifth centuries. The migration of the Vandals, Sueves, and Alans toward the Rhine in 406 went through the territories of the Alamanni and Burgundians, so they in turn also began to move in the direction of Gaul, causing the domino effect we have seen elsewhere to develop further. During the movement from Noricum to the region of the Rhine, more groups of Siling Vandals and Quadi joined the main group of tribes. Noviomagus (Speyer in modern-day Germany) and Argentoratum (Strasbourg in modern-day France) were taken by the Alamanni, and Borbetomagus (Worms in modern-day Germany) fell to the Burgundians after a long siege. The Rhine frontier, which for centuries had kept out the barbarians, was pierced in so many places that it had fallen apart, and Gaul was wide open to the Germanic tribes. Behind these were the formidable Huns, still pushing west.

BATTLE WITH THE FRANKS

On their way to Gaul, the Vandals entered the lands of the Franks, who had been paid by Stilicho to bar the passage into Gaul. According to fifth century historian Renatus Frigeridus, in a passage preserved in the history of the Frankish churchman Gregory of Tours, a great battle took place in which twenty thousand Vandals were slain, including King Godegisel. Only the timely arrival of their Alan allies saved them from complete destruction. But we must treat the words in Gregory of Tours somewhat delicately, because of his bias for the Franks. Orosius's history, written around 417, does not support these events, but instead describes a major Frankish defeat in the Rhineland that left the frontier regions open to the barbarians. However, it is clear that Godegisel somehow died in this period, and his son, Gunderic, was proclaimed king. If the Vandals lost such a great battle, this might

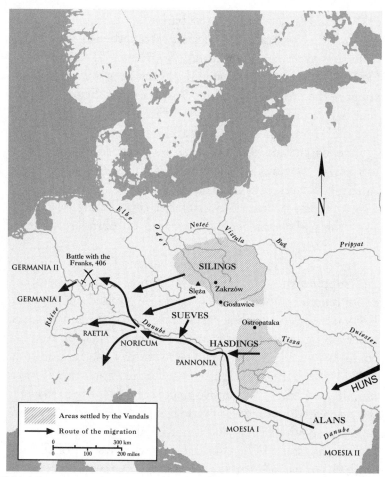

Vandal movements to Gaul.

have lost them their supremacy over the Alans and Sueves, as we see later in Spain, where the Alans appear to have been considered the strongest of the tribes.

THE ROMAN DEFENSES OF GAUL

Facing the new invaders was the Roman system of garrisoned border defenses, backed by the mobile field army. The whole concept of central reserves combined with a linear defense of the borders was aimed at protecting against everything from robbers and raiders to a massive barbarian invasion. The great number of fortresses and depots, strengthened by, among others, Emperors Valentinian I (364–375) and Valens (364–378), meant there would always be some that could support the mobile field army. Furthermore, they could prevent barbarian war bands and individuals from filtering back into their homelands with loot and slaves.

The barbarians could choose between trying to take a fortress, or moving into the empire with a more or less intact system of fortresses at their backs. To the Romans, the loss of a fortress was of little concern, as it could easily be rebuilt, since the barbarians generally focused on plundering rather than acquiring territory.

By besieging fortresses, the barbarians would waste time and supplies brought by the war bands, and new supplies could only be gained by what could be gleaned off the land. Roman troops could then easily attack the dispersed foragers, while barbarians returning to their homelands for supplies could be attacked by local garrison troops. In addition, should the barbarians engage a fortification, the Roman mobile field army could move against them. If the barbarians were defeated in a regular battle inside the empire, they were even worse off, as they would not be able to retreat past the border garrisons. When functioning, this system of defense worked against all but the greatest barbarian invasions. In fact, the situation was somewhat less than ideal. Some fortifications or garrisons were not kept at full strength because of the financial pressure on the state, and occasionally the field armies would be removed for use in civil wars, leaving the borders wide open.

The field army

The core of the new army was the mobile field armies, or *comitatenses*, which were raised by recruiting new units and pulling away parts of the border troops. Later, some elite units were termed *palatini*, and they formed the core of the central army of the emperor, later called the praesental army. *Palatini* and *comitatenses* were soon mixed in the field armies, but the *palatini* continued to have a higher status than the *comitatenses*. Some of these regular units survived even to the sixth century.

The new units created for the field armies were much smaller than the old legions, which consisted of around five thousand or six thousand men. The new units seem to have been about one thousand to one thousand two hundred strong. Most of the foot soldiers were grouped in units of about five hundred men called *auxilia*, like the allied troops of the early imperial armies.

THE BORDER GARRISONS

The remains of the old Roman legions and federate troops were combined and became static garrison troops, protecting the borders. They were called *limitanei*, because they defended the fortified border (*limes*), or *ripenses*, because they defended the great rivers (*ripa*), such as the Rhine and Danube, which made up the border. Their task was to keep small barbarian war bands out of the empire, to garrison fortresses and supply points, and to take part in collecting toll and the general surveillance of the border. As time passed, these troops turned into a form of part-time militia that was only rarely on campaign. There is a later story of a Christian soldier in Egypt who wove baskets and prayed all day, then late in the afternoon put on his uniform and went to drill with his fellow soldiers. When the *limitanei* were used on campaign, such as after the disastrous losses at the Battle of Adrianopolis in 378, they were renamed *pseudocomitatenses*.

THE SOURCES

There are a number of existing historical sources relating to the invasion of Gaul in the period from 406–411, including a variety of narratives, letters, hagiography, chronicles, and poetry. However, most of the sources speak little of the Vandals and the tribes accompanying them. One of our main sources for the invasion of Gaul is the churchman Jerome. In a letter written shortly after the invasion, he gives a long list of peoples who descended upon Gaul in 406–407: Quadi, Vandals, Sarmatians, Alans, Gepids, Heruli, Saxons, Burgundians, and Alamanni, as well as semibarbarian provincials from Pannonia, who had joined the Vandals. Jerome lived in faraway Bethlehem, but despite his distance from the events, it is believed that he was well informed through his correspondence with people all over the empire.

CROSSING THE RHINE

Because the churchman Jerome mentions Mogontiacum (Mainz in modern-day Germany) first in his list of sacked cities, we believe that the Vandals crossed the Rhine close to there in the last few days of the year 406. Again, we are frustrated by the lack of sources as well as their quality. It seems it would have been very difficult to cross the Rhine during winter, but some scholars believe that the river might have been frozen, although contemporary sources do not confirm this. Although Moguntiacum suffered, the words of Jerome that it was destroyed and thousands killed are probably overdone. Part of the Alans under their chieftain Goar appears later to have taken service under the Romans, and in 411 was still to be found among the garrison of Moguntiacum.

The combined forces of the three tribal confederations that crossed the Rhine (or four, if we count the Hasding and Siling Vandals as the separate tribes they were at this time) consisted of perhaps thirty thousand to forty thousand warriors and seventy thousand to one hundred thousand women, children, and the elderly. It would not have been difficult for such a great army to cross the Roman border.

As noted earlier, the Roman defenses were based on a large number of garrison troops' occupying watchtowers and forts along the border. But their duties were to stop small war bands from raiding. Even a few thousand barbarians would be left to the comitatensian troops, which were stationed behind the frontier. While the mobile armies took care of the intrusion, the border troops would close the frontier behind the barbarians and prevent them from filtering back after a defeat or when laden with plunder.

But the frontier defenses were not well adapted to the mass migrations that smashed through the defenses and moved on inside the empire instead of trying to return. With the comitatensian troops now engaged with the Visigoths in Italy, the Roman border forces had no chance of stopping the invasion. Two edicts, dated April 17 and April 19, 406, called on the inhabitants of Gaul to arm themselves for the peace of their country. They made it clear that the locals would have to deal with the barbarians from across the Rhine until the war against Radagaisus and the Visigoths of Alaric was over.

THE SACK OF GAUL

The migrating tribes probably split up into several groups soon after crossing the Rhine to better provide food supplies, as few places in Gaul could support such a number of people for any length of time. From the muddled description in the sources, it appears that they followed the excellent network of Roman roads through the provinces of Germania I, Belgica I and II, and plundered their way over Augusta Treverorum (Trier in modern-day Germany) to Noviomagus, Argentoratum, Remorum (Rheims in modern-day France), Samarobriva (Amiens), Turnacensium (Tournai in modern-day Belgium), Morinum (Thérouanne) and Atrebatum (Arras). From there they moved through the province of Lugdunensis Senonia to Aquitania II and Novempopulana, most likely following the roads leading from Samarobriva through Lutetia Parisiorum (Paris), Aurelianum (Orleans), Civitas Turonorum (Tours), Burdigala (Bordeaux), and toward Pompaelo (Pamplona) in Spain. They were probably stopped at the guarded passes across the Pyrenees and instead turned toward the rich lands of Gallia Narbonensis, as Roman armies were pressing them from the north. Most of the cities they came to were stormed, as only a few soldiers were left to defend the walls and some cities, like Atrebatum and Noviomagus, were unwalled. The great city of Tolosa (Toulouse) was successfully defended but suffered afterward from much famine, which was only relieved by its bishop,

Exuperius, who was somehow able to provide food for the starving. The great number of places that the sources describe as pillaged by the Vandals, Alans, and Sueves appears to be impossible to have been managed during their two-year invasion of Gaul, but most likely the sources describe the devastations caused by many independently moving subtribes.

Scholars have often asked why the great cities of Gaul fell so quickly to the barbarian invaders. No doubt the lack of soldiers to man the walls—if there were any soldiers at all—played a large part, but there was also great indifference to the invasions among the upper classes, who could move to other lands, as well as support for the invaders by the lower classes, who were oppressed by the rich, as the priest Salvian describes in his *De Gubernatione Dei*, published soon after 439:

> Meanwhile the poor are being robbed, widows groan, orphans are trodden down, so that many, even persons of good birth, who have enjoyed a liberal education, seek refuge with the enemy to escape death under the trials of the general persecution. They seek among the barbarians the Roman mercy, since they cannot endure the barbarous mercilessness they find among the Romans.

No doubt the many slaves in the region also saw the Germanic invaders as saviors and actively supported them and bolstered their numbers greatly. Indeed, many of the slaves were themselves of Germanic origin. Furthermore, the barbarians might have moved so quickly on the network of Roman roads, particularly the cavalry war bands of the Vandals and Alans, that the cities received little warning before their arrival. The devastation was great, and Bishop Orientius of Augusta Auscionum (Auch in modern-day France) said of the invasion in 407 that "all Gaul smoked as a funeral pyre," referring to the smell of burning houses and corpses. On top of this, the chaotic political situation and the pressure on the Western Roman Empire by tribes closer to Italy gave the Romans little chance to focus on the Vandals

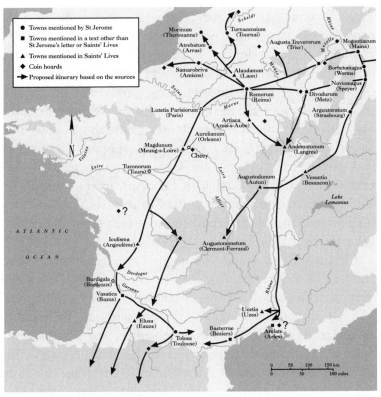

Vandal movements through Gaul.

and the other tribes rampaging through Gaul. Especially the final years of Stilicho, from 406 to August 408, when he was murdered, were troubled, as the Western government was pressing its claim to the eastern part of Illyricum. Because of this, the Eastern Empire had to fortify and defend its borders with the Western Empire just like any other border, so no help was sent from the East to the West in its time of troubles.

CONSTANTINE III

In autumn 406, while the Vandals were still marching toward Gaul, a series of revolts began in Britain. The troops stationed there mutinied and put a certain Marcus on the throne as emperor of the West. However, when he did not accept the demands of the troops, they killed him and made Gratian emperor and gave him a purple robe, a crown, and a body-guard. But Gratian did not suit them either, and after a reign of four months, he was killed. In early 407, Constantine III (407–411) was made his successor. The revolt of Britain would further increase the instability of the Western Empire, but it also aided Gaul in its defense against the Vandals and the other invading tribes. Constantine appointed Justinianus and Nebiogastes generals in Gaul and soon crossed the English Channel to Gaul with his army, leaving Britain to fend for itself. Officially, he wanted to stop the Vandals, but his real goal appears to have been to secure Gaul and Spain and thereby his throne.

He landed at Bononia (Boulogne in modern-day France) and won over the remaining Roman forces in Gaul. With his strength thus increased, he began a campaign against the Vandals, driving them before him, but without any marked successes. As the Roman troops rallied around Constantine, however, the Vandals were forced farther south, toward the Pyrenees and Aquitaine. Meanwhile, Constantine made a treaty with the Burgundians, the Alamanni, and the Franks to defend the Rhine frontier, and he accepted the existing situa-tion of their settlement there. Most likely, he preferred to spend his resources on securing his position as emperor than on throwing out the barbarians.

THE FALL OF STILICHO

The troubles of the Western Empire seemed never to end. When news reached the West in spring 408 that Eastern Emperor Arcadius had died in Constantinople on May 1, 408, and was succeeded by his seven-year-old son, Theodosius II (408–450), Stilicho made a fatal blunder. Still hoping for that regency in the East, which had been his ambi-tion since the death of Theodosius in 395, Stilicho persuaded Honorius to commission the Visigothic King Alaric to sup-press Constantine III in the West while Stilicho traveled to Constantinople to preside over the accession of the young

Theodosius II and establish a regency, thus bringing together East and West again.

While the situation in Gaul had undermined Stilicho's prestige, the deal with Alaric—giving Alaric money for helping him against Constantine III—scandalized Romans of the antibarbarian nationalist party. Rumors began to spread that Stilicho had designs for the throne, if not for himself then for his son Eucherius. The general's pact with Alaric was seen as treason. Everything that Stilicho's opponents had said about him appeared to be true. He was conniving with the barbarians, he had stood silently by while the Germanic tribes overran Gaul, he allowed a usurper to challenge the Theodosian house in the West, and the death of Arcadius had brought him to the East, instead of the West, where the troubles were. Discontent spread into the army, which revolted in Ticinum (Pavia in modern-day Italy).

On August 13, 408, Olympius, the *magister scrinii*, or master of the secretariat (a senior civil servant leading one of the three offices of the central imperial administration), led a coup against Stilicho, resulting in the execution of Stilicho in Ravenna on August 22 and that of his son soon after in Rome. Negotiations with the Visigoths again broke down, and Alaric marched on Italy to besiege Rome in November 408. After forcing a payment from the city, the Visigoths withdrew north to Tuscany.

In the disturbances that followed the downfall of Stilicho, local Romans killed a great number of barbarian federate troops and their families in Italy, thus increasing the tensions between the Romans and barbarians. The murder of Stilicho was possibly arranged by the Eastern Empire, and while it was a damaging blow to the Western Empire, it helped much to ease the tension between the two emperors.

THE INVASION OF SPAIN

While Honorius and Stilicho were occupied in Italy, Constantine III was not idle. With parts of Gaul in his hands, he sought to add Spain to his power sphere. In 408, he sent his son, Constans, and his general, Gerontius, to Spain with some of his barbarian allies. There they defeated the Roman forces which chose to remain loyal to Honorius, and had successfully defended the mountain passes against the Vandals and the other migrating tribes. After his victory in 409, Constans marched back to his father and was made co-emperor, while he left some of his barbarian allies to hold the passes. In January 409, Honorius, hard pressed by Alaric and with only a few allies left, was forced to recognize Constantine III as his colleague in the empire, thereby temporarily ending hostilities, which would soon break out again.

The troops of Constans kept a lax guard on the Pyrenean passes and appear to have been more interested in looting the surrounding countryside, and so the Vandals, Alans, and Sueves, after plundering Gaul for three years, crossed the Pyrenees and entered the rich provinces of Spain. The tribes probably felt safer moving to Spain and away from the Roman armies fighting for Gaul, gaining the eminent protection of the Pyrenees as well as new regions to plunder and to provide them with food. The statement of Jordanes that the tribes fled from the Visigoths cannot be trusted, as they were occupied in Italy, and the strange statement of Salvian that the Vandals fled Gaul to Spain out of some unnamed fear appears unreasonable too. More likely, the tribes simply felt too insecure in Gaul. This is supported by the pattern of their movements in Gaul, where they—despite their apparent strength—sought to avoid confrontations with the Roman armies. To a large extent, the Vandal migrations after they left their homelands north of the Danube and until their settlement in North Africa were determined by the political and military situation in the Roman Empire.

For the period of the Vandals in Spain, we are fortunate to have the chronicle of the Spanish Bishop Hydatius from Gallaecia, who wrote in the first half of the fifth century. After crossing the mountains from Burdigala to Pompaelo, the tribes probably marched along the Roman roads of Burgos in modern-day Spain, as well as Legio (Leon), Ocellodurum

(Zamora), Helmantica (Salamanca), and Emerita Augusta (Merida), to Hispalis (Seville). Hydatius gives the time of their crossing the mountains as September 28 or October 13, 409. Some modern historians believe that Hydatius mentions two dates because the invaders came in two groups.

While the Vandals, Sueves, and Alans were plundering Spain, the attention of the Western Empire was elsewhere. At the beginning of 410, there were six emperors and usurpers— Honorius and Theodosius II; Attalus in Rome, who had been set up by the Visigoths; Constantine III; Constans, the son of Constantine; and Maximus, a usurper in Spain. Failed diplomacy and the Roman focus on defeating Constantine allowed the Visigoths to rampage through Italy, and in 410, Rome was sacked. This led to many mutual recriminations between pagans and Christians. The pagans claimed that neglect of ancestral observances had brought about divine punishment, and the Christians in return blamed the disaster on the wicked paganism in Rome. In North Africa, St. Augustine wrote his great work, *The City of God*, to remind the faithful that the downfall of the temporal city was but a small matter compared with the eternity of the Kingdom of Heaven. Alaric did not get a chance to enjoy his victory. After sacking Rome, he marched into southern Italy, intending to invade North Africa, possibly to settle there or secure the grain supply for Italy. But he died during the journey and was succeeded by his brother-in-law Ataulf, who three years later would marry Galla Placidia (392–450), the sister of Emperor Honorius.

The disaster of the barbarian invasion of Spain was made worse by the revolt of the governor left there by Constans, Gerontius, who in 410 or spring 411 had put up his client, the Spanish aristocrat Maximus, as emperor. With an army of Constans sent to Spain to put down the revolt, Gerontius instead allied himself with the invading Vandal, Alan, and Suevic tribes and defeated the army of Constans, who was forced to flee to Gaul. While Gerontius followed up his victory by pursuing his enemy to Gaul, the Germanic tribes were left to devastate the unprotected provinces, as Hydatius describes so vividly in his chronicle. In Gaul and Britain, numerous revolts sprang up when the local nobles felt undefended against the barbarians, and the chaos in the Western Roman Empire only increased. The tribes spent the years 410–411 plundering Gallaecia, Lusitania, Baetica, and Carthaginiensis, causing widespread famine, epidemics, and misery to the provincials. The remaining part of Spain, that is, most of the province of Tarraconensis, was so far spared the devastations of the barbarians and remained in the hands of Gerontius.

THE TRIBES SETTLE IN SPAIN

In 411, hunger was again threatening, and the barbarians were eager to make peace with the Romans. The formerly rich provinces of Spain were so destroyed in this period that the price of food was soaring, and—if we choose to believe Hydatius—mothers killed and cooked their own children. The Vandals needed to end the decade of migration and settle in a revenue-producing province that could support them. In return for peace, the tribes agreed to defend Spain against the enemies of Rome as imperial federates. They received four of the five provinces in Spain to settle in. The Romans kept the fifth, Tarraconensis.

The settlement of the tribes was made by lot, but there are indications that they divided Spain according to their own preferences rather than those of the Romans. There was one major flaw in the plan, however: the settlement of the tribes in Spain was made with Gerontius and therefore with a usurpation regime. The tribes were probably not aware of this and the danger that was inherent in such a deal. The rightful emperor, Honorius, would never recognize a settlement made with a usurper and would strike down hard on any support for rebellions. Later, in 415, the tribes approached the imperial authorities for a formal recognition of their status. If their initial settlement had been officially recognized by the emperor in 411, they would not have had to do so.

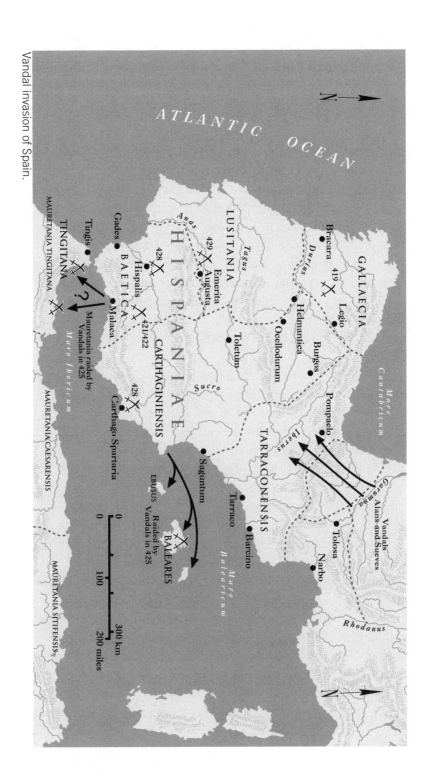

Vandal invasion of Spain.

The Hasding Vandals received the eastern part of Gallaecia (Galicia, the modern name for Gallaecia, refers to a smaller area than its fifth-century equivalent), the Sueves got the western part of Gallaecia, and the Siling Vandals received Baetica. The Alans, which were probably the most numerous among the allied tribes, got Lusitania and Carthaginiensis. This was not a random division of territory, but probably represented the relative strength of the tribes. The untaken cities and fortresses all opened their gates to the barbarians and received garrisons. However, the most important fortresses and some of the more important harbors of the Mediterranean stayed Roman, such as Hispalis and Carthago Spartaria (Cartagena in modern-day Spain). No doubt this was also to keep the barbarians from the Mediterranean. A few years later, on September 24, 419, a law was enacted making it a capital crime to teach a barbarian the art of ship-building.

Although there were about one hundred thousand Alans, Vandals, and Sueves combined, there is no archaeological evidence of their settlement in Spain. Neither do we know how they were settled. Orosius says in his *History against the Pagans* (*Historiarum adversum Paganos*) that the barbarians took to the plow after taking Spain. However, barbarians taking to the plow was a much-used literary convention in late antiquity, and because Orosius says nothing more on the matter, it is fair to doubt that they actually received lands. A more popular and believable theory is that they were billeted according to the rules for billeting Roman soldiers, and so received housing and perhaps one-third of the tax income of the provinces.

During the settlement of the Vandals in Spain, the local Roman governments continued their functions, but archaeological evidence from southern Spain shows a rapid deterioration of the infrastructure, with roads declining and bridges falling down, and a movement of housing away from the major roads into more-defensible locations. No doubt life was becoming more insecure, but for some, the invasion brought new opportunities. According to Orosius, many *coloni* (serf-like tenant farmers) fled from the Roman tax pressure and joined the Vandals.

While some scholars have believed that the modern-day Spanish region of Andalusia was named after the Vandals (Vandalusia), this is doubtful. It is much more likely that Andalusia is derived from the name the Moors used for Spain: Handalusia.

FALL OF GERONTIUS AND WAR WITH THE VISIGOTHS

The peace with the Romans would not last. Honorius had made a temporary peace with the Visigoths in 411, allowing him to send an army into Gaul. There, by spring 411, Maximus and Gerontius had defeated and killed Constans at Vienne before moving south to besiege Constantine III at Arelate.

The successor to the power of Stilicho was General Constantius, whom Honorius made master of soldiers. As he moved west with his army in 411, the Spanish troops deserted Gerontius and renewed their allegiance to Honorius, and the usurper Maximus and Gerontius fled to the barbarians in Spain. After the flight of Gerontius, Constantius took over the siege of Arelate, and after three months captured and executed Constantine III and his son Julian. Thus at the end of 411, just as Ataulf was about to leave Italy and enter Gaul with the Visigoths, there had been a significant change for the better throughout the west for Honorius. The situation improved further in 412, when Gerontius was attacked and killed by his Spanish troops because of his harsh treatment of them. Though Maximus had escaped to Spain, where he continued to rule in the mountains until 414, he was now powerless to threaten the emperor.

After the death of the Visigothic King Alaric at the end of 410, the new king, Ataulf, was turning his eyes on Gaul. In 413, he managed to suppress the usurper Jovinus, who had been proclaimed in the Rhineland with the support of the Burgundians and a group of Alans under their king, Goar.

But Honorius's General Constantius was too strong, and so in 414, the Visigoths followed the coastline into Spain and took the city of Barcino (Barcelona in modern-day Spain) as their stronghold from which they would make war on the Vandals in the coming years, sometimes for their own reasons and sometimes on the orders of Rome.

Ataulf was killed in August or September 415, and was succeeded by Segeric, who was murdered soon after, and Wallia was made king of the Visigoths. The war against the Romans was going badly, and the Roman navy was blockading the harbors of Spain and causing famine among the Visigoths. At that time the Vandals began to use the nickname Truli for the Visigoths, as they were forced to pay a gold piece for a small measure of grain, or *trula*.

CONSTANTIUS III

In the meantime at Ravenna, General Constantius was moving up in his career. He had destroyed the usurpers Constantine and Heraclianus, the Count of Africa, who had rebelled in 412, and proved himself the only effective leader in the government. So in 417, it was arranged that Constantius would marry Galla Placidia, the sister of the emperor. She protested strongly, but Honorius handed her over to Constantius, and they were married. They had a daughter, Honoria, and later, in 419, a son, Valentinian. Constantius held the empire jointly in 421 with Honorius, who rather unwillingly had appointed him co-emperor as Constantius III. Constantius, who had been the strong man in the empire for more than a decade, unexpectedly died on September 2, not quite seven months after his coronation.

DEFEAT OF THE ALANS AND SILING VANDALS

During a raid in 416, the Visigothic King Wallia managed to capture a Vandal king named Fredibal—probably the king of the Silings—and brought him to Emperor Honorius in Italy. But the Visigoths still had their eyes on the whole Iberian Peninsula. The Silings and Alans were defeated in several battles over the next three years. By 418, the Silings in Baetica were all but destroyed, and the Alans had lost their King Addac and suffered severely. The few survivors from both tribal confederations willingly joined the Hasding Vandals under King Gunderic in Gallaecia, modern-day northwestern Spain. It was probably at this time that the Vandal king began referring to himself as Rex Vandalorum et Alanorum (King of the Vandals and Alans), but the title does not appear in the sources until the time of King Huneric (477–484). It is also around this time that the name Hasding begins to be used to refer to the royal family of the Vandals, rather than the tribe of the Hasdings.

The exact status of the Alans in the tribal confederation is uncertain. They appear to have had a special, somewhat independent standing, as they alone were mentioned along with the Vandal name, whereas the Siling name disappears. Possibly they existed like the Rugi in the Ostrogothic confederation as a separate tribe, with their own laws and marrying only inside their tribe. It seems incredible that the probably difficult integration of Germanic-speaking Vandals with Iranian-speaking Alans is not mentioned by the sources, and neither are the differences in social structures, cultures, and religions. This is good evidence of the deplorable lack of sources and lack of knowledge of this important period in Vandal history, and it requires us to resort to speculation in bringing together the pieces of information we do have.

As a reward for defeating the Alans and Siling Vandals, the Romans granted the Visigoths a permanent home in Aquitania, along with the large cities of Burdigala and Tolosa. They settled there as Roman federates, but in practice ruled a virtually independent kingdom. As the Vandals later in North Africa included some groups of Goths, it is believed that small Gothic groups may have stayed in Spain and joined the Vandals when King Wallia moved to Gaul.

These Visigothic attacks of 416–418 on the Vandal coalition returned the provinces of Lusitania, Carthaginiensis, and Baetica to central Roman control. The panic created by the attacks of the Visigoths and Romans created a supergroup of some seventy thousand to eighty thousand in the Vandal coalition, which was capable of fielding an army of fifteen thousand to twenty thousand. It appears that with his new strength, King Gunderic tried to defeat the Sueves while the Visigoths were occupied in their new settlement in Aquitaine. The former allies, who had marched together for the past eighteen years, were now enemies. However, the sources are unclear on who was the aggressor in the war. It might be that because of the perceived weakness of the Vandals or pressure from Rome, which wanted to rid itself of the Vandals, the Sueves made war on the new Vandal confederation. What we do know is that Suevian King Hermanric was defeated, and the Vandals drove him and his army into the mountains of modern-day Asturias, where they were blockaded. This was the first successful pitched battle the Vandals had engaged in during their entire history, if we are to believe the sources.

CASTINUS

Only after pressure from the Roman governor of Spain, Count Asterius, and a Roman army, did the new Vandal-Alan confederacy retreat to Baetica, where it settled in the former lands of the Siling Vandals. During the retreat in 419, the Vandals were engaged by the Roman forces in a skirmish at Bracara (Braga in modern-day Spain), where Hydatius mentions that some Vandals were killed. The campaign was viewed as a Roman success, and Asterius was appointed patrician—one of the highest social ranks in the empire—soon after his return from Spain. In his stead was sent Castinus, *Comes Domesticorum* (Count of the Domestics, the military leader of the imperial guard). It appears there were then two to three years without serious warfare. No doubt the Hasding Vandals had to organize the new elements in their tribal confederation, while the Romans did not have the strength to attack them.

They were, however, not to have peace for long. In 422, the Romans sailed with a large army to Spain, and with the

Visigoths attacked the Vandals in Baetica. But as often happened in the later years of the Western Empire, jealousy and disagreements hampered the campaign. Bonifacius, the capable second in command to Castinus, refused to join the campaign because of Castinus's arrogance and instead sailed to the North African provinces, which he took over. He was later made Count of Africa.

Despite this inauspicious start of the campaign, the Romans succeeded in besieging the Vandal army in a city of Baetica, where they were on the point of surrender due to lack of provisions. But instead of waiting, the inept Castinus engaged the desperate Vandals in regular battle, where his allied Visigoths committed treachery and he was defeated. He then had to retreat to Tarraco (Tarragona). The sources mention a loss of twenty thousand Roman soldiers, although this is no doubt an inflated number. The churchman Salvian writes in *On the Government of God* that the Vandals carried the Bible as a form of standard in front of them in the battle, thereby gaining the victory. As this was the second battle victory for the Vandals in just three years, it might have done much to strengthen Christianity among them.

The exile of Galla Placidia

At the imperial court in Ravenna, intrigues continued. Empress Galla Placidia had a number of Visigothic followers who still supported her since her days as the wife of King Ataulf, and they served her as bodyguard. This close contact with the Visigoths apparently led to a charge of treason after her followers clashed with regular Roman troops during riots in Ravenna. Honorius banished her and her children, the young Valentinian and his sister, and they fled to Constantinople in spring 423. Although the East Roman emperor, Theodosius II, had never recognized Galla Placidia's late husband, Constantius III, as emperor, he did offer her sanctuary. The Count of Africa, Bonifacius, alone kept faith with her and sent whatever money he could from North Africa.

In the meantime, Honorius relied on Castinus, the master of soldiers and the emperor's leading adviser—and by virtue of that fact, Galla Placidia's open foe—to rule the Western Empire. When Honorius died at Ravenna on August 27, 423, at the relatively young age of thirty-nine, Theodosius II briefly served as emperor of a united empire and ruled through Castinus in the West. The legitimate heir, Valentinian, was in Constantinople, so at Rome, a senior civil servant named Joannes took advantage of his absence and usurped the throne of the Western Empire, supported by Castinus. Gaul, Spain, and Dalmatia supported him, and only Bonifacius in North Africa remained loyal and held his provinces against Joannes and Castinus. However, the East Roman emperor was not about to accept a usurper on the Western throne and so intervened to support the claims of the young Valentinian against the usurpation. In order to do this, Theodosius had to recognize the position of Valentinian's mother, Galla Placidia, widow of Honorius's short-lived colleague Constantius III, whom he had refused to recognize as empress, and who had now fled to Constantinople.

In 425, Theodosius II was ready to challenge Joannes and sent the masters of soldiers Aspar and Ardaburius against Italy, supported by a fleet carrying Valentinian and his mother. Joannes was defeated in battle at Ravenna, captured, and executed. Valentinian was made emperor on October 23, 425, even though he was only seven years old. His willful mother, Galla Placidia, ruled in his stead. However, the Eastern Empire continued to exercise strong influence over the government of the Western Empire, as shown, for example, by the appointment of Eastern Master of Soldiers Ardaburius as Western consul for the year 427.

THE VANDALS STRIKE BACK

The Vandals used the chaos in Italy to turn the tables and run wild over Spain, even raiding by ship the Balearic Isles and Mauretania, probably some time in 425. This is the first mention of the Vandals' using ships, which they had probably gained control of by occupying the Roman ports on the south coast of Spain. The ships were captured from the Romans, or were merchant ships or even fishing vessels that the Vandals paid for their services. The seamen were Romans, as the Vandals had no knowledge of seafaring at this time. The use of ships seriously endangered the Roman coastal cities, which had been acting as a bulwark against the barbarians because they were easy to supply and defend with the Romans in full control of the seas. The safety of the Roman islands was now also threatened, as they had no garrisons to speak of. The Vandals also attacked the province of Tarraconensis, plundering in 428 Carthago Spartaria and Hispalis, the latter of which was to a large extent destroyed.

Despite their success, the Vandals were still threatened in Spain. They had spent twenty years plundering the Spanish provinces, and since their arrival there, they had been engaged in almost continuous warfare with the Sueves, the Visigoths, and the Romans, all of whom were pressing them hard. The Siling Vandals had been all but destroyed, and the Alans had been reduced to a remnant. It was time to find new lands before famine returned, but in what direction? North was not possible, and south was only the desert of Mauretania. The new Vandal king, Geiseric, who had succeeded the recently deceased Gunderic, showed true statesmanship in hatching a plan to invade North Africa using the Vandals' newly acquired knowledge of ships and march across the desert to the fertile provinces of Roman North Africa. But how could he manage to cross over to North Africa? And what was happening in the Western Empire that made it seem an opportune time to take such a risk?

THREE

The Invasion of North Africa

"Finding a province which was at peace and enjoying quiet, the whole land beautiful and flowering on all sides, they set to work on it with their wicked forces, laying it waste by devastation and bringing everything to ruin with fire and murders. They did not even spare the fruit-bearing orchards. . . . So it was that no place remained safe from being contaminated by them, as they raged with great cruelty, unchanging and relentless."—*Victor of Vita, AD 484*

During the early fifth century, Empress Galla Placidia was the true power in the Western Roman Empire, which she ruled through her son Valentinian III, who was only a boy. She had an astounding number of important family relations: she was granddaughter of Valentinian I, daughter of Theodosius the Great, half-sister of Emperor Honorius, widow of Visigothic King Ataulf, widow of Constantius III, and mother of the reigning emperor. But her situation was precarious, and she had to rely on various powerful people at court to support her. It appears that she aimed for a balance of power at court, with no single person too dominant. She did this by playing the military and the bureaucracy against each other. The three

main powers in the years after 425 were the generals of the
three Western army groups, Felix, Aetius, and Bonifacius.

Flavius Felix was senior central field army general (*magister
militum praesentalis*) at the court in Italy and had served in the
defense of Italy from 425–429. Despite his being a powerful
factor at the imperial court and being made a patrician in 425,
little is otherwise known about him.

His rival Flavius Aetius, whom we know much more
about, was born at Durostorum on the lower Danube
(Silistra in modern-day Bulgaria) and followed in the military
footsteps of his father, Gaudentius, who had been master of
the cavalry (*magister equitum*) and Count of Africa.
Gaudentius was killed in a mutiny of his troops when holding the position of master of the soldiers in Gaul (*magister militum per Gallias*). Aetius entered the Imperial Guard but was
given as a hostage to Visigothic King Alaric for three years,
and later to the Huns. His experience with these two peoples
and their strong and weak points gave him a great advantage
later, when allied with or facing them in battle. At the death
of Honorius and the usurpation of Joannes, he supported the
faction of Joannes. Aetius had replaced Castinus, who had
commanded the army of Gaul under Joannes. Aetius reached
this position for a number of reasons, including his close connections to the Huns. When the army of East Roman
Emperor Theodosius was approaching to topple Joannes,
Aetius was sent to the Huns to buy troops. He returned with
a great Hunnish army—one source says sixty thousand men,
although that is much too great a number—three days after
Joannes was defeated. Using the Huns as a bargaining chip, he
was made master of soldiers in Gaul in return for paying the
Huns to go home without a struggle.

Bonifacius was the third strong man in the Western
Empire. He was Count of Africa and had remained loyal to
Galla Placidia during the usurpation of Joannes. Bonifacius is
first mentioned by the historian Olympiodorus in 413, when
he repelled a Visigothic assault on Massilia (Marseilles in
modern-day France). The Visigothic King Ataulf was sup-

Consular diptych of Flavius Felix, now in the Bibliothèque nationale de France, Cabinet des Medailles, Paris. The left part was lost during the French Revolution. (*Author*)

posedly even wounded by Bonifacius and had to retreat with his army, thereby freeing the city. He was in North Africa in 417 as an officer, and the next time he is mentioned by the sources is in 421–422, when the campaign against the Vandals in Spain was planned. General Castinus was in supreme command, and he refused to give the skilled and experienced Bonifacius a suitable position. At the insult, Bonifacius refused to join the expedition and instead sailed for North Africa. It appears that Bonifacius, who, during these chaotic days of the Western Empire, was a tribune, simply took charge of the provinces in North Africa and defended them succesfully against the troublesome Moorish tribes. After the death of Emperor Honorius, Bonifacius's more-or-less illegal actions in North Africa were condoned, and his rule there was made legitimate with his appointment as Count of Africa in 423. His steadfast refusal to recognize the rule of the usurper Joannes, who was supported by his former enemy Castinus, caused Bonifacius to send great sums of money to Empress Galla Placidia and to support her claims for the throne. Bonifacius's strong support for her even caused Joannes to send large forces to North Africa, thereby weakening his main armies before the battle with the East Roman forces of Aspar and Ardaburius. When Joannes was dethroned and executed, Bonifacius's future as one of the chief advisers of Galla Placidia was ensured, and in 425 he was made Count of the Domestics for his loyalty. However, he did not receive the expected promotion to central field army general, possibly because of his marriage to an Arian woman (according to the senator and poet Sidonius Apollinaris, she was a Gothic princess) and because he had his daughter baptized by an Arian priest. Instead, Flavius Felix received the title.

Consular diptych of Flavius Aetius, possibly showing Aetius presiding over circus games. Also known as the diptych of the Bourges Cathedral, it now resides at the Musee du Berry, Bourges, France. (*Author*)

For a few years, Galla Placidia's strategy appeared to work. None of the three became dominant. But it was difficult to maintain the delicate balance. Felix, who was closest to the court and perhaps the most powerful of the three, opened the conflict. In 427, he accused Bonifacius of disloyalty and ordered him to return to Italy. Bonifacius knew well what would happen and so refused the orders. In response, Felix sent an army to North Africa, but Bonifacius defeated it. This weakened Felix, and Aetius then saw his chance to enter the scene. He had defeated the Visigoths in Gaul in 426 and the Franks in 428, so his back was secure for the moment, and his successes had probably made him popular at court. In 429, Aetius was made junior central field army general in Italy. In May 430, Felix and his wife were arrested for plotting against Aetius (the details of the alleged plot are unclear), and they were executed at Ravenna. Meanwhile, the Vandals took advantage of the pre-occupation of the three generals and invaded Mauretania in 429, then went plundering along the North African coast toward Carthage and defeated Bonifacius twice in battle.

It appeared that Aetius had won the power struggle, and he soon returned to Gaul to keep the barbarians in check. But Galla Placidia had not given up her strategy. To offset the newly won power of Aetius, she recalled Bonifacius to Italy and made him central field army general. Aetius immediately marched back to Italy with an army. The two antagonists met in battle near Ariminum (Rimini) in 432. Bonifacius won the battle but was mortally wounded and died soon after. His widow later married Aetius. While Aetius retreated to his estates in the country, Sebastianus, the son-in-law of Bonifacius, tried to take up his father-in-law's position at court.

Apparently after Sebastianus failed in an assassination attempt on him, Aetius returned to the scene. In 433, he went back to Italy with great Hunnish forces, and Sebastianus was forced to flee to Constantinople. With the opposition gone, Aetius now was the strongest man in the state and was made senior central field army general. His supreme position was confirmed September 5, 435, when he was named patrician. Sebastianus would remain in Constantinople for the next decade, but would then return to the scene.

While the actions described above are the most likely course of events, our two main sources for the Vandal invasion of North Africa are the chronicle of Prosper of Aquitaine from the middle of the fifth century and that of Procopius from the sixth century, who have two other versions.

The version of Procopius, who wrote *The Vandal War* about one hundred years after the events, is the more elaborate. He ignores Felix and focuses on the rivalry of Aetius and Bonifacius. Procopius even claims that if they had not been each other's contemporaries, they might each have been called the last of the Romans, so great were their abilities, but being contemporary, they both failed. Between these two great generals and statesmen a rivalry soon arose.

According to Procopius, the rivalry appears to have started when Empress Galla Placidia bestowed upon Bonifacius the title of Count of the Domestics in 425. In response, the disappointed Aetius faked friendship with Bonifacius. But as soon as Bonifacius was back in North Africa, Aetius told Galla Placidia that he suspected Bonifacius of rebellion. She could get certain proof of this by summoning him to Italy, which he would refuse. Accordingly, Galla Placidia asked Bonifacius to come to Ravenna. Meanwhile, Aetius wrote to Bonifacius in secret that Galla Placidia was trying to get rid of him, and the proof would be that she would ask him to come to Italy without any apparent reason. Bonifacius believed Aetius's friendship was real and trusted his word. When the letter from Galla Placidia arrived asking him to come to Ravenna, Bonifacius refused. For Galla Placidia, this was proof of his rebellious designs, and in 427 he was declared an enemy of Rome.

To defend himself against the Western Roman Empire, he sent ambassadors to King Gunderic in 428, asking for the aid of the Vandals. He already knew that the Vandals were hard pressed in Spain, where they fought the Visigoths and Sueves over the now-pillaged and famine-stricken provinces. When the ambassadors of Bonifacius reached the Vandal court, Gunderic was still king, backed by his younger, bastard half-brother Geiseric. According to Procopius, the Vandals agreed to support Bonifacius, and in return, North Africa would be divided into three parts: one for Gunderic, one for Geiseric, and one for Bonifacius. But before the Vandals were ready, Gunderic died and Geiseric was proclaimed king. He maintained the agreement, and Bonifacius's fleet transported the Vandal tribes to North Africa.

A few months after the Vandals had moved to North Africa, some friends of Bonifacius, who were surprised at his sudden and unexpected rebellion, traveled from Italy to North Africa and met him at Carthage. He showed them Aetius's treacherous letter and explained his reasons for the rebellion. His friends returned to Galla Placidia and explained the case to her. She did not feel powerful enough to punish Aetius, but Bonifacius was forgiven for his rebellion. Now, however, it was too late for him to stop the Vandals. Despite being offered great rewards to return to Spain, the Vandals refused. Bonifacius fought them and was defeated, and had to retreat to Hippo Regius. In 432, after receiving large reinforcements from the Eastern Roman Empire under Aspar, he again met the Vandals in battle but was severely defeated and fled to Italy.

Despite his defeat, Bonifacius was well received at Rome, and Galla Placidia made him *magister utriusque militiae* (master of foot and horse), a title Aetius had held for three years. There was even speculation that she might make him emperor, but that did not happen. Aetius returned from the war against the Franks, and a battle between him and Bonifacius ensued. Aetius was defeated, but according to the fanciful story, Bonifacius was mortally wounded by a javelin in single combat against him. Three months later he died, and Aetius became the chief power in the Western Empire.

Prosper of Aquitaine, who lived during these events, tells a different story than Procopius. According to him, Felix declared Bonifacius a public enemy and made war on him in 427. Three generals—Mavortius, Gallio, and Sanoeces— were sent with an army against him, but one of them betrayed the others, causing the siege of Bonifacius to fail. The two other generals were killed, although the traitor soon also found his death.

According to St. Augustine, the Moors, supported by slaves and tenant farmers, also took advantage of the Roman civil war and erupted over the borders in 428, plundering the nearest settlements. Amid the chaos, both Felix and Bonifacius called in barbarians for support, as Prosper explains in this enigmatic sentence: "Thereafter access to the sea was gained by peoples who were unacquainted with ships until they were called in by the rival sides to give assistance." It is believed that one of the "peoples" mentioned were the Vandals. Since the word "peoples" is plural, it is supposed that the Gothic troops brought by Count Sigisvultus (who took over the war against Bonifacius after the deaths of the three other generals) were the other people "unacquainted" with the sea. However, too much rests on this difficult sentence. What it means exactly cannot be determined, but it must be supposed that at some time during 428, one of the sides in the struggle in North Africa called in the Vandals, who were transported in Roman ships. An Arian bishop, Maximinus, joined Sigisvultus's expedition to North Africa in the hope that he might be able to convince Bonifacius to lay down his arms. Bonifacius did not fight these forces, but instead retired to Sitifis (Sétif in modern-day Algeria). Due to the influence of St. Augustine and others, Boniface was reconciled to Galla Placidia, and Sigisvultus returned to Italy. In 429, a delegation was sent to North Africa under one Darius, and peace was finally negotiated. In 429, Bonifacius is again mentioned as being Count of Africa.

Later sources, such as the *Getica* of Jordanes, probably written in Constantinople in 551, give little evidence of one or the other of the stories. Some evidence is found in the letters of St. Augustine, who had a close relationship with Bonifacius and appears to think that Bonifacius somehow brought these calamities—that is, the Vandal invasion—on himself.

Procopius's version, although tempting in its details, is full of mistakes in the first part, such as the enmity between Bonifacius and Aetius. Aetius only became senior central field army general in 430, after Flavius Felix was executed, making it appear that Procopius simply transferred the enmity between Bonifacius and Felix to Aetius, because he was better known to him. But Prosper is, unfortunately, just as difficult to use, as, for example, he places Count Sigisvultus's expedition to Africa in 424, which is quite impossible.

It is perhaps even more surprising that Victor of Vita, a North African churchman who wrote some sixty years later on the religious persecutions of the Vandals, does not mention Bonifacius's treachery at all when he describes the invasion of the Vandals. In other places, he describes Bonifacius in positive terms. The Roman support for the crossing of the Vandals is itself unlikely. If they were to support Bonifacius or Sigisvultus in the war, why would they be transported to the farthest point in North Africa and have to suffer such a long land march that the issue of the war would be decided before they arrived? It would appear that the accounts of Procopius and Prosper are no more than stories, in line with such myths as the eunuch Narses inviting the Langobards to invade Italy in 568, and Stilicho inviting the Vandals to Gaul.

Geiseric is made king

In the early months of 428, King Gunderic died at Hispalis after taking the city. According to the churchman Hydatius, it was a divine punishment during the plundering of the treasures of a church. His younger, bastard half-brother, Geiseric, the son of Godegisel and a concubine of non-Germanic origin, succeeded him, passing Gunderic's two young sons, who were minors. He later had them murdered in North Africa to secure the succession of his own son. According to Procopius, Geiseric died at an old age in 477, and so he cannot have been born much before 390 and thus was a boy when the migrations from the Vandal homelands began. Not much is known of the circumstances of his succession. But as there is no evidence of usurpation in the sources, he was most likely elected by the Vandal nobles and the army, as was customary among Germanic tribes in the migration period. No doubt the succession of Gunderic's young sons was not acceptable to the warrior nation, which was engaged in serious wars against their neighbors.

Geiseric was to become one of the most important figures in Europe for the next fifty years. Even including the most recent victories in Spain, the Vandals do not appear to have been particularly successful in warfare until his time. They were defeated by the Langobards in Poland and the Gothic King Geberich in Moravia, defeated by the Romans on the Danube, and more recently defeated by the Franks on the Rhine. Now the Visigoths were generally gaining the upper hand in many of the battles.

Geiseric would change all this and transform the Vandals from a wandering tribe to an important power in the Mediterranean, secure from their foes, rich, and with plenty of food. He was considered cruel, but also intelligent and courageous. He is described as greedy, but this was no rare trait among the barbarians—or Romans for that matter. He was quick to act and make allies in the turmoil that was the Western Roman Empire in the fifth century, with constantly changing alliances and conditions. His Vandals would later consider him the greatest of their kings and base their royal succession on the family ties to him. The Gothic historian Jordanes described him as a man of moderate stature and limping from a fall from his horse. He was, Jordanes says, "a man of deep thought and few words, holding luxury in disdain, furious in his anger, greedy for gain, shrewd in winning over the barbarians and skilled in sowing the seeds of dissension to arouse enmity." Malchus, a Roman rhetorician of the fifth century, speaks of Geiseric's great strength for action and foresight in military matters, always keeping reserves ready to move quickly if an opportunity arose. He was an Arian Christian, but Hydatius describes him as an apostate, possibly because his mother, who may have been a Roman Orthodox Christian, brought him up in her faith. On becoming a man, he changed to the Arian faith of his people.

PREPARATIONS FOR THE INVASION OF AFRICA

In May 429, Geiseric mustered all the people of his tribes and the Alans on the northern shore of the Straits of Gibraltar. The tribal confederation included a number of Goths and Hispano-Romans. The decision to invade North Africa was probably made with the nobles. Geiseric faced a revolt of the nobility in 442, when he was much more powerful, but in 429, as newly elected king, he was probably not in any position to make dictatorial decisions. We must therefore assume there was broad agreement among the Vandal nobles to invade Africa.

The explanation by some, such as Salvian, that the reasons for the migration were religious does not ring true. The explanation offered by Cassiodorus, that they were pressed by the Visigoths, sounds more likely. Basically, the invasion of North Africa must have appeared to Geiseric and the Vandal nobles to offer a better future than staying in Spain, fending off Visigoths, Sueves, and Romans. The pressure from the Romans and their federate tribes was growing, as it appears that the Romans had set the Sueves and Visigoths in motion in 428–429 to attack the Vandals. No doubt merchants from the harbors of Spain had told the Vandals of the rich African provinces, filled with food and plunder. So the combination of Roman pressure in Spain, hunger, and the opportunity offered by the civil war in North Africa was the best chance the Vandals would have at founding a new kingdom in a safe place with enough food. The aim since the start of the migration, more than a generation ago, was still the same, but with a new geographical goal.

But the exploits of the Vandals in Spain were not finished. When Geiseric was told that Hermigarius, king of the Sueves, was plundering some of the provinces close to his marching route, he turned his army around and attacked him close to the city of Emerita Augusta. Geiseric probably felt it was inviting disaster to move his whole people with a hostile army at its back. The Sueves were defeated, and their king drowned during his flight when crossing the Gaudiana River outside Emerita Augusta. With the Sueves defeated, Geiseric turned back to the trek to North Africa.

Before embarking, possibly to organize the transport of the nation, he had all the males counted from "those who had come from the womb into the light that very day" and to the "old men, young men and children, slaves and masters," as Victor of Vita tells us. There were altogether eighty thousand males. This number has received much attention from historians as a unique example of the size of one of the migrating tribes. But the consensus is that the number is too high, and that a more realistic estimate would be around eighty thousand to one hundred thousand people all told, not just males. This range gives us a good basis for assessing the provisioning of such a multitude on the road. Even on small rations, a rough estimate would be that they would require more than 100 to 120 tons of grain every day, as well as other types of food and water. Fodder and water for the horses and animals pulling their wagons would also be needed. Emperor Julian's thirteen-thousand-man army at the battle of Argentoratum in 357, of which three thousand were cavalry, required a minimum of thirty tons of grain, twelve tons of fodder, and thirty thousand gallons of water every day. And this was only for the fighting men and horses—on top of this, slaves and the baggage train also had to be fed. Others have estimated the daily requirements for soldiers in the period to be three and a half pounds of grain per man, to be supplemented by other types of food, and nearly ten pounds of grain and ten pounds of forage per horse.

The range of eighty thousand to one hundred thousand people also helps us determine the Vandals' likely military strength. The ratio of combatants to noncombatants among the tribes in antiquity is generally considered to have been one to four or one to five, so the Vandals' strength would, at best, have amounted to twenty thousand to twenty-five thousand warriors—not a lot for taking the well-defended and provisioned North African provinces. However, because the tribes had been migrating for more than two decades, the proportion of warriors to noncombatants might have been much higher, as the weak and ill had not survived the hard life of travel.

THE NORTH AFRICAN PROVINCES

What provinces did the Vandals enter? The part of North Africa we are concerned with consisted of the coastline from the Pillars of Hercules (the Strait of Gibraltar) to western Cyrenaica. This area was divided into seven provinces, west to east: Mauretania Tingitana (capital: Tingis), Mauretania Caesariensis (capital: Caesarea), Mauretania Sitifensis (capital: Sitifis), Numidia (capital: Cirta), Africa Proconsularis, or Zeugitana, as it was also known (capital: Carthage), Byzacena (capital: Hadrumentum), and Tripolitania (capital: Tacapae). It is believed that the provinces had a combined one million to three million inhabitants, about 20 percent of whom were slaves.

Mauretania Tingitana consisted of a strip of coastline from Tingis (Tangiers in modern-day Morocco) to Sala Colonia (Salé in modern-day Morocco) in the south, and the Oued Laou River in the east, and was separated by more than two hundred miles of desert from Mauretania Caesarensis, so it was considered to be part of the Spanish diocese (an administrative division of the later Roman Empire, comprising a number of provinces). The two next provinces, Mauretania Caesariensis and Mauretania Sitifensis, were, like Tingitana, less developed than the heartlands of the Roman Empire, and there were not many settlements apart from the great city of Caesarea (Cherchell in modern-day Algeria), the former capital of the Mauretanian kings. The provinces were not poor, however, and the many villas dotting the countryside probably produced much grain. The easternmost province of Tripolitania, named for its three cities (Leptis Magna, Oea, and Sabratha), was similar, but with a long and difficult desert border, and it was constantly raided by the nomadic tribes of the desert. Tripolitania was not a rich province, with only a narrow strip of fertile lands along the coast.

The heart of Roman North Africa consisted of the provinces of Numidia, Byzacena, and Africa Proconsularis; in the latter was the center of Roman power, the city of Carthage. These lands were rich in grain, olive oil, and wine, and had been so for more than seven hundred years. The agricultural production had only increased since the Romans took the region in 146 BC from the Carthaginians in the Third Punic War, and North Africa and Egypt were the main providers of grain to Rome and Italy.

Carthage had been in ruins from the destruction of the Carthaginians in the second century BC until its refounding in the middle of the first century BC by Julius Caesar, and this had probably helped other cities of the region, such as

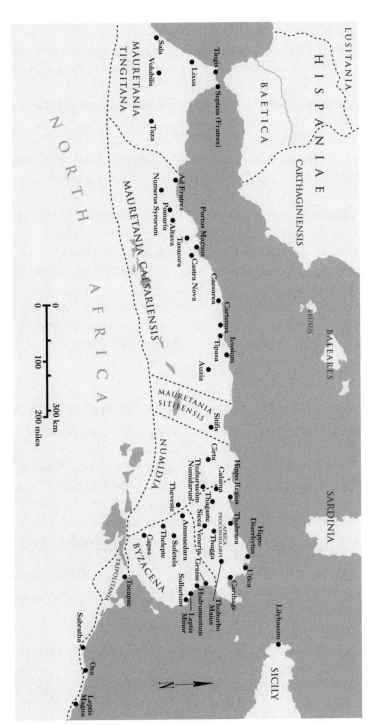

Roman provinces of North Africa.

Utica and Hippo Regius, to prosper. The three provinces were dotted with great estates, many of them owned by the emperor and farmed by hundreds of thousands of slaves from all over the empire. The constant raids of the desert tribes had not dampened the prosperity of the three core provinces of North Africa, which were at this time the richest of the Western Empire.

By the early fifth century, Carthage had an estimated one hundred thousand to two hundred thousand inhabitants and was the third largest city in the empire after Rome and Constantinople. Furthermore, it was a great cultural center, and the central economic pillar of the stricken Western Empire, producing goods for the entire Mediterranean. The revenue from North Africa was essential for the West's finances and largely paid for the great standing armed forces the empire needed to defend the remaining, more-exposed provinces in Europe. By 429, North Africa was the only part of the empire that had not been plundered in recent years.

THE NORTH AFRICAN TRADE

During the time of Julius Caesar, the province of Africa Nova, as it was called then, was already shipping fifty thousand tons of grain to Rome each year. One hundred years later, and after the emperor had assumed direct control of the provinces, it was five hundred thousand tons, and North Africa had taken over Egypt's position as the city's granary, supplying two-thirds of its needs. The fruitful districts of North Africa were also the main source of olive oil for Rome and Italy. Other than grain and olives, North Africa produced wine, figs, cattle, and horses. The enormous amount of grain, olive oil, and wine for the Mediterranean market was produced by thousands of slaves on *latifundia*, huge farms owned by the wealthy senatorial aristocracy.

The main trade was agrarian produce, although marble and pottery were also exported. The main trading centers were Carthage and Hadrumentum, the center of the olive oil trade, but a number of excellent natural ports existed, all of which were trade centers of some note.

African red slip ware vessels in the British Museum. The pot on the left is 18 centimeters high. (*Photograph by AgTigress*)

According to the *Expositio totius Mundi* (The Description of the Entire World), an account of the known world composed by an anonymous Easterner around 360, North Africa exported olive oil to almost all parts of the known world. In antiquity, olive oil was used much in cooking, but was also the primary lighting fuel and an essential component in many medicaments, soaps, skin oils, perfumes, and cosmetics. Because it was used extensively for food and personal hygiene, olive oil was of great economic importance. It is estimated that just over twenty-one quarts of olive oil were used annually per person in the provinces around the Mediterranean. Tripolitania was the main producer and exporter of olive oil, but great amounts were also produced elsewhere in North Africa.

Another major export of the region was African red slip ware, perhaps the most important type of late Roman pottery in the Mediterranean world. This pottery was produced by a number of North African workshops over a period of some six centuries, from the end of the first century AD until the seventh century and the Arab invasions. After the decline of the Italian terra sigillata industry in the early second century, North Africa began to supply the Italian fine pottery markets, and soon after covered almost the entire demand for tableware. Vast quantities were supplied to Italy and the huge market of Rome itself. From the middle of the third century to the early fifth century and the Vandal invasion, African red slip ware was the standard fine ware around the Mediterranean, despite competition from local copies.

North Africa also contained a number of state-controlled factories producing woolen and linen materials, which were dyed in the dying factories. These factories, which were staffed by state slaves, also constituted an important part of the economy of the Roman Empire.

We know the income received annually in land tax from the provinces Numidia and Mauretania Sitifensis in the mid-fifth century was 78,200 solidi (a gold coin that weighed 0.16 ounces) and 41,000 solidi, respectively, partly in gold and partly in kind. These were poor provinces. An estimate of the annual revenue for the entire diocese of Africa—that is, without Mauretania Tingitana, which belonged to the Spanish diocese—is around four hundred eighty thousand solidi, with three hundred ninety thousand solidi going to pay for the administration as well as the military forces. In comparison, Egypt, which was an extremely rich diocese, annually produced about 1.44 million solidi, or twenty thousand pounds of gold, under Emperor Justinian in the sixth century. Proceeds from the emperor's estates and the state factories went directly to the emperor's treasury.

CARTHAGE

Carthage was the undisputed capital of North Africa, lying superbly on an isthmus pointing toward Sicily and with the two-horned mountain of the Aquae Calidae (hot springs) rising to the south of it. Below was its harbor, one of the greatest centers of trade in the Western Mediterranean. To the north was the necropolis going up to the Hill of Camart. In the city itself, besides the baths, the forum, the amphitheater, and all the other usual luxuries of a Roman city, were five great temples, dedicated to Aesculapis, Saturn, Juno, Hercules, and Mercury, which in Punic times had borne the

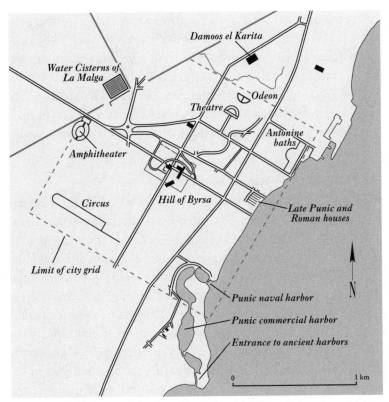

The city of Carthage in the sixth century.

names of Ashmon, Moloch, Ashtaroth, Melkarth, and Baal-Ammon. Some of these pagan temples might have been in ruins due to the zealous Christians who destroyed the old places of worship, but at least the temple of Juno Coelestis remained, for it was consecrated as a church in 425 by Aurelius, the bishop of Carthage. Carthage also contained the winter residences of the rich.

In the second century, Emperor Hadrian built a beautiful nymphaeum at the springs of Djebel Zaghouan, from which water was conducted over sixty miles by aqueduct north to Carthage, as it is today by modern pipelines to Tunis.

On a hill inside the city lay the Byrsa, the citadel of Carthage, surrounded by a wall two miles long. Here was

probably also situated the Praetorium, the palace of the proconsul of Africa. The once all-powerful proconsul had by now
been reduced to little influence by his military counterpart,
the Count of Africa. Bonifacius held this office from
423–432. Carthage was defended by the Theodosian city
wall, which Bonifacius built between 423 and 425, just in time
for the Vandal invasion. Sections of the wall have been found
by excavators.

THE CIVILIAN ADMINISTRATION

The civilian authority had, since the time of Constantine the
Great (306–337), been separated from the military authority.
The chief officials came from distinguished families and were
supported in their work by a number of lesser officials. The
chief civil servant was the *vicarius Africae* (the governor of the
Diocese of Africa), who presided at Carthage and was subject
to the praetorian prefect in Italy (*Praefectus Praetorio Italiae*),
but was appointed directly by the emperor. Below him were
the civilian governors of Tripolitania, Mauretania
Caesarensis, Mauretania Sitifensis, Byzacena, and Numidia.
The chief civil official in the proconsular province was the
proconsul, who was directly below the emperor. Mauretania
Tingitana was part of the Diocese of Hispania, so the chief
civil servant there was under the *vicarius Hispaniae*. The
provincial governor oversaw police functions, tax gathering,
and civilian and criminal justice. The taxes were mainly gathered in money or in kind. The income of the provinces flowed
to the coffers (the so-called *fiscus*) of the Count of the Sacred
Largesses (*Comes Sacrarum Largitionum*) in Rome—mainly
tolls, income from state mines and factories, and taxes, as far
as they were not used for wages for the civil administration
and the army. The Count of the Sacred Largesses had a number of civil servants in North Africa who governed the weaver
factories, the dying industry, and the collection of taxes. The
emperor also held vast areas of private property in North
Africa. After the defeat of the usurper Gildo in spring 398,
the lands taken from him, which included more than half of

the lands in Proconsularis, had to be administered by a separate official, the Count of the Gildonian patrimony.

As elsewhere in the empire, the administration of North Africa rested on the local towns. At the top of the local administration were the local councils—*ordo* and *curia*—which, apart from local administration, also were in charge of tax gathering. The highest officials in each town council were the two *duumviri*, who presided over the council and administered whatever jurisdiction the towns still preserved. Two imperial officials, the curator of the state finances and the *defensor*, had jurisdiction in smaller legal cases; greater cases would be brought before the provincial governor. The curator and the *defensor* were appointed or approved by the emperor. Their administration was supported by a number of lesser officials.

THE MILITARY ADMINISTRATION

The military administration in the provinces of Proconsularis, Byzacena, Numidia, Mauretania Sitifensis, and the eastern parts of Caesarensis was in the hand of the Count of Africa, with his seat in Carthage and under the master of the soldiers in Rome. The rest of Caesarensis, Tripolitania, and Tingitana were under separate commanders—*duces*—and in Tingitana, a *comes*. As in Gaul, a difference existed between the troops defending the border and the mobile army stationed farther inside the provinces. The borders of the provinces were separated into sections. Each section had a *castra*, or fortress, where the staff of the border troops in that section was stationed. The troops themselves were stationed in a number of smaller fortresses along the border. The troops guarding the border were called *limitanei* and were part-time peasants who farmed the lands attached to each garrison. The local troops were to handle the suppression of smaller war bands and brigands, and to perform what we now call police duties.

DEFENSES OF AFRICA

So what defenses were awaiting the Vandals in North Africa?

To aid us, we have the *Notitia Dignitatum*, a document from the early fifth century, which shows the administrative organization of the Eastern and Western empires, listing offices from the imperial court and the provinces as well as the units they commanded. It appears to describe the organization of the Western Empire around the 420s, and the Eastern Empire of the 400s. The *Notitia* lists the following forces stationed in North Africa under the Count of Africa:

> Three *legiones Palatinae* (paper strength around one thousand men each)
> One *auxilium Palatinum* (paper strength around five hundred men)
> One *legio pseudo-comitatensis* of uncertain name (paper strength around one thousand men)
> Seven *legiones comitatenses* (paper strength around one thousand men each)
> And nineteen vexillations of cavalry (paper strength around five hundred men each)

Furthermore, a considerable number of *limitanei*, probably mostly of barbarian origin, oversaw the long desert frontier, which was threatened by the restless Moors. The *Notitia Dignitatum* lists sixteen *limitanei* garrisons in Proconsular Africa, eight in Mauretania Caesariensis, and fourteen in Tripolitania of unknown strength. Together that made thirty-eight garrison units totaling perhaps at least ten thousand men, and thirty-one units of the field army with a paper strength of twenty-one thousand men. Of the thirty-one field army units, only four were top grade. However, the army was strong in cavalry, with a force of about nine thousand five hundred. In Mauretania Tingitana were units with a paper strength of four thousand soldiers. But not all the units in North Africa were at full strength. Some had been withdrawn to other theaters of war (such as fighting for the rebel Heraclianus in Italy in 413) and had not necessarily returned to their camps in North Africa or been brought up to strength. So it is impossible to ascertain the exact number of troops stationed in North Africa. But we hear from St. Augustine and the historian Olympiodorus that Bonifacius mainly had mercenary Visigoths as forces, and no regular Roman troops are mentioned. Furthermore the apparent strength of the Roman forces in North Africa can be misleading. The army was mainly constructed and positioned to absorb attacks from the desert and not from Spain. The possibility of Moorish raids made it dangerous to move *limitanei* from their border stations, and they were not first-class soldiers to begin with.

THE ROMAN FLEET

In the early empire, the defense of the African shores was entrusted to a detachment of the Syrian and Egyptian fleet, stationed in the harbor of Caesarea. It appears that this detachment was removed before the Vandal invasion, as we hear of no naval battles during that time. The fleet, which Heraclianus used in 413 to reach Italy, probably consisted of transports from the grain fleet, merchant ships from Carthage and the other great harbors of North Africa, and few or no warships. The *Notitia Dignitatum* speaks of no fleet in North Africa. However, we do know that the Roman navy operated in the Western Mediterranean against the Visigoths in Spain in 415. But in 425, it appears that the Vandals could raid the Balearic Isles without trouble.

ECONOMIC CONDITIONS

Ancient agriculture was limited in several ways, but mainly by the availability of labor and the ability to fertilize the ground. The productivity of a piece of land was not so much based on the soil itself, but more on how much labor was available to work it. Despite having quite advanced ideas on fertilizing the soil and many ways of doing so, the Romans were unable to greatly increase food production. Population levels naturally followed the level of food production, and these population levels were even dependent on locally available food, since land transport in antiquity was expensive. Transport depended on the ox, which was the most used draft animal in antiquity. Mules and donkeys were also used, but they could only pull smaller loads. A proper horse harness had not been invented, so horses were rarely used to pull wagons. Oxen, mules, and donkeys are slow animals, and having them pull loads meant having to feed them more. To put this into perspective, the transport figures in Diocletian's edict of maximum prices from 301 show that the price of a wagonload of wheat weighing twelve hundred pounds could double in about 180 miles. Shipping a load of grain from Egypt to Spain—some nineteen hundred miles—cost less than carting it seventy-five miles. In general, it appears that transport costs by sea, river, and land had an approximate relationship of 1:5:40 respectively. It was, therefore, not economic to transport anything but small and highly profitable objects over land. Because most of the necessities in antiquity, such as grain, timber, and pottery, were bulky or heavy, towns could not grow beyond what their own immediate hinterlands could provide, unless they had direct access to waterways and something to trade with. An example of the remarkable transport constraints is the major famine that broke out in Antioch in 362–363, despite the fact that grain was available only fifty miles away via a well-maintained Roman road. Only the direct intervention of the emperor saved the inhabitants from disaster.

These limitations meant the Roman economy could not develop much further than subsistence levels. The prevailing theory has been that the higher taxes of late antiquity further aggravated these conditions, meaning that life for the poor peasant population of the empire was very hard indeed. Our evidence comes mainly from historical sources documenting a fourth-century phenomenon known as the "flight of the *curiales.*" These *curiales* were the landowners wealthy enough to get a seat on their town councils (*curiae*). While a spot on the town council previously had been prestigious, the landowners in the fourth century became increasingly unwilling to serve on them. It appears that this was due to the administrative burden and costs, which the empire imposed on the *curiales.*

Accordingly, the rich landowners tried to avoid serving on the town councils, which caused the local towns to deteriorate. It appears from a number of imperial edicts that the behavior of North African *curiales* was the same as elsewhere. Laws of 373, 383, 395, 412, 413, and 429, addressed to the proconsuls of Africa, tried to deal with the standard attempts of *curiales* to evade their financial and official responsibilities.

Legal texts from the fourth century speak of the "*agri deserti*," or deserted lands. It is difficult to determine from the texts which lands they were, but a 422 law referring to North Africa indicates that three thousand square miles were included in this category. Most historians believe these were lands that peasants had left because of the tax burdens, which were increased partly to finance the defense against the Persian kingdom.

Other laws from the same period tried to bind certain categories of *coloni* to the estates where they were born, so they would not move. While there was still a distinction between *coloni* and slaves, their masters had great power over them, and a *colonus* who left the estate to which he was attached was committing a serious crime. Again, these various phenomena supported a theory that the heavy tax burden of the later empire made conditions so insufferable for the peasants that, on a large scale, they abandoned lands that had been under cultivation. This caused the deserted lands, to which the emperor then tried to bind the *coloni*. With fewer people to work the lands, less food was produced, and the general population became smaller over the years.

At the end of the 1950s, French archaeologist Georges Tchalenko began to challenge this established theory. He had surveyed lands in modern northern Syria, where a number of ancient villages had been found that could be shown to have been doing quite well in this period. Further surveys showed that this was not the only example, and that the central provinces of Roman North Africa, in particular Numidia, Byzacena, and Proconsularis, actually had a population and production increase at this time. It can now be shown that the only areas in which prosperity was not at or close to its maximum for the entire period of the Roman Empire were Italy and some of the northern European provinces, particularly Gallia Belgica and Germania Inferior, both on the Rhine frontier. Further surveys in modern southern Libya show that this period of prosperity only began to decline in the fifth century.

THE ROMAN CHURCH IN NORTH AFRICA

North Africa was a bastion of Christianity. The early ages of the religion brought such men of African birth as Tertullian, Cyprian of Carthage, Arnobius, Lactantius, and the great St. Augustine. One of the first translations of the Bible into Latin is believed to have been made by North African ecclesiastics. According to Joannes Lydus, a sixth century Roman administrator living in Constantinople, the North Africans in the early sixth century spoke Latin better than the inhabitants of Rome.

North Africa was partitioned into six church provinces, which followed the civilian administrative regions until the start of the fifth century; the only difference being that Tingitana was part of Mauretania Caesarensis, and not the Spanish diocese. The provinces were further partitioned into a great number of sees. Every province had its metropolitan, who was the bishop who had held his office the longest in the province. Only in Carthage was the bishop of the city automatically the metropolitan, no matter how long he had been bishop. The position of the North African church can be summed up in the belief of St. Augustine that the apostolic chair of Rome had great authority but was on the same level with the other sees. Only at the end of the fifth century, probably because of the persecutions of the Vandals, which had greatly weakened the church in North Africa, was it acknowledged that the bishop of Rome was the head of the North African bishops.

THE DONATISTS

The history of the church of North Africa is a troubled one. Nowhere else in the empire was sectarianism as abundant as in Africa. Donatism in particular was greatly influential because of its connection to politics and the agrarian population.

The Donatists were named after Moorish Bishop Donatus Magnus and followed a belief considered a schism by the Catholic Church. They lived in Roman North Africa, with their main seat in Numidia, and flourished in the fourth and fifth centuries. The main disagreement between the Donatists and the Catholics was over the treatment of those church leaders who renounced their faith during the Roman Emperor Diocletian's persecution of Christians in 303–305. These *traditores* ("people who have handed over"—the basis for the word "traitor") had returned to positions of authority under Constantine the Great, but the Donatists proclaimed that any sacraments celebrated by these priests and bishops were invalid, and therefore sacraments such as baptism administered by Christians who had turned over the Scriptures to the authorities to burn during persecutions were invalid. In the Donatists' eyes, there could be no forgiveness for such a sin, whereas the Catholic Church believed they should be forgiven.

The Donatist movement was born of opposition to the appointment of Caecilianus as bishop of Carthage. In 312, Caecilianus was consecrated by an alleged *traditor*, so his opponents consecrated a short-lived rival, who was succeeded by Donatus Magnus in 313. The Donatist beliefs became strong in North Africa, and Constantine the Great got involved in the dispute, calling the Council of Arelate in 314. The question of whether the acts of *traditores* were valid was debated, and Constantine decided against the Donatist belief, which was judged schismatic. The Donatists refused to accept his judgement. While the Catholics continued to see the emperor as their leader, the Donatists saw him as the devil and themselves as the true church in opposition to the

Catholics. In 317, the emperor sent troops to Carthage to suppress the Donatist movement. Persecutions of the Donatists ended in 321, but laws were issued against them by Valentinian I (364–375) after the defeat of the Donatist usurper Firmus in 375. The Donatists were suppressed through a persistent imperial campaign against them and the efforts of St. Augustine. Many Donatists converted, but the fire of their heresy continued to some extent, as is seen in the antiheresy laws of *Codex Theodosianus* in 428. Even in the sixth century, remnants of the Donatists were still to be found. They only disappeared in the seventh or eighth centuries, after the Arab conquest of North Africa. These religious troubles caused great weakness in Roman society at the time of the Vandal invasion.

CIRCUMCELLIONES, OR AGONISTICI

Another religious group in North Africa was the *circumcelliones*, as the Orthodox Catholics named them. The historical tradition around them is scanty and difficult to follow, but it seems they first appeared around 317 and claimed they were warriors of Christ. Their war cry was *"Laudes Deo"* ("Praises to God"). They were known for committing many violent deeds, and they called themselves *Agonistici* (fighters, a name that appears to stem from their belief that they were fighting for Christ). The Catholics called them *circumcelliones* (from *circum cellas euntes*) because they wandered about among the peasants. It appears that many of them were peasants themselves and were concerned with remedying social grievances, but they soon became linked with the Donatist sect. They opposed slavery and private property, and advocated canceling debts and freeing slaves.

In the sources, they also appear to have been closely connected to the Donatist worship of martyrs. The *circumcelliones* brought this worship to a fanatical level and saw martyrdom as the single true Christian virtue. The early church father Tertullian, who was from North Africa, had preached that "a martyr's death day was actually his birthday," and thus disagreed with the more common belief of the primacy of such virtues as chastity, sobriety, humility, and charity. So the *circumcelliones* sought their own martyrdom. They would attack travelers on the roads with their clubs in the hope that they would be killed during the assault. Other ways to achieve martyrdom would be to throw themselves over high cliffs. Another explanation of their name refers to their devotion to the martyr graves, which were sometimes termed *cellae*.

Pagan elements

Not only did the Christians cause unrest, but there were also still strong pagan elements in North Africa. In 408, long after the dominance of Christianity and the closing of all pagan temples and festivals, disturbances began in the city of Calama (Guelma in modern-day Algeria). Bishop Possidius, who later wrote a biography of St. Augustine, wanted to stop a planned pagan procession. In response, large parts of the population turned against him, plundered a local monastery and a nearby grain storage, and tried to set the Christian basilica on fire. A monk was killed during the unrest, and Possidius only narrowly managed to escape. While nothing more came of it, the incident shows the strength of the pagans in some of the North African regions.

The Moors

Outside the borders of the African provinces were the Berber—from the Latin *Barbari*, or as they were also known by the Romans, Moors (*Maurusi*). They lived in the mountains and steppes as well as the long stretches of deserts. Most of the tribes were nomadic and led a harsh life in the desert and supported themselves by raising livestock and raiding the Roman lands, but some were more settled and grew grain. The tribes were made up of various groups, including the blonde peoples now known as Maroccans and Cabyles. It has been suggested that these peoples are the descendants of Vandals and Moors, but there is no evidence to support this idea.

The tribes lived in poor huts and slept on the ground. They did not have bread or wine, and apart from meat and milk, they ate cakes made of barley or oats, which were baked in the hot ashes of their campfires. Militarily, they relied on surprise attacks and their massive numbers to overwhelm a foe. If this did not succeed, they were quick to retreat to their sanctuaries in the mountains or the desert. They were armed with javelins, swords, and small light shields. Their mobility was aided by horses—mainly used by the western tribes— and camels, which were much used by the tribes in Tripolitania.

Around the time of the birth of Christ, the historian Livy described an early second-century BC troop of Moorish cavalry:

> Horses and men were tiny and gaunt; the riders unequipped and unarmed, except that they carried javelins with them; the horses without bridles, their very motion being the ugly gait of animals running with stiff necks and outstretched heads.

There is no reason to suppose that this image had changed much by the fifth century.

Only by skillful use of the military forces at hand and by diplomatically playing the tribes against each other did the Romans succeed in keeping the Roman lands in North Africa generally unharmed. The tribes were often in loose subjection to the Romans, and many Moors did service in the Roman army as light infantry or light cavalry. The tribal chieftains were also accustomed to receiving their symbols of office from the Roman emperor. However, their allegiance to the Roman Empire became more and more loose, as the strength of the empire waned. Several great raids took place in the second half of the fourth century that troubled the outer provinces.

Firmus, the leader of a number of Moorish tribes, tried in 372 to take North Africa away from the empire with the support of the heretical Donatists. After taking all of Mauretania, he was defeated only with difficulty. Firmus's brother Gildo had supported the Romans in the struggle and in return was made count and master of all the troops in Africa (*comes et magister utriusque militae per Africam*). His main supporters were the tribes of the Nasamones, Garamantes, and Nazakes in Tripolitania. Later, in autumn 397, he, too, rebelled, with the support of the lower classes and Donatists in the Roman provinces. Gildo's first action of the rebellion was to stop the grain trade and threaten to starve Rome and Italy, and to declare allegiance to Constantinople. However, his brother Mascezel turned against him and turned the Moorish chieftains against him.

Also, after Bonifacius became Count of Africa in 423, he fought the Moorish tribes. Other raids threatened the Roman provinces in 428, just before the Vandal invasion, possibly because Bonifacius's attention was occupied with the struggle with Felix and his generals.

So Roman North Africa was in a serious state of disorganization at the start of the fifth century, because of the rebellions of Firmus and Gildo, religious unrest, and social problems. On top of this, with North Africa the only somewhat intact region of the Western Roman Empire, great demands were made on it to pay for the survival of the rest of the Western Empire, which was being swamped by barbarians. After the execution of Stilicho in 408, little stood between the Visigoths and Rome, which fell to King Alaric on August 24, 410. With refugees streaming from Italy bringing news of the fall of the capital, the anti-Christian forces gained credence for their beliefs that it was a punishment for abandoning the faith in the gods. In 410, possibly in response to general unrest, the tax arrears of the North African provinces were canceled. Due to further religious unrest, a Council of Carthage was held in June 411, in which 286 Catholic bishops and 279 Donatist bishops participated. There the Donatists were finally condemned, and severe laws were passed against them.

However, it was not enough. In 412, Heraclianus, the Count of Africa, was growing worried that he would be called back to Italy to answer for misadministration. His revolt began by restricting the food supply of Italy and was aimed at causing famine in Rome. He then brought his fleet of three thousand seven hundred ships—probably mainly transports from the grain fleets—against Italy to depose Emperor Honorius. But he was defeated at Ocriculum (Otricoli in modern-day Italy) and forced to flee to North Africa. In summer 413, he was captured and beheaded there. His revolt was also blamed on the Donatists, who were further persecuted.

The Vandals invade Africa

By May 429, the Vandals and Alans had gathered their tribes, and they set sail from Julia Traducta (Tarifa) in Roman fishing and merchant vessels and sailed across to the coast of Africa to Tingis or Septem Fratres (Ceuta), both in Mauretania Tingitana. Septem Fratres was the most likely landing site, only about seventeen and a half miles from Spain, and from there they could march farther on the Roman road along the coast toward Proconsularis. It is not likely, as some modern historians believe, that they split their forces and landed at both Tingis and Septem Fratres, as this would divide their strength too much at a critical point in the campaign. The forces landing at Tingis would have to go far south to cross the pass of Taza before being able to unite with the forces landing at Septem Fratres and marching on the coast road. The belief that the Vandals first landed at Tingis and later sailed to Septem Fratres because no land road existed has been disproved by archaeological finds, including a military station in the pass of Taza and inscriptions. Unfortunately, we get no hint from the sources on where exactly they landed.

It appears that there were simply not enough ships to enable the Vandals to move farther than just crossing to Africa. The numbers given by Procopius from the later invasion of Africa in 533 show that each ship carried about seventy men plus horses and supplies. Geiseric would, therefore, have required more than one thousand ships to ferry his people over in one go. But in the 460s, the expedition of Emperor

Vandal landings in North Africa.

Majorian could raise only about three hundred ships, despite gathering them from the whole of the Western Empire. In 468, it took the combined Roman Empire to gather a fleet of one thousand ships. With only the coastal province of Baetica under control, Geiseric had nothing like that at his disposal, and so would have to ferry his people across the straits. No doubt the lack of ships available to carry horses and the logistical nightmare involved made this the only option.

Transferring the Vandal people, as well as wagons and supplies, probably took around one month of ferrying back and forth. We cannot expect that there was any significant Roman resistance in Mauretania Tingitana. Most likely the few Roman garrisons would stay behind their walls and wait for the Vandals to move on.

Although we are not told so by the sources, it is possible that some fleet elements followed the Vandal tribes along the coast to facilitate supplies in the more deserted regions. We know that later at the siege of Hippo Regius, the Vandals had acquired some ships. Possibly the use of ships would also explain their ease in taking the many coastal cities along their way.

The literary sources on the movements of the Vandals are scant, but archaeological evidence suggests that the main group continued its march on the coastal road. If they marched from Tingis, the Vandals probably moved along the road to the towns of Lixus (near Larache in modern-day Morocco), Volubilis (near Meknes in modern-day Morocco), Numerus Syrorum (close to Maghnia in modern-day Algeria), and Pomaria (Tlemcen in modern-day Algeria). From there they went over the pass of Taza and on to Altava (near Ouled Mimoun in modern-day Algeria)—in total a distance of some 435 miles. If they took the coast road from Altava, it was about 745 miles to Hippo Regius, which would take about seven months. If the Vandals landed at Septem Fratres, they would have saved more than 130 miles on the march to Altava. The troubles of supplying such a multitude in one place probably caused the tribes to split up soon after the landing and move in several columns. By using the coastal road from Septem Fratres, the supply situation would have been eased somewhat.

Unfortunately, the sources say almost nothing of the long journey across North Africa. However, French historians have calculated that the Vandals moved east toward Hippo Regius at a rate of about three and a half miles a day. This must be considered quite fast indeed over such a long period. No doubt there were skirmishes or small sieges along the way, and because the Vandals were a horse people, just grazing would have taken much time. Foraging for food would also be time-consuming. The noncombatants probably traveled in ox-drawn carriages or walked. As a comparison, a day's march of the Roman army in the fifth century was around twelve and a half miles on road. Only by detaching pack animals could it be increased, and it could not be done over an extended period. According to a sermon of Bishop Ambrose of Mediolanum, the Roman army marched for three days and rested on the fourth. So altogether, the march was long and arduous, and made at quite a quick pace for such a multitude. Even with the support of the ships, the more than 1,250-mile trek across North Africa must have been hard indeed, especially as it was not only an army that traveled but women and children as well. The migration must have cost great losses among the weakest, as well as among the horses and domestic animals.

The Vandals arrived in Altava between August 14 and September 1, 429, as dated by an inscription that records the death of a provincial "by barbarian sword." The term "barbarian" must have referred to the Vandals, because the local Moors were generally known by their tribal names rather than as barbarians. From Altava, the Vandals turned toward the sea and plundered their way through Tasacora, Portus Magnus, Cartenna, Caesarea, Icosium (Algiers), Auzia (Aumale), Sitifis (Sétif), Cirta (Constantine), Calama, Thagaste (Souk Ahras), Sicca Veneria (El Kef), and Thuburbo Maius (Kasbat). The local inhabitants were killed or taken as slaves, and their villas and houses burned. The Catholic churches and monasteries were also sacked. Papal rescripts—responses of the pope to questions of individuals—written shortly after the invasion make it clear that those who did not manage to flee the barbarians faced death or mutilation, and one rescript regards the status of consecrated virgins who had been raped during the invasion.

It appears that the towns and cities fell easily, probably because of a lack of provisions and garrisons. Some cities did not have walls and so fell more easily. We might be surprised at the success of the Vandals, who had no previous knowledge of taking fortified cities. According to Victor of Vita, the Vandals piled corpses around the walls to force the inhabitants to surrender because of the stench and disease. This seems unlikely, however, because the Roman authorities would know that corpses posed no danger of disease from beyond city walls. The Vandals may have used the local population as living shields when they assaulted the walls, and theirs may be the corpses Victor describes as having been piled up around the walls.

No doubt as in the case of other barbarian invasions, the Vandals were joined by runaway slaves and the lower classes, who saw a way to change their conditions. This might cause treachery in the cities and aid the besieging Vandals. We also see evidence of the Vandals making full use of their cavalry to ride fast and attempt to surprise the Roman cities. While conducting the military campaign, Geiseric also had to ensure supplies for perhaps more than sixty thousand noncombatants—a number swelled by deserters, slaves, Arians, Donatists, and *coloni*. No doubt ships were also used to ease the supply situation.

By the early part of 430, only Cirta and Hippo Regius had managed to hold the walls against the Vandals, but a Vandal attempt at surprising the garrison of Carthage had failed. The rest of the cities had been sacked, and Cirta would soon fall, but we do not know exactly when. After the failed attempt on Carthage, a part of the Vandals turned south into Byzacena, which they raided in the second half of 430, and the main body turned back toward Hippo Regius, over Utica, Hippo Diarrhytus, and Thabraca. In the region of Hippo Regius, Count Bonifacius felt strong enough to meet the Vandals in open battle with the forces of North Africa and his bodyguard, but he was defeated and had to retreat into the city itself. Bonifacius might have had troubles with his Germanic troops (mainly Visigoths) being Arian, and thus perhaps ready to desert to the Vandals.

The Vandals pursued Bonifacius, arrived before the walls of Hippo Regius at the end of May or June 430, and immediately initiated a siege. Bonifacius's aim was to delay the Vandals—who were forced to continually move to keep their unwieldy mass of noncombatants fed—and wait for possible support from Rome and the Eastern Empire. For Geiseric, this was the opportunity to destroy the Roman commander in North Africa with most of his troops, taking the second city of North Africa and a great harbor to secure his supplies.

St. Augustine

Hippo Regius was the city of the bishop Augustine and the place where he wrote his many books, including his greatest work, *The City of God* (*De Civitate Dei*). He was informed of the Vandal invasion and told of the burnings, the massacres, the torn-up fruit trees, and the devastated churches. Many bishops asked him whether to stay or flee to safer places. Possidius, the bishop of Calama who was with Augustine and later wrote a life of the saint, has him saying as his first advice, "Remain with your flocks and share their miseries." North African Bishop Honoratus argued against this in a letter to Augustine: "What is the use of our remaining, whilst before our eyes the men are murdered, the women raped, the churches burned, and then to be tortured ourselves, to make us disclose the hiding places of treasures which we have not?"

The bishops pleaded the words of Christ, "When they persecute you in one city, flee into another." Augustine reflected on the examples of Cyprian and Athanasius, who had for a time left their sees, and with some hesitation and some limitations, he consented to the request. We may or may not believe that these were the words of Augustine, but they give a sense of the desperation felt by the Roman provincials at the time. Augustine would die on August 28, 430, in the third month of the siege, at age seventy-six. He had often said that a Christian should not depart the world except in a state of profound penitence for all sins committed after baptism, and so as he lay on his deathbed, he had the penitential Psalms of David copied for him by his friends and set up on the walls in front of his bed so he could look at them constantly. He also ordered that nobody should enter his bedchamber except the doctor and the boy bringing his meals so he could use all his waking thought in prayer. In this fashion, perhaps the most influential of the church fathers passed away with the Vandals besieging the walls around him.

For fourteen months, from May 430 to July 431, the Vandals besieged Hippo. But the defense was successful, probably because of the Vandals' lack of skill in taking walls and because of their lack of means to provision any greater force in the same place for an extended period. Burdened with so many noncombatants, the Vandals were forced to live off the land and so could not stay long in the same region. The fact that they could maintain the siege of Hippo for so long is a testament to the fertility of the African provinces. And so, pressed by famine, the Vandals broke off the siege in July 431.

The conditions at the time are described in the writings of Bishop Capreolus of Carthage, who had to explain to the bishops at the Synod of Ephesus on June 22, 431, why none of the North African bishops could attend:

> For the prompt ability of any that could travel is impeded by the excessive multitude of enemies and the huge devastation of the provinces everywhere which presents to eye-witnesses one place where all its inhabitants have been killed, another where they have been driven into flight, and a wretched vista of destruction spreading out far and wide and in every direction.

END OF BONIFACIUS

The Western Romans responded to the desperate situation of North Africa, and in 432 sent large forces to relieve Bonifacius. These were joined by forces sent from the Eastern Roman Empire under a young but veteran chief general, Aspar, who was of Alan descent. With the added forces and the unsuccessful siege of Hippo Regius, Bonifacius and Aspar tried to decide the war with a pitched battle in front of the walls of Carthage in 432. But the Romans were again defeated by the Vandal light cavalry and the military ability of Geiseric. Procopius alone mentions this battle, so it might have been only a skirmish.

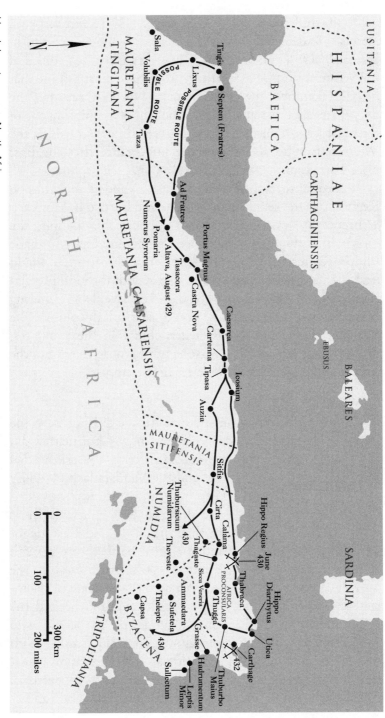

Vandal route across North Africa.

Bonifacius was recalled to Rome in 432 to face his rival Aetius. He defeated Aetius but died of wounds incurred in the battle. On January 1, 434, Aspar was appointed consul of the Western Empire in Carthage, and so we must assume that he had taken over the government of North Africa after the departure of Bonifacius. The symbolism of appointing one of the most important men of the Eastern Empire consul of the Western Empire also shows the importance that the East placed on keeping North Africa Roman.

According to Bishop Possidius, the Vandals took Hippo Regius after the setback at Carthage and burned it. However, archaeological evidence does not support this. Despite the sack, which might not have been so severe, Geiseric made Hippo Regius his residence. Until 435, the Vandals would lead an inconclusive war against Aspar, with the local population of North Africa being killed and enslaved, and suffering from famine. The Vandals would particularly punish the Catholic clergy and the Roman nobility in the provinces, probably not for religious reasons but because they were the richest and staunchest supporters of the empire.

Peace with the Romans

The court at Ravenna understood that it did not have the power to defeat the Vandals—at least now—but neither did the Vandals have the power to take Carthage. Geiseric needed to consolidate his conquests, and the Vandals' lack of ability to take city walls would keep him out of the well-defended Carthage indefinitely. According to Procopius, Geiseric reflected on the possibility that the West and East might again unite against him and that two battles were enough chances taken, as a single defeat could prove fatal to the Vandal cause. It can also be speculated that despite his victories, casualties must also have been heavy, and he had the responsibility of all the noncombatants of his people, who were probably suffering from almost constant famine. With war in the provinces going on for so long, provisions must have been exceedingly scarce, and again, as it appeared in Spain, there was nowhere else to go to find food. The Vandals

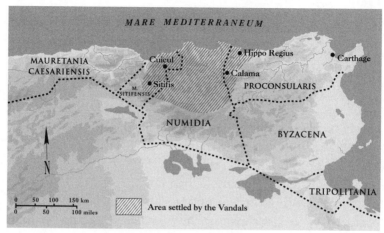

Area under Vandal Rule at the peace of 435.

had to settle in North Africa or be destroyed, and peace for even a few years would secure their hold over the Roman lands. The years of warfare had also depleted his warriors. After three years of stalemate, on February 11, 435 (some sources say 436), peace was concluded in Hippo Regius between the West Romans and Vandals. The conditions were apparently these:

+ Carthage was to be left free of raids.

+ Part of the proconsular province taken by the Vandals that lay immediately around Carthage was to pay a yearly tribute to the Romans (probably including grain and olive oil for Rome).

+ The Vandals were allowed to live as Roman federates in the regions already conquered (which was probably the remainder of the proconsular province, Byzacena, and Numidia; the Mauretanias and Tripolitania appear to have stayed Roman).

As in Spain, the Vandals were most likely billeted according to the rules of *hospitalitas*, that is, the Roman regulations for quartering soldiers, and so received housing and an amount of the local taxes for their support. The main part of the Vandals was settled in Numidia, close to the sea and with Hippo Regius the seat of King Geiseric. Aspar most likely left North Africa when the treaty was made in 435, as he was needed for other tasks in the East.

Only two years after the peace, trouble arose with the Catholics. Some bishops had disturbed the Arians in their church services, and Geiseric punished the unruly Catholic churchmen—including Possidius of Calama and the Bishops Novatus of Sitifis and Severianus of Cera—with banishment. As a Roman federate he had no jurisdiction over them, but this shows how little it meant to be a federate in the fifth century—to a large extent, the Vandals could do as they pleased. Although no systematic persecution of Catholics had begun, Geiseric tested the loyalty of five noble Romans who had joined his court while the Vandals were residing in Spain. He asked them to show their faith and loyalty to him by converting to Arianism. The nobles—Arcadius, Probus, Paschasius, Eutycianus, and Paulillus—refused to convert, so their properties were confiscated and they were banished. When they tried to return from banishment, four were tortured to death. While religion officially was the cause, there were no doubt other, underlying reasons, and Geiseric had to put down any possible traitors or power factions that might conspire against him.

The Vandals seem to have been somewhat restless in their new settlements, as they raided Sicily by sea in 438. This also shows that the Vandals were using ships again, no doubt crewed by Roman sailors, willingly or unwillingly. In 2001, excavations of Olbia in Sicily revealed a fleet of eleven cargo ships, dated from the fifth century, that had been burned in the harbor, which might be a remnant of the 438 Vandal raid or later ones. That the Romans were well aware of the danger of the restless Vandals is seen from a sermon by Quodvultdeus, bishop of Carthage, sometime after the peace of 435:

> You [the Vandals] do not believe in keeping the true
> faith of the universal church, you who teach that faith

with the Romans is not to be kept. . . . Even now you know what you are: of what sort you are you make evident. Do you wish to know what you are? While you avoid or cast off the struggles to lend assistance, you are neither brave in war, nor are you faithful in peace.

CAPTURE OF CARTHAGE, 439

The troubles for the Western Roman Empire continued. While Aetius managed with Hunnish help to destroy the Burgundian kingdom on the Rhine in 436–437, the Visigoths were also active, and in 439, Roman General Litorius was severely defeated at Tolosa in Gaul. This setback enabled the Sueves in Spain to take the former Vandal provinces of Baetica and Carthaginiensis, which were fully occupied by 441.

All in all, Aetius's achievements during the 430s were prodigious. Franks and Alamanni were pushed back into their cantons beyond the Rhine, the Burgundians and Bagaudae were thoroughly subdued, the Visigoths' pretensions were reined in, and much of Spain was returned to imperial control. For good reason, then, Aetius was considered by some to be the last true Roman of the West. The connection between the two parts of the empire was further strengthened on October 29, 437, when Valentinian III married Licinia Eudoxia, daughter of Theodosius II, at Constantinople. Before returning to Rome, he ceded the city of Sirmium in Illyricum to Theodosius. But then Carthage fell in 439.

While the West Romans with Aetius at their head were fighting the Visigoths in southern Gaul, Geiseric suddenly attacked Carthage and took it on October 19, 439. One explanation for the ease of the city's capture is that the Romans were taken by surprise, expecting that the barbarians would keep the treaty. But the Romans had a great deal of experience with the barbarians' disregard for treaties if they were not backed up by brute strength. A more logical explanation might be that there was too small a garrison guarding Carthage due to the other troubles of the Western Empire at the time.

The city was sacked and suffered the usual atrocities. A sermon by Bishop Quodvultdeus just after the taking of Carthage describes the scene:

> Where is Africa, which was for the whole world like a garden of delights? . . . Has our city [Carthage] not been punished cruelly because she did not want to draw a lesson from the correction handed out to the other provinces? . . . There is no one to bury the bodies of the dead, but horrible death has soiled all the streets and all the buildings, the whole city indeed. And think on the evils we are talking about! Mothers of families dragged off into captivity; pregnant women slaughtered . . . babies taken from the arms of their nurse and thrown to die on the street. . . . The impious power of the barbarians has even demanded that those women who were once mistresses of many servants, have suddenly become the vile servants of barbarians. . . . Every day there comes to our ears the cries of those who have lost in this assault a husband or a father.

While the quote contains the usual theme on the sacking of a city, this sermon was given to the people who actually experienced it. No doubt it would have to contain at least some measure of truth.

Again, those treated most harshly appear to have been the Catholic clergy and the Roman nobility, probably because they were the classes who most resisted the Vandals and had the most riches to take. In 439 or 440, all property of the Catholic Church was confiscated, and the clergy, including Bishop Quodvultdeus, were put on badly maintained ships and sent to Italy. According to Victor of Vita, it was expected that the ships would sink and so rid the Vandals of the bishops. The nobility was mostly banished. No doubt Geiseric recognized the danger of having a strong Roman nobility in what he intended to make his capital. Among the exiled senators was Gordianus (the grandfather of St. Fulgentius), whose sons later returned to North Africa and got back from the Vandal king the family lands in Byzacena.

The churches were sacked, but later, in 455, when Bishop Deogratias ransomed Roman captives by selling the church plate—church objects made of precious metals—it had clearly been replaced already. All the churches in Carthage were closed, and some—including the Basilica Restituta, the Cathedral of Carthage, and the Basilica Maiorum—were given with their properties to the Arian priests.

So important was the capture of Carthage to the Vandals that October 19, 439, was made the start of a new Vandal calendar, as year 1. The Vandals now also controlled one of the busiest ports of the Mediterranean, and they would make full use of the ships, shipyards, and maritime experience available there. After thirty-nine years of migration, the Vandals were now undisputed masters of North Africa, and Geiseric seems for the first time to be entitled King of Africa. The Vandals had found a new homeland, which they would occupy until the end of their existence as an independent people. The Romans saw the danger of this new kingdom. According to the Paschal Chronicle (*Chronicon Paschale*, a seventh century Byzantine chronicle of the world), in 439, Emperor Theodosius II had walls built on the seaward side of Constantinople, possibly in response to the Vandal threat. Such an action seems a very fast response to the taking of Carthage, and it might also have been in response to the peace of 435, or the Vandal raid on Sicily in 438.

FOUR

The Vandals in North Africa

"So the Vandals, having wrested Libya from the Romans in this way, made it their own. And those of the enemy whom they took alive, they reduced to slavery and held under guard."—*Procopius, mid-sixth century, describing the defeat of Bonifacius and Aspar before the walls of Carthage in 432*

The Western Empire had been subjected to severe barbarian invasions since the start of the fifth century. Every devastated province and every loss of territory—even temporary—reduced the revenue of the empire, which it needed to maintain its armies. Gaul had been sacked repeatedly since 406 and produced little revenue. The invasion of rich and unplundered Spain in 409 was a severe blow from which it had not recovered. Now the most important parts of North Africa, which was the greatest source of revenue to the Western Empire, had been lost too. The Western Empire was facing an acute financial crisis. Expenses were soaring and the tax base dwindling. Even the landowning elites, the rulers of the Roman state, faced a new reality. Their main incomes were based on their land holdings, spread all over the empire, and it was now apparent that their interests were best served by making an accommodation with the Germanic federates settled in the provinces.

The financial disaster for the empire and the importance of the loss of revenue can be traced in the laws of the following years. In 440–441, the empire sought to maximize the remaining existing revenues. A law dated January 24, 440, withdrew all existing special imperial grants of tax exemption or reduction. A law of June 4 the same year aimed to curtail the practice of imperial officials taking an extra percentage for themselves when collecting taxes.

On March 14, 441, it was decreed that lands that had been rented annually from the imperial properties, with tax privileges attached, were now to be assessed at the normal rate, as were all church lands. The law also reduced the privileges of the higher dignitaries by removing their exemptions from a number of burdens, such as "the building and repair of military roads, the manufacture of arms, the restoration of city walls, the provision of the annona [in this case, most likely subsidies paid to barbarian kings in return for their cooperation], and the rest of the public works through which we achieve the splendor of public defense." Emperor Valentinian III was frank in his justification:

> The emperors of a former age ... bestowed such privileges on persons of illustrious rank in the opulence of an abundant era, with less disaster to the other landowners. ... However, in the difficulty of the present time, this practice is obviously not only inequitable, but also ... impossible.

THE IMPORTANCE OF THE NORTH AFRICAN GRAIN SUPPLY

Valentinian III and Aetius, who actually governed the Western Empire, were forced to take a number of desperate steps to finance the empire and its defense. With chiefly the Huns and the Visigoths pressing the remaining provinces, the West needed a great army. The important trade in the Mediterranean was disrupted by the loss of Carthage and the raids of the Vandal pirates. Furthermore, the loss of North Africa cut off the essential grain supply to Rome and left only Sicily and Sardinia to feed the population of Rome.

To what degree Italy and Rome depended on the grain of Africa is shown by the wars between Vespasian and Vitellius in 69, and Septimius Severus and Pescennius Niger in 193–194. Vespasian planned to take Italy only after taking North Africa and Egypt, the two main suppliers of grain. Septimius Severus sent an army to North Africa to avoid its occupation by Pescennius Niger. In 395, the rebel governor Gildo closed the African harbors for grain trade with Italy, and the same was done during the rebellion of Heraclianus in 412–413.

Despite the depopulation of Rome after the sack in 410, Rome was still the greatest city of Europe, with more than five hundred thousand inhabitants. But with the grain supply at best disrupted, the population no doubt decreased more and more. Feeding this population was difficult, as large numbers still qualified for free daily rations of bread, olive oil, and wine. The enormous ports of Rome—such as Ostia, Portus, and Tibur—show the scale of import that was needed. On the other side of the Mediterranean, continuing excavations at Carthage by the United Nations Educational, Scientific and Cultural Organization (UNESCO), which started in 1974, show the huge port facilities needed for the grain and olive oil ships for Rome. With the grain and olive oil supplies in the hands of the Vandals, the Western Empire could be held hostage at their pleasure.

THE VANDALS STRIKE FIRST

Because of the pressure from the Huns and Visigoths, the Western Romans could not do anything immediately, but instead asked the Eastern Romans for help to retake North Africa and restore the fortunes of the empire. The marriage of Valentinian III and Licinia Eudoxia in 437 worked to the West's advantage, and help was promised. But the collection of an army would take time.

While the Western Romans were considering their options, Geiseric struck. He knew they could not accept the loss of their main source of revenue and food for Rome, so he prepared himself for a counterstrike by striking first. Again Geiseric showed his strategic insight and ability. To protect his people against the Romans in the best manner, he needed a fleet. Despite their lack of seafaring knowledge, the Vandals became the first Germanic tribe to maintain a fleet and soon possessed the most formidable navy in the Western Mediterranean. The basis for the fleet were probably cargo ships and warships captured in the surprise attack on Carthage, supplemented by ships brought from the migration from Spain and the other parts of North Africa, as well as new ships built in the great shipyards of Carthage. The crews were native Romans, but the officers may have been Vandals. Perhaps Geiseric was inspired by the expeditions undertaken to the Balearic Isles and the invasion of North Africa, both conducted in borrowed ships. His quick action also proves there must have been a number of ships readily available.

By striking at Sardinia and Sicily, and further controlling the grain supply for the Western Empire, Geiseric could secure the existence of the Vandal kingdom. As the Vandal king collected his great fleet in the harbor of Carthage, Valentinian III granted a special license to Eastern traders on March 3, 440, to guarantee food supplies for the city of Rome. Also that month, the emperor ordered the repair of the walls and towers of Rome, and master of the soldiers Sigisvultus began making preparations to defend the coast. Inscriptions have been found recording the repair of the fortifications of Neapolis (Naples in modern-day Italy) and the walls of Terracina from the 440s—no doubt all part of Sigisvultus's efforts.

A crisis was looming, and on March 20, the emperor issued another law asking for recruits for the army and threatening anyone who harbored deserters with severe punishment. The Western Romans did not know where the Vandal fleet would make landfall, and on June 24, 440, an imperial edict was sent out authorizing the inhabitants across the empire to once again carry weapons and to be ready to defend themselves. Furthermore, they were to support the army of Aetius and the troops of the Eastern Empire moving to the defense of the West. The inhabitants of the empire had been kept unarmed for centuries to avoid unrest, so this was indeed a desperate measure. The law explained that the carrying of arms was necessary "because it is not sufficiently certain, under summertime opportunities for navigation, to what shore the ships of the enemy can come."

Sicily was the Vandals' goal. They landed, presumably at Lilybaeum (Marsala), the nearest point to Carthage, without encountering any significant resistance. After capturing the city, they marched, plundering through the island, and besieged Panormus (Palermo), which put up stiff resistance. According to Hydatius, local Catholics were persecuted. War bands even entered the region of Bruttium in south Italy, where they were stopped by a defense organized by the local magnates.

It was probably never Geiseric's plan to incorporate Sicily into his kingdom. The island did not suffer any permanent damage, particularly not the countryside, and by the 490s it was again supplying Italy and Rome with grain. In 441, however, the emperor was forced to remit six-sevenths of the Sicilian taxes because of the Vandal devastations, furthering the economic troubles of the empire.

Vandal raids

From this time until Geiseric's death in 477, the Vandals made the coasts of Italy, Sicily, Illyricum, the Peloponnesus, and the islands of the Aegean unsafe by their piratical raids. Even Gallaecia in Spain was raided. Procopius tells the story that once, when the fleet was lying ready in the harbor of Carthage, Geiseric came limping down from his palace. When he entered his ship, the pilot asked for orders where to go. "Plainly against those with whom God is angry," he replied, and left the goal to be decided by the winds and the currents.

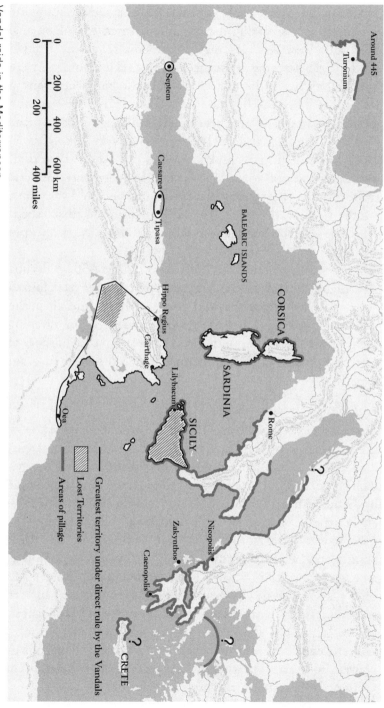

Vandal raids in the Mediterranean.

As we have seen, the Vandals did not suddenly appear overnight as a seafaring nation. The seamen were Romans. The raids were troublesome for the empire, as the Roman border defenses now could be bypassed. The Romans were also well aware of the danger of seaborne barbarians, and a law in the Theodosian code promised to burn alive anyone teaching barbarians the art of shipbuilding. Most of the recorded Vandal naval exploits were raids in Viking style: quick hit-and-run attacks, with forces put ashore to raid an area before troops could be collected against them. Geiseric made a point of attacking places that did not hold garrisons. At the time of the great Roman expedition against North Africa in 468, the Vandals had more than forty years of experience in naval operations.

In a poem recited on New Year's Day 456, Sidonius Apollinaris described the Vandals' coastal raids as a fourth Punic War, coming as they did from Carthage. Initially in the years after taking Carthage, Geiseric focused on ravaging Sicily, probably because it was closest to the harbor of Carthage and it allowed him to damage the Roman grain supply.

THE SEBASTIANUS AFFAIR

News reached Geiseric in Sicily of the arrival of Sebastianus, the son-in-law of Bonifacius, in Carthage. After Bonifacius died in 432, Sebastianus took over his position as *magister militum praesentalis* but was soon forced to flee to Constantinople by Aetius. After an exile in Constantinople, Sebastianus traveled to the Visigothic King Theodoric in Toulouse, where he tried to get some position at court, without success. As it turned out, Sebastianus did not come to Carthage in 440 as an enemy, but as a fugitive. He had landed in North Africa to offer his services to Geiseric. No doubt his previous history caused Geiseric to mistrust him and consider him a danger to his kingship. On the advice of one of his Arian bishops, Geiseric, who had returned from Sicily, asked Sebastianus to convert to Arianism to show his faith. When he refused, Geiseric later had him executed on a pretext.

THE ROMAN COUNTERSTRIKE

The expected Eastern Roman fleet arrived at Sicily in 441. It consisted of one thousand one hundred ships carrying a great army of perhaps twenty-five thousand troops. Pentadius, the Roman official in charge of the logistics of the expedition, was later promoted for dealing with the enormous administrative task of dispatching the expedition. Its aim was to retake North Africa, or at least curb the piratical Vandals. The Western Empire appeared to have been saved from the brink of disaster. But the army was commanded by five generals—Areobindus, Ansila, Inobindus, Arintheus, and Germanus—who spent their time idly quarreling about the conduct of the campaign and accomplished nothing during the year. In 442, the Persians and, especially, the terrifying Huns under Attila and Bleda were threatening the borders of the Eastern Roman Empire, and the army was recalled without having done anything in Sicily. The Hun invasion required Aetius's attention for a long period. Aspar, who had crossed swords with the Vandals in the early 430s, commanded the Eastern troops facing the Hun invasion in 442–443. Northeastern Illyricum was devastated, and possibly also parts of Thrace. Because of the Vandal threat, which had the highest priority for the Eastern Empire, Theodosius II was forced to conduct a weak policy toward the Huns. For his lack of success against the Huns, Aspar himself temporarily lost favor with the emperor, who kept him from any important military commands until the end of his reign.

THE PEACE OF 442

With no support from Constantinople and new and more urgent barbarian troubles, Western Emperor Valentinian III was forced to make peace with Geiseric in 442. The peace acknowledged Geiseric's control of the richest provinces of North Africa. The Vandals were given Proconsularis, Byzacena, and parts of Numidia and Tripolitania; the great city of Hippo Regius; and Gaetulia (probably a name for the southern parts of Byzacena). In return, Geiseric agreed to continue to supply North African grain to Italy from the provinces now controlled by the Vandals. The peace with Valentinian III probably did not keep Geiseric from raiding other parts of the Mediterranean coasts.

From imperial edicts and Victor of Vita we are informed that the devastated provinces of Mauretania Caesarensis and Sitifensis, parts of Numidia around Cirta, as well as Tripolitania remained Roman. Legal evidence confirms that the empire was subsequently administering the three Mauretanias—Tingitana, Caesarensis, and Sitifensis—and the easternmost part of Numidia. Although our main source for this peace, Victor of Vita, does not mention it, the Vandals also probably took control of the coastal strip of western Tripolitania. In 435, the Vandal lands had been surrounded by Roman lands, but by 442 that was no longer the case.

By acknowledging the right of the Vandals to the provinces, the Western emperor recognized the independence of the Vandal kingdom. From an "enemy of our empire," in a Roman law of June 24, 440, after 442 Geiseric had become a formally recognized client king of the empire, with the title *Rex Socius et Amicus*: Allied King and Friend. But after the peace of 442 and until the death of Valentinian III in 455, the Western Romans still spoke ill of the Vandals and their devastations. They even mention in laws that the North African lands must be retaken as soon as possible.

This was the first fully independent Germanic kingdom established on former Roman soil. In return, Geiseric gave his son, Huneric, as a hostage to the Romans to seal the peace. It has been suggested that Huneric had already been given as a hostage in connection with the peace of 435, but most historians now believe it happened in 442. In 442–443, Huneric was betrothed to Eudocia, a daughter of Valentinian III's—clearly a political engagement, as Eudocia was only five years old when the treaty was signed. In 445 or 446, Huneric was returned. The betrothal was a massive break with tradition, as it was the first legitimate marriage contemplated between barbarian royalty and the imperial family. It also shows how important the grain of Africa was to the ailing Western Empire.

The Vandal kingdom

Geiseric now settled his Vandals and Alans in Proconsularis and Carthage, probably to occupy this richest province and keep the Vandal army together and ready for war and expeditions. Few Vandals settled elsewhere in the kingdom.

We do not know much about how the Vandal kingdom functioned administratively. Procopius says:

> And among the Libyans all who happened to be men of note and conspicious for their wealth he handed over as slaves, together with their estates and all their money, to his sons Huneric and Genzon. . . . And he robbed the rest of the Libyans of their estates, which were both very numerous and excellent, and distributed them among the nation of the Vandals, and as a result of this these lands have been called the Vandal Allotments [*Sortes Vandalorum*] up to the present time. And it fell to the lot of those who had formerly possessed these lands to be in extreme poverty and to be at the same time free men; and they had the privilege of going away wheresoever they wished. And Geiseric commanded that all the lands which he had given over to his sons and to the other Vandals should not be subject to any kind of taxation. But as much of the land as did not seem to him good he allowed to remain in the hands of the former owners, but assessed so large a sum to be paid on this land for taxes to the government that nothing whatever remained to those who retained their farms. And many of them were constantly being sent into exile or killed. For charges were brought against them of many sorts, and heavy ones too; but one charge seemed to be the greatest of all, that a man, having money of his own, was hiding it. Thus the Libyans were visited with every form of misfortune.

Procopius is supplemented by Victor of Vita on the question of the land settlement: "He [Geiseric] also made an arrangement concerning the individual provinces: Byzacena, Abaritana and Gaetulia, and part of Numidia he kept for himself; Zeugitana and the proconsular province he divided up as an allotted portion for his people."

Although the proconsular province was the smallest of the African provinces, it was doubtless the richest. A province named Abaritana is not known, but it was probably a small district in the proconsular province.

What Procopius and Victor of Vita describe is the great royal domain of the king. As we see from Victor, this consisted of almost the whole of Numidia and Byzacena, as well as part of Proconsularis. These lands were cultivated by slaves and their former masters, the great Roman landowners. Thus the wealthy aristocracy was reduced to servitude, probably not as farmhands but as overseers and stewards. These lands were probably mainly part of the imperial *fisc*—the lands of the Roman emperor. Slaves and tenants merely changed masters, and probably did not notice much difference. It might even be speculated that the slaves and some of the *coloni* did not view the Vandal invasion as a threat to their livelihood, but as a path to improving their conditions. The enormous royal lands created the financial and social foundation for the Hasding royal family and cemented its power over the nobles. The role and position of the king in Vandal society had changed radically.

The second class of lands was the so-called Vandal Allotments, which were divided, along with cattle, slaves, and *coloni*, among the Vandal warriors. The estates were hereditary, as we hear from Victor of Vita, but probably carried with them the obligation to serve in the royal army. They were exempt from taxes. For the *coloni*, there was only the difference that the rent was now paid to their new landowners. We see in this system the emergence of the feudal system of the Middle Ages, with a burdened lower class and a warrior aristocracy above it that received lands in return for military serv-

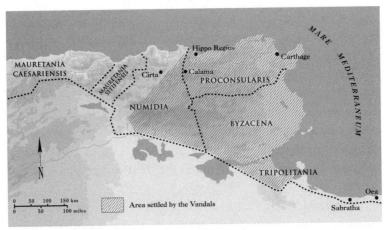

Area under Vandal rule at the peace of 442.

ice. This spared the Vandals the huge costs of paying an army, but it also made the army more territorial because it was more difficult to station troops away from their lands for any extended time.

The Vandal Allotments were mainly found around Carthage, the center of the Vandal power. The Vandals were too few to dominate the whole of the kingdom with the vast Roman population estimated at between one million and three million, outnumbering the invaders by almost forty to one. So to create stability, Geiseric had to settle the greatest part of his followers in a small, but wealthy, part of the kingdom and leave the rest to the Roman provincials. This was like the Ostrogothic kingdom of Italy, where the Ostrogoths were concentrated in north Italy, Ravenna, Rome, and Neapolis. No doubt the Arian Church was given the lands of the Catholic Church, and perhaps also confiscated lands from the Roman nobility.

One line of argument holds that the Vandals were allocated portions of the state's land-tax revenue rather than full ownership of actual pieces of real estate, as during their settlement in Spain. But decisive contradictory evidence is provided by the fact that Victor of Vita refers to Huneric as launching a persecution of Catholic Christians in the Vandal Allotments in 484. Proof, surely, that the Vandal Allotments were pieces of land.

The poorer land was left in the hands of the heavily taxed Roman provincials, according to Procopius. Since the poorer lands were closer to the borders, they were probably also more open to attacks from the desert tribes, now that the Roman fortified border was no longer guarded. The Vandals themselves did not initially care much for their borders toward the south.

The land settlement was probably made soon after the peace of 442. The Vandals took over the remaining Roman towns in the Mauretanias and Tripolitania no later than the death of Valentinian III in 455. By 455, the Balearic Isles, Sardinia, and Corsica had also been taken over by the new naval power, which would then hold all the major grain-producing areas of the Western Mediterranean: North Africa, Sicily, and Sardinia.

ADMINISTRATION OF THE KINGDOM

The administration of the kingdom was, as in most of the other barbarian kingdoms, left in the hands of Roman officials. No doubt the Vandals could more or less do as they wanted, but Roman law still existed. The Vandals undoubtedly saw the value of some kind of administration to tax the population, regulate trade and industries, as well as to administer the law for the Roman population. Again, we do not know the exact system of the remaining bureaucracy, but we hear of a proconsul of Carthage and a *praepositus regni*, a form of prime minister, in Victor of Vita, and a *primarius provinciae* (possibly a form of provincial governor) in the *Life of St. Fulgentius*.

Despite the violence and oppression of the Roman subject population that the sources describe, the situation was probably not as financially oppressive as it had been under the imperial government. Procopius informs us that when Emperor Justinian destroyed the Vandal kingdom in 533, it was no longer possible to find the tax registers in the public archives because Geiseric, at the beginning of his reign, had destroyed the registers, without which the population could not be taxed effectively. Since the same author tells us that the landowning classes were burdened by taxes, we may safely assume that he is speaking of the great landowners' estates and not the farms of common people. Possibly only the Vandal Allotments were meant. However, we know that Bishop Fulgentius (467–533) as a young man had served as a procurator, or tax collector, for the Vandal government until he resigned in disgust at the brutal methods he had been ordered to employ.

VANDALS AND "VANDALISM"

It is impossible to avoid the question of the connection between the Vandals and the word "vandalism," meaning senseless destruction of culture and property. It is generally now believed that the negative term, which first appeared in the seventeenth century, is based on myths and stories.

In contemporary sources, particularly biased Catholic writers, the Vandals are described as barbaric murderers and destroyers of culture. This historical tradition was followed in the Middle Ages. Christians in Europe studied the history of Victor of Vita, the *Life of St. Fulgentius*, and similar anti-Vandal Catholic sources, and saw the Vandals as pagan or heretic marauders. In the eleventh century, when Gregory of Catino wrote a history of his monastery in Farfa, Italy, he deduced that the Langobards, late benefactors of his monastery, could not have destroyed Farfa in the sixth century, and so accordingly the Vandals must have been responsible. Numerous French churches invented stories of the Vandal invasion in Gaul and their destruction or miraculous saving. In 1517, the famous painter Raphael wrote a letter to Pope Leo X condemning the builders of modern Rome, who plundered the ancient ruins to find statues and other objects to beautify their houses, describing them as "Goths and Vandals"— clearly referring to the sacks of Rome by those two tribes.

Confusion also arose from the identification of the Vandals with the Vinedi, the German term for Slavs, which became much diffused in the Middle Ages. From this mixing of names was derived a right of rule over the Slavonic-Vinedic regions around the Baltic Sea. Thus in early modern Swedish and Danish royal titles, the Vandals, or Vender, can be found alongside Swedes, Danes, and Goths. Only in 1973 did the Swedish king drop the title King of Vandals—which was symbolized by the third crown in the national arms of Sweden—although he retained the crown.

But the negative connection with the Vandal name stems to a large extent from the Age of Enlightenment. Bishop Henri-Baptiste Gregoire of Blois, France, in 1794 used the word "Vandalism" to critizice members of the French Revolution for their destruction of churches and their works of art, possibly thinking of the Vandals' plundering of Gaul, sack of Rome, or actions against the Catholic Church in North Africa. From then, the term entered common usage, and by 1798 it was listed in the *Dictionnaire de l'Académie Française* (Dictionary of the French Academy). Since then the negative meaning has existed in many languages, including English, German, Spanish, Italian, Danish, and Portuguese. Some people have tried to change the popular opinion of the Vandals. For example, German scholar and writer Friedrich Meyer of the late eighteenth century defended the Vandals and asked the French to end the unjust degradation of a proud and free Germanic people.

And indeed, the Vandals were no worse or more barbaric than the other migrating tribes, such as the Franks and Alamanni, whose names received no such treatment. Only the terms "Hun" and "Goth" are, in some languages, used in a pejorative sense, but nothing like on the scale of "Vandals." Many of the harsh words aimed at the Vandals in contemporary sources are based on the struggle between the Arians and the Catholic Church. For the Catholics, there was nothing worse than persecutors and heretics. No doubt the church and the Roman nobility had cause to make the Vandals out to be worse than they were, so that the common people would not be enticed into converting to Arianism and the slaves to run away to join the invaders.

The Vandals pillaged the countryside and towns, killed or enslaved people, and burned cities. We even hear of fruit trees being rooted up, but this was probably done to deny the enemy provisions or to prevent the local inhabitants to live off the land and conduct guerrilla warfare against the invaders. But these terrible deeds were common to all the barbarian peoples of the time and, we might add, the Roman army when at war. Only in the Vandal persecutions of the Catholics do we see an aspect that is unfamiliar to us. Churches were burned and desecrated, bishops and priests were tortured or sent into exile, and people were forcibly converted to Arianism. No doubt our understanding of Vandal history would be different if Arian or Vandal sources had survived—sources which may have described the Catholics and their actions in similar terms.

RELIGION

The Vandals were, like almost all Germanic nations, Arians, in the manner of the great Bishop Ulfilas. Being considered heretics by the Romans, they were naturally opposed to Orthodox Catholics. We do not hear much of the religious fervor with which they carried the banner of Arianism until they reach the North African provinces. But it was inevitable that a conflict would arise, as North Africa was known for its strong—perhaps even fanatical—religious beliefs. Even the names of the Catholics were of a highly religious nature: Quod-vult-Deus, Deo-gratias, A-deo-datus (What-God-Wills, Thanks-to-God, Given-by-God).

Another example of the fanatical religious beliefs in North Africa is that of the great Donatist controversies, which arose during the persecution of Diocletian and his successors. A hundred and twenty years had passed since then, and it might have been expected that purely personal issues, such as whether this or that bishop, under threat of death, had delivered up sacred books to imperial officers, would have been lost to memory. But the Donatists had long memories and still eagerly discussed the election of Caecilianus to the see of Carthage, as if that event had happened yesterday instead of more than a hundred years ago. As already noted, the conflict ended in the victory of the Catholic Church, which started a campaign to root out the Donatists in North Africa.

Most of the imperial laws against the Donatists are from the reign of Honorius (395–423) and the first twenty years of the fifth century, and clearly show the religious hatreds of North Africa at the time of the Vandal invasion. For example, a fine was instituted for higher officials found to be Donatists, such as a count, who would have to pay two hundred pounds of gold, a huge sum. According to the imperial laws, the Donatists—"whom the patience of our clemency has preserved until now, but who ought to be branded with perpetual infamy, and shut out from all honorable assemblies, and from every place of public resort"—were not allowed to buy, sell, or give property. Their churches were taken away from them and given to the Catholics. Such treatment of people who worshipped the same god, but in different ways, created a tense religious environment, which the Vandals faced when they entered North Africa.

VICTOR OF VITA

Much of what we know of these events comes from the *History of the Vandal Persecution* by Victor of Vita. Around 484, Victor, a native of North Africa, wrote about the religious persecutions of the Catholics from the arrival of the Vandals in 429 until 484, where his history ends. He gives a minutely detailed account of the atrocities inflicted by the Vandals on the Catholics in the kingdom. He describes the Vandals as sadistic in their treatment of their Catholic opponents, and is thus in strong opposition to, for example, Salvian, who not long after the arrival of the Vandals expressed happiness that they were cleaning up the lax Roman sexual practices that were rife in North Africa.

We know little of the passionate Victor, although from the subject and his vehemence we might expect that he was part of the Catholic clergy. Some think he may have been the bishop of the town of Vita in North Africa, whose name around 484 was indeed Victor, but other parts of his story disprove this. The text itself implies that he was a priest, but not a bishop, probably from Carthage, as he shows great knowledge of the city and access to the archives of the see of Carthage. However, he was not among the 4,966 clergy exiled by King Huneric, because he describes himself as able to visit them in their confinement.

He describes in great detail how the Vandals of Geiseric would burn churches and basilicas of the Catholics and put the bishops and priests to death. Often they would suffer torture until they handed over whatever gold and silver they or their church had. Random women, children, and old men were killed, and Victor describes in his usual partisan manner how the North African towns were emptied of inhabitants because of the persecutions. In Carthage, the Temple of Memory was destroyed and other public buildings burned. Catholic churches were destroyed or converted to Arian churches. It is this destruction and desecration of churches and the Christian sources' focus on it that, more than anything, has made the term "vandalism" synonymous in later days with senseless destruction.

But Victor's presentation of the persecution is exaggerated. Although two bishops appear to have been burned to death during the reign of Geiseric, it can be conjectured that it was the work of pillaging barbarians rather than part of any organized persecution. In 439, after the capture of Carthage, the bishop of Carthage, Quodvultdeus, and many of his clergy were put on board unsound ships and set out to sea, but they managed to arrive safely in Campania. Again, this does not appear to have been an attempt to do anything more than send them into exile. If the Vandals wanted them dead, they could ensure this in other ways. Victor's *History of the Vandal Persecution* is full of killings, but ignoring those who were slain for political motives and discounting the more fantastic tales of mass murder, which other sources do not confirm, we are left with just five martyrs, of which only one certainly died. Out of a population of several million, this cannot be said to be many. Victor also complains that Geiseric ordered the burial of the dead Catholics to be conducted without the singing of hymns. We might deduce from the description that takes such a prominent place in Victor's history that apart from the general violence and pillaging of the Vandals, religious persecution was not as severe and cruel as he tries to make it appear.

The persecutions of Geiseric

Another of Victor of Vita's stories shows perhaps a more realistic image of Geiseric's persecution. A delegation of Catholic bishops asked the king to give them churches to worship in, but was strongly rejected. They were forced to depart and had to make do with what buildings they could find. For some years, it appears, this unobtrusive worship of the Catholics was permitted, although not expressly sanctioned. Then came denunciations and calumnies, especially against those priests who officiated "in the regions which paid tribute to the Palace." (Unfortunately, we do not know the identity of the regions.) If one of these priests, in his sermons, mentioned the name of Pharaoh, Holofernes, or Nebuchadnezzar, or any similar Biblical tyrant, he was accused of speaking against the person of the king and was immediately sentenced to banishment. Most likely the Catholic Church was trying to rouse the people against the king during the sermons. For this reason, a whole group of bishops were banished and their sees left empty.

Supported by the Arian Church, Geiseric ordered various high-ranking persons, particularly at the Vandal court, to convert to Arianism. If they refused this test of loyalty, they were exiled, tortured, or murdered. In the end, the king commanded that the court and the followers of his sons all had to be Arians. The command is understandable, as the Vandal rule was still not secure and this was a means of achieving the obedience of his and his family's advisers. Thus it was not the religious reasons behind Arianism that were important, but the fact that being Arian meant being Vandal, or at least not being Roman Catholic. However, if we look at the facts behind Victor's accusations, the following conclusions can be drawn about the persecutions under Geiseric:

- The churches were generally handed over to the Arians or destroyed.
- The bishops were generally exiled, and it was forbidden to reelect successors.

Catholics were generally, but not individually, persecuted because of their faith. Only in some cases were high-level officials punished, possibly because the king saw it as an insult to him that his closest advisers did not share his faith. There appears to be no record of a general attempt to convert the middle and lower classes—such as the farmers, traders, and artisans in the cities—to Arianism.

At length, on the urgent entreaty of Emperor Valentinian III, and probably because Geiseric wanted to further the possible marriage between Huneric and Eudocia, he permitted the Orthodox Church of Carthage to ordain for itself a bishop in October 454, the gentle and charitable Deogratias, who for three years governed the see with general approval. On the death of Deogratias, the see was again left empty, until 475, in the final years of the reign of Geiseric, when, on the intercession of Emperor Zeno (474–491), the surviving bishops were permitted to return from their exiles.

It appears that at least initially, Geiseric targeted the North African Catholic Church because of its wealth and opposition to his rule, and not because of any particular religious fervor. The threat of persecution of the Catholics was also later used as an instrument against the Romans in foreign politics.

PLOT AGAINST GEISERIC

There was a traditional struggle for power between the nobility and the monarch in Germanic kingdoms, and the Vandals' was no exception. With Geiseric's founding of the kingdom in North Africa, his power and prestige reached astounding heights. But jealousy and the resulting loss of power among the nobility also caused resentment and even treachery. The advantageous peace treaty with the Romans in 442, and the great lands that Geiseric reserved for himself, caused several Vandal nobles to form a conspiracy against him in 442. In their eyes, he had become too arrogant and powerful. But the conspiracy was revealed before their plans were ready, and it was bloodily suppressed. Prosper of Aquitaine wrote that it caused more dead Vandals than a lost war. The suspicions and jealousy caused by this conspiracy was a hard blow to the Vandal kingdom, and the nobility would never again reach the position they had before and during the migrations. Indeed, the king's position was strengthened greatly at their expense. To support himself against the rebellious hereditary nobles, Geiseric now appointed new nobles for the royal administration. These nobles owed their position to the king and had to take an oath of allegiance to him.

THE DESTRUCTION OF CITY WALLS

To further secure his power, Geiseric caused all the city walls in the kingdom to be destroyed, apart from those at Septem, Caesarea, Hippo Regius, and Carthage. This would prevent rebels from taking a city and holding it against the Vandals, and it would force them to meet the Vandal army in open battle, where the Vandals would be at their strongest. However, this novel scheme left the provinces wide open to the Moors and forced the provincials to construct more-primitive defenses, as the Vandal army could not be everywhere to defend them. Procopius says Geiseric was praised for the scheme in his lifetime but was later ridiculed for it, as it made an invasion of the kingdom much easier. No doubt also, the Moors felt the cities and towns were easier to raid without their fortifications. But given the situation, weighing the pros and cons, it was probably a wise decision, and it can be argued that it appears the Vandals faced no rebellions until the final year of the kingdom. Traces of the demolished city walls can still be seen in such places as Tipasa.

THE ECONOMIC SITUATION OF THE WESTERN ROMAN EMPIRE

The Western Roman Empire was in dire straits after the peace of 442. Most of the taxes from North Africa had been lost, and the rest much reduced. On June 21, 445, Valentinian issued a tax edict regarding the remaining Roman-held provinces in North Africa, which reveals that Numidia and Mauretania Sitifensis were now producing only one-eighth of their previous tax revenues. A law from 444 provided for a new sales tax of 4 percent to help pay for the army.

To give an idea of the magnitude of the damage done to the Western Roman Empire, we can calculate that the tax lost from Numidia and Mauretania Sitifensis was 106,200 solidi a year. From the sources, we know that a regular comitatensian infantryman cost approximately six solidi per year, and a cavalry trooper around ten and a half. This means that the yearly tax lost from these two provinces alone equaled the loss of yearly wages for about eighteen thousand infantrymen, or about ten thousand cavalry. Including the much richer provinces of Proconsularis and Byzacena, the figure is closer to around forty thousand infantry, or more than twenty thousand cavalry. These were on top of other economic losses caused by the sacks of Gaul, Spain, Sicily, and Italy. The Western Empire was simply no longer capable of paying the forces needed to protect the remaining provinces.

For the Roman landowners in North Africa, the Vandal invasion and the peace of 442 was also a disaster—both financially and personally. The emperor did what he could to alleviate their situation. On October 19, 443, Valentinian III suspended the normal operation of financial laws in the case of Romans from North Africa, who "are despoiled, needy and exiled from their own country." Moneylenders were not allowed to sue them for money borrowed since their exile until they recovered their own property, unless they had other sources of income elsewhere. Furthermore, they could not be pressed on financial matters pertaining to the period before their exile, and they could not be charged interest on any loans. Presumably, many of the great landowners borrowed money after their flight in 439, as most expected North Africa to be retaken soon. But after the peace of 442, this could no longer be expected, and the emperor had to protect the exiles from their debtors. The problem did not go away, and on July 13, 451, Valentinian decreed that "wise provision shall be made for the African dignitaries and landholders who have been despoiled by the devastation of the enemy, namely, that in so far as it is able, the august imperial generosity shall compensate for that which the violence of fortune has taken away."

The emperor granted a five-year tax remission on thirteen thousand units of land in Numidia, in the hope that this would bring the untilled lands back into production. Cash grants were also provided. Those who had lost their lands in Proconsularis or Byzacena were given priority in the leasing-out of public lands in Mauretania Caesariensis and Sitifensis, and other landholders, who were not as bad off, were expelled from their existing leases. In this fashion, a few of the great landowners were able to regain some of their fortunes in Mauretania. Only in the later part of the reign of Geiseric did some of the Roman nobility return to their lands in North Africa, particularly after 455.

Foreign relations of the Vandal kingdom

That the Vandal kingdom was recognized as a new power in the West is also seen in the fact that the Visigothic King Theodoric sought them as allies and offered his daughter to Huneric, the son of Geiseric, some time between 440 and 444. The connection did not last long. When Geiseric suspected that his daughter-in-law planned to poison him, he sent her back to her father, probably in 444—after cutting off her nose and ears, according to the Gothic historian Jordanes.

But the split between Huneric and the Visigothic princess appears to have been caused more by the prospects of Huneric marrying Eudocia, the daughter of Valentinian III, which was being negotiated. The story about poisoning might simply have been an excuse to end the connection. No doubt the Romans feared an alliance between the Visigoths and the Vandals, which would threaten the empire, and they would try their utmost to keep them apart diplomatically. For his part, Geiseric probably realized that the safety of his kingdom rested more on his connections to the Western Empire than to the other Germanic kingdoms. After the cruel treatment of the Visigothic princess, and the failure of the alliance between the Visigoths and Vandals, the Visigoths sought the alliance of the Suevian King Rechiarius after 446. Only the mutual danger of the Hunnish invasion in 451 caused the Romans and Visigoths to work together again.

Hydatius records that Vandal ships raided Turonium on the coast of Gallaecia and captured many slaves around 445. We don't know why this long-range raid on the Suevian kingdom was carried out, but it may have been to ensure Huneric's return from being a hostage at Rome, as he went back to Carthage sometime in 445 or 446. Archbishop Nestorius's *Book of Heraclides*, written in 451, mentions Vandal attacks on Italy and Rhodes. However, the text cannot be considered entirely trustworthy, as it also states that the Vandals attacked the area of the Ganges River in India. Likewise, the anonymous *Life of Daniel the Stylite* mentions that the inhabitants of Alexandria feared a Vandal attack, even though there were never any attacks on Egypt. In this period when Roman naval power in the Western Mediterranean was falling apart, provincials would turn to piracy. It is possible that any piratical attack was considered "Vandal" no matter the actual people behind it.

After the raid in 445, and until the death of Valentinian III in 455, we hear nothing of further Vandal raids on the

Western Empire. It is therefore believed that during these years, Geiseric tried to appease the Western Empire in order to marry his son Huneric to the daughter of Valentinian III. A panegyric by the fifth century poet Merobaudes on the third consulship of Aetius (446) mentions that the invader of Africa had dared to enter into close connections with Rome, so Huneric and Eudocia are believed to have been already connected by 446. For Geiseric, it was a major goal to become connected to the imperial house and the Western Roman Empire, as it gave more legitimacy to the Vandal kingdom. To further please the Romans, Geiseric gave permission to instate a new bishop for Hadrumentum, and later, on October 24 or 25, 454, the empty see of Carthage was filled by Deogratias on the request of the emperor. At the same time, several exiled Catholic bishops returned to their sees.

Geiseric managed to come from the difficult period of invasion and settlement to making a more stable kingdom, which was respected as a major power in the Western Mediterranean. With the unruly nobles cowed, his kingdom stabilized, and the internal struggles in the Western Empire blossoming again, Geiseric was ready to play his greatest role in Roman history.

FIVE

The Sack of Rome

"Year 455. Forty-third in line of the Roman emperors, Marcian, now in the fourth year of his reign, ruled alone. ... Geiseric entered Rome—according to an evil lie spread by rumour he had been summoned by Valentinian's widow before Avitus became Augustus—and having looted the wealth of the Romans, he returned to Carthage, taking with him Valentinian's widow and two daughters, and the son of Aetius, who was named Gaudentius."
—*From the Chronicle of Spanish Bishop Hydatius, who wrote in the first half of the fifth century*

The menace of the Huns, which had played so great a part in the massive migrations of the fourth and fifth centuries, was curbed in 451. Attila had invaded Gaul with his army and destroyed a great number of cities, but was finally brought to battle by Aetius around June 20, 451, at the Catalaunian Fields, near Chalons-en-Champagne in modern-day France. After a hard and difficult fight, Attila was forced to retreat from the empire. We hear nothing of the Vandals in the list of his allied Germanic tribes. For Aetius, the success meant that his fame was at the high point of his career. Although Attila would later attack Italy, the Huns' force was spent, and when

Attila died in 454, his empire fragmented. This was an opportunity for the subject Germanic tribes, and they rose up and defeated the Huns in the battle of Nedao in 454. The Vandals are not mentioned in the short description of the battle by Gothic historian Jordanes, although Sueves and Alans are mentioned. Any remaining Vandals in the Danube and Silesian regions would also have gained their freedom then, but they were probably subject to other stronger tribes, such as the Gepids.

Aetius murdered

Aetius was not to enjoy his triumph over Attila for long. In 454, Valentinian III contrived to kill him while they were in the palace examining proposals to bring in more money for the bankrupted empire. While Aetius was calculating the total collected from taxes, Valentinian charged him with planning to take over the Western Empire and stabbed him to death with a sword. This was the inglorious end of the one known as "the last of the Romans."

On March 16, 455, some followers of Aetius killed Emperor Valentinian III to avenge the murder of their master. Valentinian was only thirty-seven years old, but he had been emperor for thirty years. The next day, the patrician Petronius Maximus, who according to some sources might have had a hand in the murder of Aetius, was proclaimed emperor, without the acceptance of the Eastern Emperor. To consolidate his position, he forced Valentinian's widow Empress Eudoxia to marry him. Her daughter Eudocia, who was bethrothed to Geiseric's son Huneric, was instead forced to marry Petronius Maximus's son Palladius, who was named caesar, indicating the line of succession to emperor after his father.

Empress Eudoxia appeals for Vandal aid

In despair, the widowed Empress Eudoxia asked Geiseric to help her in her need and to send forces to Rome to avenge the murder of her husband by the usurper Petronius Maximus.

Solidus of Licinia Eudoxia struck at Ravenna sometime between 437–439. (*Author*)

Geiseric, who saw that his plan to marry Huneric into the imperial family was falling apart, did not need much convincing. Furthermore, the chance to plunder was too good to refuse for his avaricious heart. He officially declared the treaty of 442 with the Western Roman Empire void on the death of Valentinian III. That Eudoxia asked the Vandal king to come to her aid is believed by most scholars to be a fanciful story, as no contemporary sources mention this as anything but a rumor. It is more likely that Geiseric was drawn in because of the severing of the connection between Huneric and Eudocia, as well as the chance for plunder. No matter the reason, he collected his forces quickly and, less than two and a half months after the death of the emperor, at the end of May 455, Geiseric set sail for Rome with an army of Vandals and Moors. This is the first time the Moors appear as auxiliaries for the Vandals. Either Geiseric or another Vandal fleet captured Sardinia at this time. Victor of Vita tells us that Sicily, Corsica, and the Balearic Islands were also captured around this time. Except for short periods, Sicily remained Vandal until the end of the Western Empire, and only around 477 was it ceded to Odoacer, the barbarian ruler of Italy, on the stipulation that he pay an annual tribute to Carthage.

THE SACK OF ROME

The fleet reached Portus, the harbor of Rome, in the early days of June 455. Many Romans, particularly the nobility, fled at the news of the approaching Vandals. When Petronius Maximus also attempted to flee instead of preparing Rome's defenses, he was killed, on May 31, 455, by Ursus, a Burgundian soldier of his bodyguard, because of his cowardliness. The body of the unpopular usurper was then torn apart by the mob and thrown into the Tiber River. No attempt was made to organize a defense of the city or to buy the Vandals off. On June 3, three days after Petronius Maximus was killed, Geiseric arrived in Rome and was met at the Porta Portuensis gate by Pope Leo, who pleaded with him for the life of the inhabitants of the city in return for willingly turning over all the church plate of Rome.

Perhaps the Vandals were daunted by the walls of the city and welcomed some opportunity to take it without a struggle. Geiseric well knew that his army was not great enough to hold the city and that Africa was wide open to attacks if he stayed too long. Perhaps he also did not want to face too much resistance from the population, which still numbered perhaps five hundred thousand—probably around fifty times the size of the Vandal army. So the Vandal king conceded to Pope Leo that there would be no killing, no burning of either private or public buildings, and no torture to force people to give up their hidden treasures. With this agreement in place, the Vandal warriors entered the city. The story of the pope's intercession might be apocryphal, because the sermon he gave on July 6 celebrating the retreat of the Vandals mentions nothing of the fact, and only attributes the saving of the city to the grace of God.

For fourteen days, the Vandals slowly and leisurely plundered the city of its wealth. Everything was taken from the Imperial Palace on the Palatine Hill, and the churches were emptied of their collected treasures. Even the Temple of Jupiter Capitolinus, the greatest temple in the Roman world, was emptied of its treasures, and half the roof, which was made of copper coated with gold, was stripped off. Emperor Domitian (81–96) had spent twelve thousand talents of gold (more than 387 tons) on the gilding, and it was probably the mistaken belief that the roof was solid gold that led the Vandals to tear it down. Most likely they soon found out that it was not real gold and left the other half. Also, the treasure taken by Emperor Titus (79–81) in 71 from the sack of Jerusalem and the Jewish Temple was now transported to North Africa. Many priceless statues of the great city were also taken to the Vandal ships. Of the whole Vandal treasure fleet, only the ship carrying the statues of the Roman temples and palaces sunk on the voyage; it still awaits discovery on the bottom of the Mediterranean. Despite the great indignity of the sack of Rome, it appears Geiseric was true to his word and did not destroy the buildings. Also, we hear nothing of any killings. Despite the negative connotation their name now carries, the Vandals conducted themselves much better during the sack of Rome than did many other invading barbarians.

The marriage of Huneric

When the Vandals left around June 16, they took a great number of Roman citizens with them as slaves. The Vandals were particular to pick out the most skillful craftsmen, administrators, and laborers. But they also brought other captives: several senators; Empress Eudoxia and her two daughters, Eudocia and Placidia; and Gaudentius, the son of Aetius. For Eudoxia, it must have been a shame of the greatest magnitude, but it probably also saved her from the revenge of the inhabitants of Rome, who were the real losers in her power struggle with Petronius Maximus. Eudoxia was a very important person, as she was the widow of two emperors and the daughter of a third. For Geiseric, the noble captives, if we may call them that, were an enormous political success. The oldest princess, Eudocia, was given in marriage to Huneric. Eudoxia and the youngest daughter were treated in the best manner at Carthage, but they were held as hostages and only given back after seven years, on the strong and repeated request of East Roman Emperor Leo. Until then, they were potential bargaining tools. We hear no more of Gaudentius. When the Vandals returned to Carthage, some of the captives were given to the Moors and others kept by the Vandals. A number of captives were ransomed by Deogratias, the Catholic bishop of Carthage, in return for the church plate of the city.

EMPEROR AVITUS

For two months, the Western Roman Empire was in such chaos that a new emperor could not be chosen. Finally, on August 14, 455, word came that on July 9 in Arelate (modern-day Arles, France) the Gauls had confirmed Avitus, a nobleman of Auvergne, emperor. He entered Rome on September 21, and on January 1, 456, the poet Sidonius Apollinaris gave a panegyric in his honor predicting the reconquest of North Africa. Clearly, the Romans wanted revenge.

Avitus, who was about sixty years old, came from a noble family in Gaul. When he was younger, he had served under Aetius in his campaigns in Gaul, Noricum, and on the lower Rhine and the Danube. After several commands in the military, he was made praetorian prefect of Gaul and held this high office from 439 to 445, before retiring to his estates. He was already on friendly terms with King Theodoric and acted as the main ambassador between the Western Empire and the Visigothic kingdom. This alliance had stopped the mighty Attila in 451 at the battle of the Catalaunian Fields. It appears that the alliance was dissolved when the Huns retreated. But the murder of Valentinian III probably revived the idea of an alliance between Visigoths and Romans. The usurper Petronius Maximus had taken Avitus out of retirement and made him general of all the forces in Gaul. In the three months of Petronius Maximus's reign, Avitus succeeded in pushing back some barbarian raids on the lower Rhine. Given all this and his popularity with the army, he was an obvious choice to become emperor when news came that Petronius Maximus had been slain and the Vandals had sacked Rome.

Avitus supported by the Visigoths

Apart from the dissolving Western Roman Empire, there were four powers in the Western Mediterranean: the Vandals, the Visigoths, the Burgundians, and the Sueves. The Vandals ruled North Africa; the Visigoths ruled southwestern Gaul, with their capital at Tolosa; the Burgundians occupied the Rhône Valley, with their capital at Lugdunum (Lyons in modern-day France); and the Sueves held large parts of southern and western Spain, which they ruled from Asturica Augusta (Astorga in modern-day Spain). The Vandals and Visigoths had been enemies since their time in Spain, broken only by the brief marriage of a Visigothic princess to Huneric. Relations naturally did not improve with Geiseric's treatment of his Visigothic daughter-in-law. The Visigoths and Burgundians distrusted each other and often raided each other's territory. The Sueves were somewhat on the sideline. After the Vandals left Spain, they occasionally tried to take parts of Roman Spain, but were at peace with their Visigothic neighbors, in part because King Rechiarius had married a sister of the Visigothic king.

So Avitus and the Visigoths decided to form an alliance. Avitus would be made emperor with the backing of the Visigothic armies. In return, Avitus would condone the Visigoths' attacking the Sueves, officially on behalf of the Romans. The Burgundians would be given more land in the Rhône Valley if they supported the Visigothic forces in attacking Spain. The way this all happened was not so simple.

The Visigoths threatened to invade Roman Gaul. Avitus gathered all his forces to defend against the invasion, but first he tried to negotiate with the Visigoths. When they met at Tolosa for the negotiations, they were informed that Petronius Maximus was dead and Rome captured, which suited their plans well. Officially, the Visigothic King Theodoric accepted keeping the peace, but only if Avitus was made emperor. Feigning reluctance, Avitus accepted the terms and was made emperor by his forces in Gaul. The Visigoths then attacked the Sueves with their newly found Burgundian allies and soundly defeated them at the river Urbicus on October 5, 456, capturing their king, Rechiarius, whom they killed a little later. The Suevian kingdom was thus weakened severely for many years. This is a splendid example of the important role the barbarian kingdoms played in Roman politics in this period.

No support from the East Romans

It appears that Geiseric's strategy was to keep the Western Empire down through raids and disruption, as well as by controlling the grain trade. So one of the first tasks of Avitus's reign was to send a delegation to Constantinople to ask for aid from Emperor Marcian. Without the ships of the Eastern Empire, he could not transport the Visigoths and his own army to North Africa. But Marcian did little. He demanded the return of the imperial captives—Empress Eudoxia and her two daughters—and an end to the Vandal raids but offered no ships, thereby dooming the Western Roman response. Possibly this weak response was the plan of the powerful Arian patrician Aspar, who still ruled behind the Eastern Roman throne.

Marcian's inactivity was later the foundation of a story, told by Procopius, that as a young man before he became emperor, Marcian participated in the campaign with Aspar against Geiseric in North Africa and was captured in the defeat of the Romans in 431. When Geiseric was reviewing the prisoners, he noticed an eagle hovering over Marcian and shading him from the heat of the midday sun. Believing that this was an omen that one day this young officer would become emperor, Geiseric freed him on oath that he would never again fight against the Vandals. It was also rumored of Aspar that he had become friendly toward the Vandals after his campaign in North Africa in the first half of the 430s, and was unwilling for the Eastern Romans to fight and destroy them.

With no Eastern help forthcoming for Avitus, Geiseric took his time in occupying the remaining Roman provinces in

North Africa, and the Moorish tribes in these regions submitted to him. In 463, an inscription employing a distinctively Vandal dating system was put up in Cuicul, on the provincial border between Numidia and Mauretania Sitifensis. This indicates that the region, which lay well within the imperial zone in 442, had been taken by the Vandals twenty-one years later.

RICIMER

Meanwhile, other forces inside the empire would ensure the downfall of Avitus. Despite the fact that the Romans focused more on an expedition to Pannonia, the Roman General Ricimer gained a victory over the Vandals in Sicily. In 456, Geiseric had sent a fleet to raid Sicily and South Italy. Count Ricimer moved quickly against the landing and defeated the Vandals at Agrigentum (Agrigento) in Sicily. He achieved a second important victory the same year against another Vandal fleet at Corsica. Sixty Vandal ships had sailed from Carthage to Corsica, probably to raid Italy and Gaul. The capable Ricimer followed them there, outmaneuvered them, and won a great victory. But this victory caused more problems for the Western Empire than it solved. After his victories, Ricimer became popular in the army and one of the most powerful men in the Western Empire, and he had no regard for the alliance between the Visigoths and Avitus. Ricimer was the son of a Suevian father and Visigothic mother, so he may have also objected to the destruction of the Sueves. His rise to power could not be denied, and Ricimer would be kingmaker at Rome for the next sixteen years.

AVITUS DEPOSED

Avitus would not last long on the throne. A revolt started in Rome caused by famine—no doubt because the Vandal strategy to cut off the food supplies from North Africa was effective—gave Ricimer the pretext he needed, and he went into rebellion. When Avitus fled to Gaul, Ricimer deposed him, saying he was unfit to rule the empire in those troubled times.

Avitus did not reach his home, but was captured at Placentia (Piacenza in modern-day Italy) by Ricimer, who was now master of the soldiers. In a surprising and strange act of charity, Ricimer made Avitus bishop of Placentia—although he killed his supporters. Ricimer then made General Majorian his puppet emperor on April 1, 457, with the blessings of the new Eastern Roman emperor, Leo I (457–474), who had been placed on the throne by Aspar on February 7. Until the final years of the Western Empire, Geiseric remained their foe.

Majorian

When Majorian became Western Roman emperor, he had two main tasks. The first was to reestablish the authority of the empire in Gaul, as the Visigoths and Burgundians had rebelled when Avitus, their candidate for the throne, had been removed. The second task was to defeat the menacing Vandals, who held a stranglehold on the grain supply of Rome.

Majorian soon achieved the first success of his reign by defeating an Alamanni war band in Raetia. We learn from the poet Sidonius Apollinaris that he then went to Campania in south Italy in 457 after receiving news that Geiseric was raiding the region again. Sidonius relates that the enemy fleet was in a river mouth, most likely of the Liri or Volturnus. Majorian arrived while the Vandal troops were dispersed in pillaging the area. A skirmish was fought in which the Vandals were defeated, and they retreated to their ships. With horses and men trying to reach the ships while pursued by the enemy, everything was in confusion. Among the killed was Geiseric's brother-in-law. The Vandals were forced to abandon the expedition and return to North Africa. The defeat appears to have had no real importance, and so might only have involved a few hundred warriors. But the presence of Geiseric's brother-in-law might indicate a larger force of perhaps one thousand warriors, which we might term a thousandship, for want of a better word.

In 457, Majorian again lifted the prohibition against civilians carrying arms, perhaps a sign of the difficulty of defending the long coastline against the Vandals. But the emperor, now supported by the Burgundians, also had to battle the Visigoths. He spent 458 and 459 in war against them, and defeated them. With his back secure, Majorian could now turn his eyes to the south, to avenge the sack of Rome and restore the city's grain supply.

PREPARATIONS FOR THE CAMPAIGN

According to his panegyrist, Sidonius Apollinaris, Majorian "felled the forests of the Apennine and filled the harbors with Roman triremes." The eloquent Sidonius compared the preparations of the expedition with the ones made by the Persian King Xerxes against the Greeks in 480 BC. Strangely, Majorian did not make an invasion straight to the North African heartland or via Sicily, but chose instead to go via Spain, possibly because he was informed of disaffection among the Moorish tribes in Mauretania and Numidia, who were allied with the Vandals. Another possibility is that he wanted to avoid fighting the formidable Vandal fleet, which he could do by approaching North Africa from farther west. He made Carthago Spartaria his main base and collected there his navy of three hundred ships in the spring of 460. His army arrived in Spain in May. No help appears to have been sent from the Eastern Romans. Probably unnerved by this great gathering of forces, Geiseric sent ambassadors to treat for peace in 460, but without success.

Geiseric was well aware of the danger and did not rely on diplomacy alone. He took his fleet along the coast of the Mauretanias, plundering and devastating his own provinces along Majorian's possible line of march. He also poisoned the wells. After all, he had himself taken this route and knew of its difficulties. Then, by some unknown stratagem, he destroyed or captured Majorian's three hundred ships, somehow aided by traitors. Unfortunately, the sources of this turbulent period are so scanty and difficult to use that we have no idea how he managed to eliminate the strong Roman fleet. Three years of preparations were lost, and the invasion of the Vandal kingdom was canceled in May 460. An ignoble peace for the Romans was made in which the Vandals were to abstain from raiding, and the Romans from invading Africa. Also, Majorian was required to give up his alliance with General Marcellinus, the semi-independent ruler of Dalmatia and Illyria, who was hostile to the Vandals.

For Majorian, this was the end. He had proved too active for Ricimer, who deposed him on August 2, 461, near Tortona. Five days later, Majorian was murdered. On hearing the news, Geiseric considered the peace with the Western Romans void and began again to raid the coasts of the empire. We know that the Vandals raided Sicily in 462, 463, and 465, but were defeated in 465 by the General Marcellinus, who later played a great role in the wars against the Vandals. On November 19, 461, Ricimer made the elderly senator Libius Severus emperor. He died on August 15, 465, and we know almost nothing of his reign. It appears that Ricimer had found the type of emperor he wanted.

GEISERIC AS WOULD-BE KINGMAKER

The emperor of the Eastern Empire, Leo, was not pleased about the murder of Majorian and the elevation of another of Ricimer's puppet-emperors. When the Western Romans asked for ships to replace the fleet destroyed at Carthago Spartaria so they could defend themselves against the Vandal raids, they were coldly told that the existing treaties with the Vandals would not allow such a thing. The East did send one or two embassies to Geiseric, asking him to stop raiding Italy and Sicily. Of course, the Vandals ignored the pleas and continued their profitable business.

The Vandals were also unhappy about Ricimer's power in the West, as Geiseric now had a candidate for emperor. Since the sack of Rome in 455, the Eastern Empire had asked for the return of Empress Eudoxia and her two daughters who had been taken back to Carthage. Finally, after seven years,

Geiseric sent the empress and her younger daughter, Placidia, to Constantinople in 462. Princess Eudocia, the wife of Huneric, was to stay. Her mother and sister were used as bargaining tools to get a treaty with the East. In Constantinople, Placidia married Senator Anicius Olybrius, making him the brother-in-law of Geiseric's son, Huneric. It was Olybrius whom Geiseric wanted to put on the throne of the Western Roman Empire. Because of Eudocia's marriage to Huneric, Geiseric also claimed the property of her father, the murdered Emperor Valentinian III, and of Aetius. It is unclear why he also claimed the property of Aetius, but it was no doubt connected to his taking the son of Aetius as prisoner to Carthage after the sack of Rome. He sent many embassies to Ricimer, who of course denied the preposterous request. Accordingly, the Vandals raided mainly the southern coasts of Italy every year for plunder and slaves.

THE TROUBLES OF THE WESTERN ROMAN EMPIRE

Ricimer was also for a short time threatened by an alliance between the Vandals and the master of the soldiers in Gaul, Aegidius, who had been a close friend of Majorian's. To avenge his murder, Aegidius sent ambassadors to the Vandal court to seek an alliance, but he fell in battle with the Visigoths in 464, before anything came of it.

Ricimer had other enemies, including Marcellinus, the ruler of Dalmatia and Illyria, who was a former counselor to Majorian. He had fought the Vandals in Sicily as general of the Romans. When he discovered that Ricimer was bribing his troops, and with little money to counter this, he retired to Dalmatia and set up his own little principality. In 465, however, the Eastern Roman emperor asked him to stop warring against Italy and join forces with him against the Vandals.

ANTHEMIUS

Libius Severus had died on August 15, 465, and for a year and eight months, Ricimer felt no need to appoint a new emperor. There were two candidates—Anthemius, who was supported by the Eastern Empire, and Olybrius, who was supported by the Vandals. Ricimer finally chose Anthemius, son-in-law of the late Eastern Roman Emperor Marcian. Geiseric was furious at the choice, but Ricimer made his decision on the condition that the Eastern Empire would give him massive support for the destruction of the Vandal kingdom. Furthermore, to strengthen their connection, Anthemius's daughter Alypia was to marry Ricimer when Anthemius arrived in Italy. In spring 467, Anthemius landed with a great army in Italy; he was made emperor on April 12 near Rome. The fleet that brought him was commanded by Marcellinus, who in 466 had attacked Vandal Sardinia and reclaimed it. The marriage was concluded as planned. In 467, Marcellinus continued his efforts to stabilize the Western Empire and recaptured Sicily, which the Vandals appear to have captured some time after the death of Majorian.

Emperor Leo, Ricimer, and Marcellinus joined forces in 468 to make the campaign to end the troublesome Vandals once and for all. If North Africa could be regained, the Western Empire might still have a chance to recover and survive. After the elevation of Anthemius, Geiseric directed his piratical attacks against the Eastern Empire. Greece, Illyricum, and the Greek islands felt the heavy hand of the Vandal fleet. While Geiseric was occupied in raiding Greece, Marcellinus tried to land in North Africa but was turned back by contrary winds. However, the appearance of the Roman fleet caused envoys from the Visigoths and Sueves, sent to Geiseric to negotiate an alliance against the Western Romans, to give up their task and turn back. Geiseric also negotiated with the Ostrogothic troops in the Balkans under Theodoric Strabo to attack Constantinople, but the negotiations did not bear fruit.

ASPAR AND LEO I

The kingmaker and man behind the throne in the Eastern Roman Empire was Aspar, who had crossed swords with the Vandals in the early 430s. He was a former consul and easily the most powerful man in the Eastern Empire. The sources even say that he would have been emperor himself if he had not been Arian and a barbarian. He had earlier placed his bodyguard (*domesticus*), Marcian, on the throne in 450. In 457, when Marcian died, it was expected that Anthemius would succeed him, but instead Aspar and his son Ardaburius chose their *curator* (household overseer), Leo. Over the next thirteen years, Leo slowly distanced himself from Aspar. Still, Aspar's position was so strong that one of his three sons could have succeeded Leo, who had no sons of his own.

Leo strengthened his position by befriending some of the Isaurian mountain people from the highlands of Asia Minor who were in Constantinople. He gave his daughter Ariadne in marriage to one of them, Tarasicodissa, who later changed his name to Zeno. Now Zeno was in a position to gain the imperial throne, and so he became Leo's greatest supporter against Aspar and his party. Another contender for the throne was Basiliscus, the brother of the emperor's wife, Verina, who was also well connected to Aspar. Because of the political climate in Constantinople, the situation was now a disaster waiting to happen.

THE AFRICAN EXPEDITION

In 468, preparations for the strike on the Vandals were finished, and an Eastern Roman army was ready. Marcellinus came from Dalmatia, and the Western Empire supplied troops and gold for the expedition. Another army would march from Alexandria and attack Tripolitania.

The capable Leo spared nothing to make the war a success. The sources say there were a thousand ships, manned by seven thousand sailors, and one hundred thousand fighting men. The number of sailors seems low, but that might indicate that there were really fewer ships, and while the number of fighting men is impossibly high, it signifies a force quite out of the ordinary, so we might cautiously estimate it at perhaps thirty thousand. Leo also collected sixty-four thousand pounds of gold and seven hundred thousand pounds of silver.

The cost of such an expedition equaled or even surpassed a year's imperial revenue.

But the choice of overall general, Basiliscus, Leo's brother-in-law, was to be the undoing of it all. Basiliscus showed the full extent of his ineptness, so much so that some historians believe he was bribed by the Vandals or Aspar to fail as greatly as he did.

Initially, the three-pronged campaign went well. Marcellinus had brought his troops to Sardinia and Sicily and defeated the Vandals there. A force under Generals Heracleius of Edessa and Marsus the Isaurian marched from Egypt on the coastal road, defeated the few Vandal forces in Tripolitania, and from there moved toward Carthage. The main attack was conducted by Basiliscus and moved straight against the Vandal heartland. After defeating part of the Vandal fleet, he landed at Mercurion, a town some thirty-five miles from Carthage, on the Promontorium Mercurii (Cape Bon in modern-day Tunisia). The historian Procopius says it was believed that if he had moved immediately against Carthage, he would have taken it at once, as Geiseric was terrified at the enormous force brought against him. But Basiliscus did not move from Mercurion, and it was later thought that he might have been cowardly or treacherous. More likely, he was simply a bad general.

Meanwhile, Geiseric reacted immediately, arming as many troops as he could and putting them on ships. Other fast ships were made ready to be used as fire ships. He then asked Basiliscus for a five-day truce, pretending he was about to surrender. Basiliscus agreed. Geiseric needed the five days for the wind to be favorable to his plan. As soon as the wind changed, the Vandals sailed against the Roman fleet, towing the fire ships. When they came near the Roman ships, they ignited the fire ships and sent them against the tightly packed Roman fleet. The first Roman ships caught fire, and, aided by the wind, the fire spread quickly to the others. Amid the confusion, the rest of the Vandal fleet struck, ramming ships and hurling javelins at the Roman sailors, as Procopius stirringly narrates:

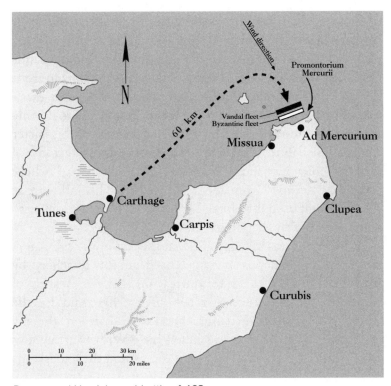

Roman and Vandal naval battle of 468.

As the fire advanced in this way the Roman fleet was filled with tumult, as was natural, and with a great din that rivaled the noise caused by the wind and the roaring of the flames, as the soldiers and the sailors together pushed with their poles the fire-boats and their ships as well, which were being destroyed by one another in complete disorder. And already the Vandals too were at hand ramming and sinking the ships and making booty of such of the soldiers as attempted to escape and of their arms as well.

The Romans could not fight back effectively, and despite the courageous defense of the Roman second in command, Joannes, the fleet lost great numbers of ships. Only half the fleet managed to reach Sicily. With the Vandals in command

of the sea, there was no possibility of supplying the great
Roman army in North Africa. Heracleius and Marsus
retreated to Tripolitania, which remained in Roman hands
until 470, when the troops were required on the Balkan frontier and for the political infighting at court. Basiliscus extri-
cated himself and returned to Constantinople, where he only
escaped execution because of the entreaties of his sister
Verina. The failure of the 468 expedition and the great loss of
money threw Constantinople into turmoil. Aspar, whose
power had declined from about 466, regained his influence at
the court and used it to force Leo to fulfill his old promise to
name Aspar's son Patricius caesar and Leo's successor.

Marcellinus was killed in Sicily at the end of the campaign,
sometime in 468, possibly in a battle or by treachery by
Ricimer, but the sources are unclear on this. On hearing of
Marcellinus's death, Geiseric is supposed to have said that the
Romans had cut off their right hand with their left, thereby
intimating that Ricimer had killed him. With Marcellinus's
forces leaderless, the Vandals soon recaptured the lost islands
of Sicily and Sardinia.

Despite this setback, Leo attempted to conquer the
Vandals through another naval expedition in 470, under the
command of Heracleius and Marsus, employing troops from
Egypt and the nearby desert areas. The expedition disem-
barked and captured a number of cities in Tripolitania before
Leo recalled the force due to fear of Aspar. One source says
that in Leo's 470 invasion, troops landed in Africa and
attacked Carthage, forcing Geiseric to negotiate, but that Leo
was compelled to retreat due to political problems in
Constantinople. We do not know if there were, in fact, two
separate operations in 468–470 or one united operation,
mixed up by the sources. But Aspar's resurgence was only
temporary. He and his son soon fell from power, and they
were executed in 471, some say because of his alleged support
for the Vandals. The chances of Basiliscus's ever becoming
emperor grew slim indeed. The Vandals probably signed a
formal peace with the Western Empire in 470, but it appears

that peace with the East was only made in 472. We do not know the exact terms of the peace settlements, but it may have been to return to the status quo before the war.

FALL OF ANTHEMIUS

With the defeat of Basiliscus's expedition, the Western Empire was lost. It had no money, and the Eastern Romans could not finance another expedition on such a scale. The West had fragmented and had no sources of revenue for the army, which had to defend the empire against Vandals, Burgundians, Visigoths, Sueves, and other barbarian tribes. In 470, Anthemius's harsh response to a suspected conspiracy alienated Ricimer. In spring 471, a rift appeared between them, and Ricimer called six thousand Germanic veterans who had served in the Vandal War to join him in Mediolanum (modern-day Milan). Ricimer proclaimed the former Vandal candidate Olybrius emperor in April 471. This may have neutralized Eastern Roman support for Anthemius, because Olybrius was allied with the imperial family.

It was now clear that the Vandals were the dominant power in the Western Mediterranean. After an attempt at negotiations between Ricimer and Anthemius, civil war erupted in Rome in late 471 or 472. For five months, Ricimer besieged Anthemius in Rome, and famine was rife among the inhabitants. Finally, on July 11, 472, Ricimer took the city— some say helped by treachery within the walls—and Anthemius was beheaded by Ricimer or Gundobad, who was Ricimer's nephew and a Burgundian prince. Ricimer died, apparently of some disease, only five weeks later, on August 19, after having been the de facto ruler of the Western Empire for sixteen years. Gundobad took over his position.

EMPEROR OLYBRIUS

Anicius Olybrius had all the makings of a successful emperor. He was the husband of the great-granddaughter of Emperor Theodosius, on good terms with the Eastern Roman emperor, and supported by the powerful Vandals because of his relations to Geiseric and Huneric, Geiseric's son. Finally, Geiseric had managed in his goal to put a Vandal-backed emperor on the Western throne.

But only three months after the death of Anthemius, Olybrius died, on October 22 or November 2, 472. During his short reign, Olybrius had gained the support of Gundobad, who was backed by the Germanic troops after Ricimer's death. Gundobad, who was now in power, left the throne empty for five months before making Glycerius, a former Count of the Domestics, emperor on March 3, 473. Gundobad did not remain in Italy long, for in 473, he inherited the throne of the Burgundian kingdom after his father, Gundioc, died. Eastern Emperor Leo did not recognize Glycerius and instead chose Julius Nepos, a former general in Dalmatia, as the Western emperor. Nepos deposed Glycerius, who was made bishop of Salona (Solin in modern-day Croatia). Nepos was proclaimed emperor of the West in Portus, the harbor of Rome, on June 24 or 29, 474.

Fate of Eudocia

Eudocia had fled the kingdom for Jerusalem in 472, after sixteen years of marriage to Huneric, and left her children at Carthage. Officially, she left because of troubles with the religion of her Arian husband. But it is difficult not to connect her flight with the political events in the Western Empire, particularly because neither Huneric nor Geiseric appear to have made much out of her leaving. That it was due to her husband's Arianism may just have been a story told by the Catholic sources. More likely, it was the price for the Eastern Romans to accept Olybrius on the Western throne. When she died, Eudocia was buried in the sepulcher of her grandmother in Jerusalem.

Emperor Zeno

Leo I died January 18, 474, and Zeno succeeded him. The Germanic Vandals believed that treaties functioned as personal agreements between individuals and not binding contracts between states, and so they erupted once again in raids against the Eastern Romans. Because Zeno faced serious internal problems in his empire, he was forced to settle with the Vandals. In 474, he sent the patrician Severus to North Africa to negotiate a peace. To force an advantageous settlement, Geiseric attacked the Greek city of Nikopolis, as well as the island of Zakynthos, and possibly also Rhodes. Procopius says that when trying to land at Taenarum in Peloponnesus, the Vandals were repulsed by the Romans. In response, Geiseric landed on Zakynthos, plundered it, and took five hundred inhabitants prisoner. These were said to have been taken out to sea, chopped to pieces, and thrown into the ocean.

Despite the attacks, peace was concluded with the Eastern Empire in summer 474. The peace of 474 was a so-called eternal peace, not connected to the ruling emperors, as was usual, and was to last for more than two generations. The Vandals stopped their raids. Many Roman slaves were returned and others ransomed. Geiseric promised that the exiled Catholic clergy could return and that the Catholics in Carthage would not be persecuted for their beliefs. But the appointment of a new bishop of Carthage was not allowed.

With the peace, the independence and recognition of the Vandal kingdom of Africa was ensured. It was the height of the reign of Geiseric, who had succeeded in almost all his major goals. And the much-needed peace allowed Emperor Zeno to focus on troubles much closer to home.

The years 475 and 476 brought the climax of the struggle between the disgraced general Basiliscus and Zeno in the East. With the aid of his sister Verina, Basiliscus pushed Zeno out of Constantinople and gained the throne himself. In January 475, Zeno fled to his home province of Isauria. In August 476, he returned to Constantinople and retook his throne with the aid of Harmatius, a treacherous officer in Basiliscus's army. Basiliscus and his entire family were sent to die in Cappadocia.

ROMULUS AUGUSTULUS

On August 28, 475, the Western emperor, Julius Nepos, made Roman noble Flavius Orestes, a former secretary to Attila the Hun, master of the soldiers. This was an unfortunate choice, as Orestes soon deposed Nepos, who fled to Dalmatia. Orestes then put his son, Flavius Romulus (surnamed Augustulus, or little Augustus, because he was so young), on the throne with the help of the Germanic mercenaries in Italy and their powerful commander, the Scirian Odoacer. Romulus Augustulus was the ninth emperor proclaimed in Italy between 455 and 475, although only four of them were officially recognized in Constantinople. In 475 or 476, with both the Western and Eastern empires in turmoil, Orestes made peace with Geiseric, probably permanently ceding Sicily and Sardinia to the Vandals in return for their support against the Eastern Romans.

FALL OF THE WESTERN EMPIRE

Because the imperial treasury was now bankrupt, the Western soldiers, who were mainly Germanic mercenaries, demanded land in Italy in return for their services. When Orestes refused, their commander, Odoacer, killed him on August 28, 476. Orestes's son, Romulus Augustulus, was removed but allowed to live out his life in the south of Italy as a private citizen and given a yearly allowance of six thousand solidi.

With Odoacer now in power, one-third of Italy was given to his barbarians, and the Senate sent envoys to Emperor Zeno in Constantinople asking for Odoacer to be appointed patrician and entrusted with the administration of Italy. The envoys brought the imperial regalia and stated that there was no need for a separate emperor in the West, as Zeno's rule was considered sufficient for both parts of the empire. In reality, Italy would be ruled independently by Odoacer. In 476, the Vandals gave Sicily to Odoacer in return for a yearly tribute, but they kept a part of the island—probably the important harbor and fortress of Lilybaeum, which could also function as a bridgehead for retaking the island, if necessary. We do not know why Geiseric gave Sicily away. Possibly he did not have the strength to hold the island against an aggressive Odoacer, or perhaps he sought the prestige of receiving tribute from the ruler of Italy.

THE CONDITIONS OF THE CATHOLICS IN AFRICA 455–476

The conditions of the Catholics mentioned in the peace of 474 make it reasonable to look at their conditions since the death of Emperor Valentinian III in 455. Initially, the Catholics were treated better, no doubt because they were more peaceful toward the Vandal rule and the Arians. This influence was possibly due to the political insight of Bishop Deogratias in Carthage. However, on his death in 457, conditions worsened. With Geiseric occupied in foreign wars, the Catholic clergy conspired against the Vandals, possibly also supported by Constantinople. When the conspiracy was discovered, several bishops were exiled, including Felix of Hadrumentum and the bishops from Girba, Sabratha, and Oea in Tripolitania. It was ordered that if any of the exiled bishops died during his exile, a replacement could not be appointed. No doubt unrest in the outlying province of Tripolitania was a cause for concern at the Vandal court, as it could spark other uprisings. The remaining one hundred sixty-four bishops in Proconsularis were maltreated, and the church plate confiscated, according to Victor of Vita. The Catholic churches of Carthage, which had been given back to the Catholics, were again closed, and no new bishop of Carthage was appointed. When the Catholics defied the king and still tried to conduct services in the closed churches in the kingdom, they were severely punished. The strong reaction was probably due more to the act of defying the king than because of the religious significance of the services. Most likely, the Vandal king sought to curb or destroy the leadership of the Catholic Church in North Africa, making the Catholics easier to control and perhaps even to convert.

DEATH OF GEISERIC

On January 25, 477, Geiseric died. For almost fifty years, he had ruled the Vandals and taken them from a wandering tribe of little significance to masters of a great kingdom in the rich provinces of Roman North Africa. Even in his final years, he appears to have had the same energy and restlessness of his younger life. Geiseric had for two generations embodied the Vandal nation, and soon after his death, the energy and activity that he had pressed upon the Vandals began to wane. Geiseric's success made him one of the greatest kings of the Germanic migration age; he was also recognized as one of the cleverest of all the Germanic kings of this period. His ability to establish a fleet and use the grain and olive oil supply as a strategic weapon against the Western Roman Empire were strokes of genius. His military abilities are undisputed, although unfortunately, the sources give us few or no descriptions of his strategies or the course of the battles in which he was involved.

Despite the apparent success of Geiseric in foreign affairs, the Vandal kingdom had no allies when he died. By his aggressive foreign policies, the Vandals were forced to stand alone in the Mediterranean world. His ambitions were initially expansionist, and then, when his limits were reached, he chose to conduct an offensive defense. Geiseric had attempted to exert military power over more than the North African provinces by expanding into Sicily and other Mediterranean islands, but the kingdom simply didn't have the power to control such a great area and population. Prudently, he withdrew from most of Sicily, while still keeping a foothold—most likely to have a base from which to retake it when he had the strength for it—but kept the remaining islands. Later, however, the Vandals would find themselves hard pressed even to defend their African lands.

Geiseric's successes in internal politics were more lasting and, perhaps, more important. He quelled the ambitions of the nobility and created a new nobility that owed its status to the king. To modern eyes this might not seem important, but at the time it was a completely new way of defining the role of a king in a Germanic society. He also managed the transition from the difficult phase of initial settlement to a more stable kingdom, settling his Vandals in the rich lands around Carthage and heralding a form of feudalism. He may have been the architect of organizing the Vandals into thousand-ships, which were not only military units but also administrative groups. And he ensured by his laws that the Hasding lineage would rule the kingdom until its end.

The two main internal enemies to the kingdom during his reign were the Catholic Church and the Roman nobility. By his harsh treatment of both groups, Geiseric was able to quell any uprisings and threats to the new kingdom. Some modern scholars have seen the destruction of tax registers as an attempt at a social revolution to gain the support of the *coloni*, but this appears to be an overinterpretation of Procopius's statement that Geiseric had the registers destroyed.

The third major threat to the kingdom in North Africa was the Moors. Relations with them were good during Geiseric's reign. Moors were brought on his raids and given booty, and they may have been kept in check mainly by Geiseric's reputation as a superb general rather than by military force. By using them as allies, he was also able to project more strength outside the borders of the kingdom, as he did not need to guard his borders so carefully.

Geiseric's greatest achievement was to be the first Germanic king to carve his own stable kingdom on former Roman soil and to make a lasting peace with the Roman Empire, thereby creating a sovereign state. But he failed to create a bond between the Romans and Vandals, as Theodoric the Great later tried so eagerly to do in his Ostrogothic kingdom in Italy. Until the end of the kingdom, the Vandals remained a small military nobility—a form of warrior aristocracy reminiscent of feudal society in the Middle Ages. The Vandal kingdom comprised Vandals, Alans, Moors, Goths, Romans, and many other ethnic elements in the tribal confederation. But there was no ethnic basis for the kingdom, and because Geiseric did not forge a bond between the Roman population and his people, the kingdom would eventually fall.

In his will, Geiseric said that royal power among the Vandals should always fall to the oldest of his male descendants, a succession system known as agnatic seniority. Thus, as the oldest of Geiseric's sons, Huneric succeeded his father to the Vandal throne. But under Geiseric's system, Huneric's brothers, Theodoric and Genzon, were next in line, rather than Huneric's son Hilderic. It is surprising that Geiseric did not create a dynasty as the other Germanic kings had done, and knowingly prevented Hilderic from succeeding Huneric. Geiseric may have wanted to ensure that there was always an experienced adult governing the kingdom.

Geiseric's enormous—and almost religious—importance to the Vandals is seen in the speech of the last Vandal king, Gelimer, before the battle of Tricamarum in 533, in which he asked the Vandals to fight bravely and not to shame the memory of Geiseric. While the words might have been invented by Procopius, we may believe that Procopius felt that these could have been the words spoken.

Even the final struggle for the Vandal kingdom was intertwined with the will of Geiseric. In a letter to Emperor Justinian, King Gelimer replied that he had deposed the reigning King Hilderic because he had to prevent him from making a revolution against the spirit of Geiseric. The Romans used this usurpation as a pretext for invading the kingdom, leading to its destruction in 533.

SIX

The Later Kingdom

"For after the death of Geiseric they [the Vandals] had fallen completely into softness and had maintained neither the same strength for action nor the same military establishment which he had kept ready for use, so that he always moved more quickly than his opponents calculated."
—*Malchus, Roman rhetorician of the late fifth century*

Huneric was older than fifty when he succeeded his father in 477. He was married to the daughter of Valentinian III, Eudocia, but she had already left him by 472. Nothing is known of his time as a hostage at the imperial court, but it does not appear to have changed his character remarkably. We can trace some influences of his stay in the Roman Empire in the fact that, for example, he renamed Hadrumentum as Huniricopolis, in the common imperial fashion.

Apart from some small skirmishes with Roman trade ships from 477–478, we no longer hear of Vandal pirate raids against anyone after the peace with the Eastern Romans in 474 and the death of Geiseric. It may be that problems with adversaries within and close to his kingdom kept Huneric otherwise occupied, and the focus of his reign turned away from the foreign policies of his father and toward domestic challenges. The Vandals' former allies the Moors had supported them out of fear of Geiseric, but now they began a long struggle for the outer parts of the kingdom.

BATTLES AGAINST THE MOORS

The Vandals had in a way been too successful, conquering more territory than they could control with their limited numbers. They simply did not have the forces needed to exert control over more than the central parts of the kingdom. As the outer parts of the Vandal kingdom began to dissolve, the Moors moved into the vacuum. Already by 484, the Moors dwelling in the mountainous Aures region—which lay some thirteen days' journey from Carthage in Numidia in the east of modern-day Algeria—had revolted. Because of the difficulty of fighting with cavalry on the steep rocky slopes, this region never again came under the Vandals. During almost his entire reign, Huneric fought the Moors in the Aures region without any decisive results. During the latter part of the fifth century, inscriptions show an adaptation of the imperial rhetoric of power by the tribes of the Aures Mountains. One inscription in Little Kabylia celebrates the self-proclaimed *Rex gentis Ucutamani* (King of the Ucutamani people). On another, the Moorish King Masties laid claim to the successive titles of *dux* (duke, a military commander of forces stationed in a frontier province) and *imperator* (emperor). Farther west, the third and most famous inscription is from Altava from 508. It shows that the region around the towns of Safar, Altava, and Castra Severiana in Mauretania Caesarensis was under the control of the Moorish King Masuna, who styled himself *Rex Maurorum et Romanorum*— King of Moors and Romans. In 484, this area was still a Vandal possession, but evidently not twenty-four years later.

The loss of Vandal prestige under Huneric affected relations with the Eastern Empire. Huneric had asked to have the property of Eudocia and of her father, Valentinian III, handed over. Minor hostilities had also erupted, and it appears that the Vandals had captured some trade ships. In response, Emperor Zeno sent Alexander, the head steward of the household of Huneric's sister-in-law, Placidia, to negotiate. Huneric accepted the weakened position of the Vandal kingdom and withdrew his demands in 478, compensated the Roman traders, and declared that the Vandals would live in friendship with the Roman emperor. As reason he gave the honorful treatment of his sister-in-law, the wife of Olybrius, at the imperial court. According to the Roman rhetorician Malchus, Huneric's response was due to the Vandals having adapted to the lifestyle of the rich Romans and grown soft from luxury. Huneric also agreed to allow the filling of the seat of the bishop of Carthage, which had been vacant since the death of Deogratias in 457, and to give the Catholics in North Africa more freedom. Probably around the end of 480, Eugenius was elected bishop of Carthage.

In return for all this, Huneric asked that the Arians in the Eastern Empire be allowed to freely conduct their services. The difficult Catholic clergy in the kingdom refused to acknowledge Huneric's demands and caused much trouble, until they were persuaded by the Roman envoy Alexander and the population to accept the conditions. The reason for the milder treatment of the Catholics was probably Huneric's concern about the powerful Eastern Empire, and not some intention to reach out to the Catholics, as we see from his later persecutions. Instead, he turned with fearful force on the Manicheans, whose successful propaganda among the Arian clergy provided him with a cause for retaliation.

STRUGGLES AMONG THE HASDINGS

Huneric needed peace with the Romans, not only to deal with the Moors but also with the Hasding royal family, to ensure the succession of his son, Hilderic. In his attempt to create a dynasty, he turned his anger on the families of his brothers, Theodoric and Genzon, who were closer in line for the throne. This attempt to ensure a direct line of succession instead of following the will of Geiseric met with great disapproval from the nobles. Some of the nobles were punished severely, and Heldica, the prime minister, was executed, as was his wife. Huneric then focused on his brother Theodoric, who, according to the law of Geiseric, was next in line for the throne. He may have also been at the center of the opposition against Huneric, willingly or not. Theodoric's wife was executed on a false charge, and his oldest son soon followed his mother to the grave. Theodoric and the oldest son of Genzon, Godagis, were then exiled, where they later died. The young son of Theodoric and his two daughters were punished by being ridden on a donkey through Carthage and were afterward exiled.

Other followers of his brothers, as well as many other nobles, were killed, and the Arian Patriarch Iucundus, who was the spiritual guide of Theodoric, was burned alive in Carthage because he objected to Huneric's succession wishes. Other clergy were thrown to the wild animals or executed. By 481 or 482, most of the opposition was dead. But when Huneric died unexpectedly of a disease in 484, his nephew, rather than his son, succeeded him, thwarting his plans.

Religious persecutions

When Huneric perceived around 481–482 that the Roman Empire was threatened and weakened by trouble inside and outside and thus was little threat to the Vandal kingdom, he began to reassert pressure on the Catholics. He was strongly supported in his actions by the Arian clergy, including the fanatical Patrich Cyrila, who had replaced Iucundus as head of the Arian Church. Even though we have only pro-Catholic sources, the best of whom is Victor of Vita, who had many reasons to present the persecutions in as bad a light as possible, there is no doubt that Huneric moved against the Catholics with great hatred. While the Catholic sources see the persecutions as religious, it is possible that Huneric also—or perhaps mainly—like his father saw them as politically motivated measures to strike down the strongest anti-Vandal groups in the kingdom. An edict stated that all people who held public office had to convert to Arianism. If they refused, their property was confiscated and they were exiled.

However, a plan to confiscate the property of bishops who died and ask five hundred solidi to replace the bishop with a new one, was canceled on the recommendation of his advisers. At the start of 483, he began the persecution of the Catholics in earnest and struck hard at the heart of Catholicism in North Africa. About five thousand bishops, priests, and others were gathered in the cities of Lares and Sicca Veneria in Proconsularis. From there they were marched through Byzacena to the Moorish desert, where they were to live in exile. The hardships of this event are seen in an inscription from south of Sicca Veneria, which lists names of martyrs and confessors.

Many died during the march south. This brutal action caused Emperor Zeno to send an ambassador to Carthage to ask for milder treatment of the Catholics, but to no avail. Huneric showed his contempt for Zeno in 483 when he announced harsher measures while the envoy, Reginus, was in Carthage. It appears that the emperor's request may have spurred the king on to further persecutions. On May 19, 483, a royal edict was read aloud in Carthage and sent by couriers around the kingdom, stating that all Orthodox bishops were to gather in Carthage on February 1, 484, to debate the truth of their doctrine with the Arian clergy. Four hundred sixty-six bishops went to Carthage from throughout the kingdom, including bishops from the Balearic isles and Corsica. No doubt they suspected an ulterior motive behind the edict and the convenience of gathering all the Catholic bishops of the kingdom in one place. The king rejected a request that bishops from outside the kingdom participate. Probably he feared that they would not be cowed so easily. To further his plan, the brightest and most able of the Catholic bishops were exiled beforehand or maltreated. The Arian bishops did not show up, and so the debate was canceled, but the Catholic bishops made a statement of their beliefs, the so-called *Book of the Catholic Faith* (*Liber fidei Catholicae*), in which they tried to prove through biblical examples that the Father, the Son, and the Holy Ghost were of one substance and essence.

With the excuse that the debate was canceled because of the troublesome Catholics, Huneric closed all the Catholic churches in North Africa on February 7, 484, and ordered that they remain closed until the debate was taken up again. On February 25, Huneric issued another edict, denouncing all Catholics as heretics if they did not convert to Arianism before June 1. Referring to the great persecution of the Nicene belief conducted by the Tetrarchs in the early fourth century, he cited as additional authority for the right of Arianism the twin councils held in 359 at Ariminum and Seleucia-in-Isauria (Silifke in modern-day Turkey), at which Emperor Constantius II had secured a victory for the Arian faith. Religious ceremonies were forbidden, the churches were kept closed, and Catholic clergy were not allowed to stay inside the borders of the kingdom. All Orthodox books and texts were to be burned. All the property of the Catholic Church was to be handed over to the Arians. Indeed, the Catholic churches remained closed until August 10, 494, and only then could the clergy return from exile.

The bishops collected in Carthage were thrown out of the city, and they gathered before the walls. When the king, during a morning ride, was asked why he was treating them as he did, instead of answering, he ordered them to be ridden down. Soon, however, he opened the possibility of the bishops reentering their sees if they took an oath to recognize the future elevation of his son, Hilderic, to the throne and agreed not to conspire with other countries against the Vandals. Here, perhaps, we see the real reasons behind the severe persecution. Only 25 of 46 refused and the rest took the oath. Those who refused were exiled to Corsica, to chop wood for the king's fleet. Those who took the oath were allowed to work as farmers near their sees.

GENERAL PERSECUTION

Only after June 1, 484, did a general persecution of Catholics begin. Although Huneric tried to avoid martyrs, he was also pushed by the Arian clergy, who saw the opportunity to rid themselves of their hardest opponents. Important figures such as Bishop Laetus and the proconsul of Carthage, Victorianus, were martyred during the persecutions. Thousands of others were beaten and maltreated in various cruel ways, such as cutting out the tongues of the confessors. One reason for the violent persecution was probably that the Catholics were continually provoking the Arians by proselytizing in their regions. A further embassy by the Eastern Romans in 484 had no success in quelling the bloodthirst of the king, and Huneric even forced the envoy, Uranius, to witness atrocities.

Although Geiseric also had conducted persecutions, they were mainly aimed at influential individuals and threats to his power. In 484, Huneric appears to have expanded the persecutions to include more ordinary people. The persecutions under Huneric came about because of political motives, religious fanaticism, and, perhaps, desperation. In many cases the clergy appear to have conspired and actively defied the king's commands, which might have been the case with Victorianus, the proconsul of Carthage. With his power less secure than Geiseric's, it is possible that Huneric felt the need to show his power to the Roman population, who outnumbered his Vandals greatly. Even the slightest show of weakness could spark revolts.

No doubt the persecutions also increased the number of converts to Arianism. While the Catholic sources make a point of saying how few Arians there were, the evidence is much different. The aim of the Lateran Synod on March 13, 487, in which thirty-nine Italian and four North African bishops took part, was to find a solution to what should happen to Nicene bishops and clergy who had converted to Arianism, and how to return them to Catholicism. No doubt many did not see the religious arguments as important enough to risk their lives. Catholicism in North Africa was perhaps shaken, but the death of Huneric on December 23, 484, saved the situation from becoming worse.

GUNTHAMUND

Following the succession law of Geiseric, at the death of
Huneric, Gunthamund, a son of Genzon's, was next in line
for the Vandal throne. By fleeing Huneric's wrath, he had
saved his life and was now made king. His older brother,
Godagis, had already died in exile. The persecutions of the
Catholics were continued for a while, but that soon changed.
By 487, Bishop Eugenius of Carthage had been brought back
from exile, and it appears that the Catholic churches were
allowed to reopen and four bishops were allowed to participate in the Lateran Synod of 487. The church of the martyr
Agileus in Carthage was even given back to the Catholics in
487. There are indications, however, that the Arian clergy on
their own continued sporadic persecutions of the Orthodox,
and in 496, there is still evidence of the Catholics being under
pressure.

It is not clear why the new king changed Huneric's religious policies. There was no real pressure from the Eastern
Roman Empire, but perhaps Huneric's persecution of his
own family caused Gunthamund to change his policies. He
may have thought Huneric's harshness toward the Roman
population was unwise, and he wanted to gain more support
among the common population. But Gunthamund also faced
enemies on his borders, which may have caused him to focus
elsewhere. The Moors were increasingly causing trouble on
the borders and inside the kingdom.

During his reign, Gunthamund focused on the war with
the Moors and fought them in numerous battles. The Moors
settled on the borders of Byzacena raided the province and
attacked the inhabitants. Their plight was great, as they had
no walls behind which to defend themselves, and they were
forced to flee or turn their houses into little fortresses. While
Gunthamund appears to have been successful in some of the
battles, the Moors were not completely defeated, as an
inscription from 495 found at Tipasa shows. It refers to a
Catholic exile buried in the city who was killed in a "Moorish
war."

Meanwhile, Italy had been brought into a great war when the Ostrogoths of Theodoric the Great entered the still rich and fertile lands in 489 and made war on Odoacer and his Germanic troops. It was a great opportunity for the Vandals to retake Sicily from Odoacer, but Gunthamund failed in this completely. A Vandal expedition to Sicily was defeated—possibly after some initial successes—by the Ostrogoths, and Gunthamund was forced in 491 to ask for peace with the Ostrogoths. The tribute from Italy to the Vandal kingdom was stopped, and the Vandals lost their foothold in Sicily. It is possible the Vandals were not strong enough to keep an army in North Africa and Sicily at the same time. Despite the important events that took place during Gunthamund's reign, we know very little about them because there are almost no sources for this period.

THRASAMUND

The unfortunate Gunthamund died around September 3, 496, and was followed by his brother Thrasamund (496–523), who was well respected for his abilities and good education. The new king quickly showed that he did not accept his brother's religious policies. Unlike his predecessors, Thrasamund was interested in religious issues and theological debate. His assault on the Orthodox Church was founded in the deeply held belief that it was his duty to expunge the Nicene Creed from North Africa while at the same time maintaining the stability of the Vandal kingdom. So Thrasamund strengthened the campaign to spread the Arian faith, but he did not treat the Orthodox as harshly as his predecessors did. Converts were given gifts, honors, and jobs in the administration or at court. Criminals who converted were pardoned. It appears that this strategy created many more converts. Troublesome Catholic bishops were removed from their sees and exiled. In 508–509, sixty Catholic bishops ignored a previous royal edict that forbade the consecration of new bishops, and they were exiled to Sardinia. Among these was the renowned bishop of Ruspe, Fulgentius.

Thrasamund engaged himself deeply in theology, and around 516–517, he brought Fulgentius to Carthage from his exile in Sardinia in order to debate religious issues. Sardinia had become the spiritual center of the North African church in exile. Sardinia even created two popes during the Vandal period: Hilarius, who was bishop of Rome from 461–468, succeeded despite the wars and the Vandal presence, but the other, Symmachus (496–514), was no doubt helped by the sudden surge in Christian life in Sardinia. Several monasteries were founded by the exiles in Sardinia, and Fulgentius appears to have been a leader among the Catholic bishops on the island. While Fulgentius was in Carthage, extensive effort and resources were put into converting the Catholic congregations in Sardinia to Arianism. When Fulgentius managed to convert some Arians in Carthage back to Orthodoxy, he was exiled again in 518–519, after two years of freedom. He and his exiled friends had to stay in Sardinia until the time of King Hilderic (523–530).

The *Life of St. Fulgentius*, probably written by his disciple Ferrandus shortly after Fulgentius's death, is the most important source on the religious life of Vandal North Africa after Victor of Vita's *History of the Vandal Persecution*, which ends around 484. Ferrandus describes Thrasamund as a persecutor, but one quite unusually concerned with the intellectual foundations for his actions and one who appears eager to debate theological details with Fulgentius. But Thrasamund could also be harsh against the Catholics when he felt it was needed. Among other actions, he issued an edict stating that empty sees were not to be refilled, and more than sixty bishops were exiled to other countries, including Eugenius, the bishop of Carthage.

However, the exiles inside the kingdom were treated fairly well and were allowed to communicate with the rest of the population. Also, Pope Symmachus was allowed to send gold and clothing to the exiles. Surprisingly, Thrasamund did not move against the Catholic monasteries, and Fulgentius even founded two monasteries in North Africa, placed on land given to them by wealthy Romans. Indeed, after the banishment of the bishops under Thrasamund, the monasteries appear to have become centers of faith more than before. They increased in number and were particularly concentrated on the east coast of Byzacena. While the argument between the Arians and Niceans might seem to be of a somewhat difficult theological nature, one source tells us that the nature of the Trinity was now a popular topic at dinner parties among the nobles of the kingdom. This shows how Romanized the Vandal elite had become—almost all of whom had been born after the migration years.

THRASAMUND MARRIES AMALAFRIDA

By 493, Theodoric the Great had secured his hold on Italy and created an independent Ostrogothic kingdom. The Ostrogoths were also Arian, and Theodoric worked to make treaties with the other Germanic kingdoms. He approached the Vandals, whose fleet would be a great asset to him, as he had none to oppose the Romans and needed the grain from North Africa and Sardinia to feed the population of Rome. The Vandals would gain greater security from the alliance and revenue from the trade with Italy. To cement the alliance, around 500, Thrasamund, whose wife had died without children, married Amalafrida, who was the sister of Theodoric the Great and a widow. The marriage strengthened the ties between the two kingdoms. The marriage was made on a great scale, and one thousand Gothic nobles and five thousand mounted warriors went with her to Carthage as a bodyguard. Theodoric even handed over the city of Lilybaeum on the west corner of Sicily to Thrasamund as part of her dowry. We may in this see a return to the situation in Sicily before the war with the Ostrogoths in 491. However, the great number of armed Ostrogoths following Amalafrida to Africa must also have raised some eyebrows and caused some concern in the Vandal nation, even if they, as some modern historians believe, were a kind of military aid to the Vandal kingdom. A border stone in Sicily, which is now lost, attested to the island's division at the marriage of Thrasamund, carrying the inscription *"Fines inter Vandalos et Gothos"* (border between Vandals and Goths).

In Ostrogothic Italy, it seems that the marriage was used politically to legitimize the rule of Theodoric. In a panegyric dated 507, poet and Bishop Ennodius speaks of the "obedience" of the Vandals to Theodoric's rule. In the same year, Cassiodorus, the prime minister of the Ostrogothic kingdom, implied that the enemy of Italy had been curbed by Gothic diplomacy. However, we do not see any evidence of the Vandals being subservient to the Ostrogoths. Quite the contrary, the Vandal fleet and the threat of a stoppage of grain supplies put the Ostrogoths at a disadvantage, as they had no way of retaliating without a fleet.

Battles with the Moors

The continuing battles against the Moors did not go well. Cabaon, an experienced warlord, ruled the Moors in Tripolitania. He heard that the Vandal army was moving against him and prepared himself accordingly. We know of this campaign against Cabaon through Procopius, who describes it in detail. When the Vandals camped on the first day of the campaign, they used the local Catholic churches as stables for their horses and other animals. They beat and mistreated the Catholic priests they came across and forced them to do various menial tasks for the Vandal warriors. Cabaon then instructed his troops and spies to do the opposite when they marched through the regions in which the Vandals marched. They were to clean the Catholic churches and help the priests, and so gain the support of the local population.

When informed by his spies that the Vandals were near, Cabaon prepared his army for battle. He made a circle in the plain where he wanted to make his palisade and put camels twelve deep around the palisade, while placing women and children and their possessions in the middle. The Moorish warriors were to stand between the camels and cover themselves with shields.

When the Vandals came to the camp of the Moors, they were perplexed. They were all horsemen and did not know how to go into battle on foot, but neither were they good with javelins and bows, preferring to fight up close with spears and swords. The horses were afraid of the smell of the camels, and so refused to charge the camp, and the Vandals could do nothing at a distance. The Moors, on the other hand, hurled javelins against the enemy from their safe defensive position until the Vandals' losses caused them to retreat. When the Vandal forces began to flee, the Moors came out against them and killed and captured many. According to Procopius, only a remnant of the army returned to Carthage, and it was considered the greatest defeat the Vandals had suffered against the Moors. The other Moorish tribes were inspired by this defeat, and so they, too, rose in revolt, and Thrasamund was forced to evacuate the farmers of the southern part of Byzacena. The Moors could easily replace their losses in these battles, but for the Vandals, whose army almost literally was their kingdom, it caused great concern. They may also have been alarmed by the fact that Cabaon might be supported by the Catholic Romans, whom he continued to treat kindly during the campaigns. It may have been this disastrous campaign that caused Thrasamund to ask for Gothic military aid while he was regaining his strength. But this is speculation, and it is difficult to establish a chronology of events from the poor sources.

Relations between the Ostrogoths and the Vandals

Thrasamund continued the focus on keeping back the Moors, while entertaining the friendship of the most powerful nations around the Mediterranean: the Romans, the Ostrogoths, and the Visigoths. Thrasamund was like Gunthamund—a quiet monarch who focused on the inner workings of the kingdom. He kept up peaceful foreign politics and did not raid the other nations around the Mediterranean. The relations between the Vandals and Theodoric the Great and the Ostrogothic kingdom of Italy were quite friendly until the final years of his reign, but were somewhat strained in the years 508–511. In the battle at Campus Vogladensis (Vouillé in modern-day Provence, France) in 507, the Visigoths had been severely defeated by the Franks. Their king, Alaric II (484–507), was killed, and they were forced out of Gaul by the Frankish king Chlodowech. The Ostrogoths moved into Gaul in the following year to retake Provence and support their kinsmen. With the Ostrogothic army fighting the Franks, a Roman fleet appeared off the coast of South Italy and raided Calabria and Apulia. Theodoric the Great sent an embassy to the Vandals to ask for their support as promised in their treaty after the marriage of Amalafrida, but Thrasamund did nothing. Furthermore, it is known that he courted the friendship of Emperor Anastasius in the same period, and it appears that the Vandals might have made some sort of secret agreement with the Romans. However, the Ostrogoths were successful in Provence, and no further harm was done by the Romans, who did not have the strength to invade Italy.

Gesalic

In Visigothic Spain, the usurper Gesalic (507–511) caused a great deal of trouble. Although he was soon dethroned and had to flee from his capital at Barcino, he was still to cause more troubles for the Visigoths and the Ostrogoths. From Barcino he sailed to Thrasamund in North Africa, where he was kindly received in 510 and provided with large sums of money so he could return to try his luck at the Visigothic throne again. When Theodoric was informed of this surprising Vandal support for the usurper, he wrote a strongly worded letter in 511 to Thrasamund in which he also told him that he could not possibly have asked the advice of his wife, Amalafrida, who undoubtedly would have kept him away from such a hostile action toward the Goths. Thrasamund accepted the letter and the rebuke, and sent ambassadors with large presents to the Ostrogothic court at Ravenna. Theodoric accepted the apology for his actions but did not accept the presents. Gesalic himself was soon defeated and killed, but a crack in the relations between the two kingdoms had appeared. After these events, the two kingdoms appear for a while to have returned to more friendly relations, and in 519, Thrasamund sent wild beasts to the circus games in Rome when the entrance into the consulate of the noble Eutharich, the son-in-law of King Theodoric, was celebrated.

RELATIONS TO THE ROMAN EMPIRE

The reign of Thrasamund was characteristic of a movement toward Roman culture, and Thrasamund was on friendly terms with Emperors Anastasius and Justin (518–527). On the death of Anastasius in 518, there was much doubt about who would succeed him. After long debates and deliberations, the Senate chose Justin, against the wishes of the Imperial Guard and others at the court. Justin was a surprising choice. He was an Illyrian peasant who had risen from the ranks in the army and was now, at about age sixty-five, chief of the palace guards (*comes excubitorium*). He had no administrative experience or cultural education, and his main abilities lay in his respectable, if not distinguished, military career. Some sources even describe him as being illiterate. Justin soon took steps to improve the conditions of the Catholics in North Africa by sending embassies to the Vandals and continuing the good relations started by Anastasius.

HILDERIC IS MADE KING

On May 6, 523, Thrasamund died; he was succeeded on May 7 by his elderly cousin Hilderic, the son of Huneric and Eudocia. Due to the succession law of Geiseric, the throne had passed to his nephews on the death of Huneric, and Hilderic had waited almost forty years to succeed to his father's throne. He was born roughly between 456 and 472, and so was at the time around fifty or sixty years old, and an example of one unfortunate aspect of the succession law of Geiseric—that the king would always be quite old. It was believed that he was influenced by his Catholic mother, and Procopius relates that Thrasamund, on his deathbed, had

50 denarii coin of Hilderic with a reverse showing a personification of Carthage and the legend FELIX KARTG, "Fortunate Carthage." (*Author*)

ordered him to swear that he would never use his royal power to restore the churches to the Catholics. He swore, but cleverly tried to escape the oath. So after Thrasamund died, but before Hilderic was crowned, he issued orders for all exiled Catholic bishops to return, to open the closed Catholic churches, and he made Bonifacius bishop of Carthage. In this way he had not used his royal power to help the Catholics. These were the first signs of a radical political change toward the Roman Empire.

Hilderic permitted the holding of two Catholic provincial councils in 523, in which Fulgentius also participated. On February 5, 525, the great Council of Carthage was held for the entire kingdom, but the bishops of Byzacena boycotted it because they did not acknowledge the primacy of the bishop of Carthage, the newly appointed Bonifacius. Only sixty-one bishops participated, compared to the four hundred sixty-six at the religious discussion of 484. The smaller number was probably due to the Byzacenan boycott and the wars with the Moors, which made the roads unsafe. For example, other than the bishop of Mina, none of the bishops from Mauretania Caesarensis were able to attend, because of Moorish invasions. The quick holding of the Catholic councils are clear evidence that Hilderic had contemplated his change of policy toward the Catholic Church before becoming king. New Catholic churches were also being consecrated in Proconsularis, including a new basilica in the town of Furnos Maius built in 528.

In foreign politics, Hilderic turned away from the Ostrogothic kingdom and turned toward the Roman Empire. Hilderic was on friendly terms with Emperors Justin and Justinian (527–565), who was governing the Empire for his uncle, who was old and inexperienced in matters of state. This radical turn is also seen in the minting of Vandal silver coins with the image of Justin. We may speculate what would have happened if Huneric had managed to put Hilderic on the throne so many years before.

Revolt of Queen Amalafrida

But the Arian Amalafrida, who had been queen of the Vandals for some twenty years, was not going to accept this change in foreign relations and the new religious policy of the kingdom, and she started a rebellion in 525. She may have been spurred on by the Ostrogoths, who feared an alliance between the Romans and Vandals. No doubt this complete reversal of the Vandal kingdom's religious policies and foreign relations also caused many to support her. The rebels asked for help from the Moors, who eagerly came with an army. At the city of Capsa, some three hundred miles south of Carthage, on the edge of the desert, a great battle was fought between the rebels and the Vandals. Hilderic was victorious, and Amalafrida was captured and taken to Carthage. The remains of her Ostrogothic bodyguard of six thousand were executed for supporting the rebellion. The Ostrogothic king, Theodoric the Great, would not accept this grave insult and gave the order to build one thousand ships and gather crews to create an Ostrogothic navy. The collection point was to have been Ravenna on June 13, 526. His death on August 30, 526, ended this plan, but the prospects of the expedition would have been bleak, as the veteran Vandal navy probably would have easily put the inexperienced Ostrogothic fleet to flight. The Ostrogoths also lacked knowledge of logistics, which would have caused great problems for an invasion. Furthermore, the Romans would not have accepted an assault on a friendly king.

THE MURDER OF AMALAFRIDA

Until the death of Theodoric in 526, Amalafrida was kept a prisoner in Carthage. After Theodoric died, Hilderic put her to death for her rebellion. The Ostrogothic Queen Amalasuntha, daughter of Theodoric the Great who ruled on behalf of her young son Athalaric, was greatly angered by the murder of one of the Ostrogothic royal family. The already dismal relations between the two kingdoms now turned even worse. But a military stalemate existed, as neither of the two peoples was capable of a serious attack on the other. The Roman statesman Cassiodorus, the prime minister of the Ostrogothic kingdom, wrote an angry letter of complaint to Hilderic on behalf of the queen. Ambassadors carried the letter to North Africa asking for an explanation. Hilderic claimed that Amalafrida had died a natural death on account of her old age, but this appears not to have been believed. It is not clear what happened next. The Ostrogoths probably threatened war, and the Vandals undoubtedly answered back with threats of raids by their powerful fleet, but nothing happened. It would take the Ostrogoths a long time to prepare an expedition, and without a fleet, they could not seriously harm the Vandals. But Queen Amalasuntha would soon find a way to punish the Vandals.

THE DECLINE OF HILDERIC

Hilderic was a strongly pro-Roman and pro-Catholic ruler, but his Vandal subjects did not like his policies and considered him a weak king, as he did not have the military abilities of his predecessors. Although he beat down the rebellion of Amalafrida, his position continued to weaken. For several years, Hilderic's subjects, who valued military prowess, watched his rule with ever-greater impatience. Because of

Hilderic's age, his first cousin once removed, Gelimer, was
expected to become king soon. Gelimer was the son of
Geilaris, who was the son of Genzon, who was the son of
Geiseric. But Gelimer could not wait, and took over more and
more of the tasks of the king, which Hilderic, in the spirit of
friendliness—and probably to appease the "nationalistic"
party—gave him. But it appears from a later letter Gelimer
sent to Emperor Justinian that Hilderic might have thought
to change the succession rules of Geiseric in order to put one
of his popular nephews, Hoamer or Hoageis, on the throne.
It does not seem unreasonable for the son of Huneric to try
again to change the succession—after all, Hilderic had waited
more than half a lifetime to reach his father's throne.

VANDALS DEFEATED BY THE MOORS

Hilderic was a well-educated ruler, but he could not stand
warfare, and according to Procopius even disliked hearing of
it. Accordingly, his nephew Hoamer led his armies against the
Moors. The elderly king was most likely also physically unfit
for war.

Apart from the capital, Mauretania Caesarensis was now
entirely in the hands of the Moors. Mauretania Tingitana was
long gone, apart from possibly Tingis and Septem, and by
525, southern Numidia and Mauretania Sitifensis had also
been lost. The rise of the Moorish chieftain Antalas in the
southern parts of Byzacena caused particular problems.
During a raid in 528 or 529, the Moors of Antalas were
pushed into the mountains, where they fortified themselves.
Meanwhile, the Vandal warriors led by Hoamer—or
Hilderic, according to the panegyrist Flavius Cresconius
Corippus (which seems unlikely because of his age and lack
of interest in warfare)—were suffering from thirst and left
their positions to get water from a nearby river. The Moors
attacked the Vandals while their army was in disorder and
soon routed them. In the difficult terrain, the Vandals lost
many warriors. For the Vandals it was a disaster. They held
their kingdom through their army, and a defeat would only

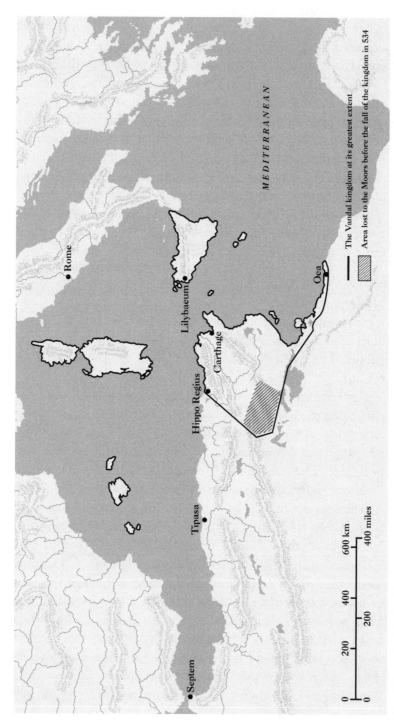

The Vandal kingdom at its greatest extent

Area lost to the Moors before the fall of the kingdom in 534

Vandal area lost to the Moors.

inspire revolts among their Roman population and further raids by the Moors. After the defeat, the eastern coast of Byzacena, with Ruspe, Hadrumentum, and Thapsus, was subject to severe Moorish plundering expeditions.

THE FALL OF HILDERIC

The defeat was the opportunity Gelimer had been awaiting. A Germanic king was not allowed defeat in battle. It was more or less accepted that a militarily unsuccessful king could be removed. Hilderic had lost a great battle against the Moors and was, according to Gelimer, conspiring to give the kingdom to the Romans. No doubt, Hilderic's religious and pro-Roman policies were also exasperating the nobles of the kingdom, who saw a chance to regain their power over the kingship, which they had lost during the uprising of 442 and the steady decline since then.

Accordingly, Gelimer, backed by the Vandal nobles, deposed Hilderic on June 15, 530, and threw him into jail with his followers and family. Among the former were several who came from the Roman nobility and naturally leaned toward the pro-Roman king; among the latter were Hilderic's nephews Hoamer and Hoageis. Gelimer, an able warrior and general, was then made king. Gelimer knew what would have become of him if Hilderic had succeeded in changing the rules of succession. Since Gelimer was the legitimate heir next in line after Hilderic, Hoamer or Hoageis would no doubt have murdered him if one of them had come to power. While the Roman sources describe the elevation of Gelimer as usurpation, there is little doubt that most of the Vandals objected to the Romanized and unwarlike ways of Hilderic, and his better treatment of the Catholics. Furthermore, the pressure of the Moors made it natural to choose a king who was more capable in war than Hilderic. There is no evidence that any Vandals supported Hilderic, despite Roman attempts during the later war with the Vandals to propagandize against Gelimer. If any opposition to Gelimer existed, it would surely have been mentioned by our anti-Vandal sources. Neither was Vandal resistance to the later Roman invasion less bitter. However, the deposition of Hilderic and the elevation of Gelimer would have far-reaching consequences, and they signaled the beginning of the end of the Vandal kingdom.

SEVEN

The Roman Invasion

"Before all things [is] this, which now Almighty God has deigned to indicate through us on behalf of His praise and name; this has exceeded all miraculous works which occurred in the present age: that Africa should recover her freedom through us in so short a time, having been captured by the Vandals one hundred and five years ago—Vandals who were at once enemies of souls and bodies."
—*The opening sentences of Emperor Justinian's edict on the Praetorian Prefecture of Africa, issued at Constantinople in 534*

In the Roman Empire, which now consisted of the lands of the former Eastern Empire ruled from Constantinople, a new emperor had come to power who would change the fate of the Vandal kingdom. Emperor Justin's favorite nephew was Petrus Sabbatius, whom he adopted and gave the name Justinian. The choice of his nephew was not surprising, as he had several times been selected for various important missions and had been steadily promoted within the imperial administration. When Justin became too weak to rule, he turned the daily business of the empire over to Justinian. Both of them were on friendly terms with King Hilderic. In spring 527, Justin became dangerously ill, and the Senate asked him to name Justinian as his colleague and successor. The ceremony was performed on April 4; on August 1, Justin died, leaving Justinian emperor of the Roman Empire.

Justinian was highly religious, energetic, and often worked late into the night. He was able to choose able generals and ministers, some of whom he promoted from low station. He came from a poor background, from the peasants of Illyria and Thrace. His wife, Theodora, who played an important part in his rule, was a former dancer from a poor family.

Above all, Justinian was Roman in spirit, and he boasted that Latin was his native tongue—he did not even speak Greek up to the standards of the imperial court. He was well acquainted with Roman history and revived many old Roman customs while also trying out new thoughts and ideas. His main aim appears to have been to restore the Roman Empire to its ancient glory by recovering the provinces of the Western Empire, particularly Rome, the center of the ancient empire. For the Roman Empire, it would be the last chance to recover the lost provinces; time was passing, and fewer and fewer of the citizens of the former Western Empire remembered the old days of the empire before the Germanic kingdoms established in the fifth century. In the case of North Africa, few— if any—would have experienced the time before the Vandal rule, and so the population might be less eager to support the return of the legions. After all, they had lived in the Vandal kingdom all their lives. So for Justinian, it was time to act.

Procopius and Corippus

We now enter a period of Vandal history where our sources, mainly Procopius and Corippus, are much better, and so we are able to go into greater details on the Vandal kingdom and the campaign that ended it. Procopius was the secretary of General Belisarius, who was commanding the expedition to retake the Roman lands in North Africa. During and after Belisarius's campaigns, Procopius wrote about events he observed firsthand and those he learned about through talks with Vandals and Goths. His vivid and detailed descriptions of Justinian's wars and Belisarius's life are our best sources for the period.

Procopius was born at Caesarea in Palestine late in the fifth century and became a lawyer. In 527, he reached the position of legal adviser and secretary to Belisarius, and followed him during his first command against the Persians. He accompanied him again in 533 in the war against the Vandals, and in 535 against the Ostrogoths. Based on the events he describes and does not describe, it can be calculated that Procopius died sometime after 558. Procopius's greatest work, *History of the Wars*, tells of the Persian Wars of Justinian down to 550, the Vandal War, and the later events in North Africa (532–546),

Mosaic of Emperor Justinian in the Church of San Vitale in Ravenna, Italy. The church of San Vitale was founded in 526 and dedicated in 548. (*Author*)

as well as the Gothic War against the Ostrogoths in Sicily and Italy (536–552). Later events are also sketched until 554. Procopius was a diligent and fairly critical narrator of facts and developments, although his knowledge of remote historical events was somewhat limited. His work is abundant in details on people and places, and he boldly criticizes Emperor Justinian and his own master, Belisarius.

Corippus wrote an epic poem, *Iohannis*, or *de Bellis Lybicis* (The Libyan War), in the sixth century. Its main subject is the reconquest of North Africa by Emperor Justinian, and more specifically the campaigns undertaken by his general, John Troglyta, who fought to suppress the Moorish revolts after the fall of the Vandal kingdom. The poem describes the political and military situation in North Africa before and during the campaigns. While its aim clearly is to laud the exploits of John, which is done in panegyric tones, it still provides a wealth of information.

Corippus was born in North Africa, probably in the beginning of the sixth century, as he was an old man when he wrote a panegyric on the accession of Emperor Justin II in 565. We do not know exactly where he was born, but it appears to have been in the countryside, not far from Carthage, to which he later moved. He was a teacher in the earlier part of his life and wrote poetry before he wrote his great epic, although none of that has survived. There is little doubt that he witnessed many of the events he describes, but we cannot know for certain that he followed John on his campaigns. We know he lived in Carthage after the Vandal War in the 530s, but later moved to Constantinople, where he may have been a scribe at the court. There he wrote his panegyric for Emperor Justin II, possibly in 567. After this date, we hear nothing more of him, and being at an advanced age, he probably died soon after.

Preparations for the invasion of North Africa

On the eastern borders of the empire, Justinian would fight against the Persians to maintain a status quo, but he had no ambitions for conquest there. His general objective seems to have been to use only the money and soldiers necessary to keep the Persians from any major invasions, thus freeing him to reconquer the lost provinces of the West. When he became emperor, he acted according to these principles, actively carrying on the war against the Persians while continuing negotiations for a settlement.

In 528, he began to set his grand plan into motion. A series of changes were made to further the efficiency of the Eastern military commands, and soon afterward the whole line of border defenses was moved forward. New fortresses were constructed close to the Persian border to strengthen the Roman military presence and their defenses.

He then reinforced the Roman army of the East, bringing it up to about twenty-five thousand men, and appointed two new generals, Sittas and the young but able Belisarius, who would later play a great part in the fall of the Vandal kingdom. With these changes, the war, which had so far gone badly for the Romans, took a more favorable turn. In 530, Sittas defeated a Persian army at Theodosiopolis (Erzurum in modern-day Turkey) and at Satala (Sadak), both in Armenia, and Belisarius won a great victory at the heavily fortified city of Daras (Oğuz in modern-day Turkey), on the Persian border. The following year, however, the Persians invaded the Roman territory in the neighborhood of the city of Callinicum on the Euphrates (Ar-Raqqah in modern-day Syria), with the aim of attacking Syria and the principal city of the East, Antioch. The armies clashed at Callinicum, and the battle was a stalemate, with great losses on both sides. Nevertheless, the Persians were forced to retreat without having taken any Roman city or stronghold.

PEACE WITH THE PERSIANS

The Persian King Cabades died in autumn 531. His son, Chosroes, who wished to focus on possible trouble at home, agreed in spring 532 to sign a Treaty of Eternal Peace. The territorial status quo before the war was restored. Furthermore, Justinian agreed to pay Chosroes eleven thousand pounds of gold for the latter's abandoning all claims to an old subsidy toward the defense of the strategic pass named the Caspian Gates. The pass of the Caspian Gates was the traditional invasion route of the northern barbarian tribes, and both nations were to contribute to its defense. The death of Cabades and the peace (for at least some years) on the Eastern frontier fit Justinian's plans very well. The emperor was now free to start the first stage of the reconquest of the West.

GELIMER IS THREATENED

When Justinian was informed of the overthrow of Hilderic in 530, ambassadors were sent to Gelimer. They carried a letter stating that Gelimer had done wrong in deposing the rightful king, according to the will of Geiseric, particularly as Gelimer would gain the throne soon anyway. Justinian went on to recommend that Gelimer keep Hilderic as king in name at least, while he took care of affairs of the kingdom himself, until Hilderic's natural death when Gelimer would become king. Doing so would keep relations with the Romans friendly.

But Gelimer coolly ignored the letter and sent away the ambassadors. Hoamer was then blinded, and the aged Hilderic and Hoageis were kept in closer confinement, as Gelimer charged them with planning to flee to Constantinople. Blinding was a custom sometimes used to prevent a person from becoming king or emperor, and has been interpreted by some as an indication that Hilderic had been planning to put Hoamer on the throne instead of Gelimer.

When Justinian heard of the mistreatment of the deposed king, with whom he was on friendly terms, he sent another embassy with a letter to Gelimer, as he had fewer other options to react. In the letter he requested that Hilderic, Hoamer, and Hoageis be released and sent to Constantinople. No doubt Justinian believed that if Hilderic could be secured, a war on Gelimer could be made with the pretext of reinstating the rightful king and creating a focal point for all who would oppose Gelimer. He ended the letter by threatening that he would not let the matter rest, and that the treaty with Geiseric made in 474 would not prevent him in this. With a wonderful twist of words, the emperor said that the Romans would come, not to make war on the person who had succeeded to the kingdom of Geiseric, who was Hilderic, but to enforce the law of Geiseric.

To this Gelimer replied that he had not usurped the king-ship, but prevented Hilderic from making a revolution against the spirit of Geiseric. Hilderic was dethroned by the Vandal people, not by him. With Hilderic removed, Gelimer was the next in line according to the will of Geiseric, and he had simply taken his rightful place as king. He then went on to tell Justinian not to meddle in the affairs of the Vandal kingdom and not to break the treaty made between Emperor Zeno and Geiseric in 474. If the Romans were to come, the Vandals would oppose them with all their power. The open-ing sentence of the letter was written as one king to another, probably to irritate Justinian, as Gelimer put himself on the same level as the emperor.

Justinian was greatly angered by the insolence of the Vandal king and so was eager to punish him and move his plan for retaking the West forward. Accordingly, when the war with Persia was concluded, he began preparing to invade North Africa. While his main strategic goal was to take Rome and Italy, he knew this could not be done without holding North Africa. The Vandal navy would be able to disrupt the supplies for the Roman armies in Italy, and the population of Rome would soon starve. Grain

A 50 denarii coin minted around 530 featuring Gelimer. (*Courtesy, Classical Numismatic Group*)

and olive oil from North Africa and Sardinia were needed to hold any conquests in Italy.

The general of the East, Belisarius, was summoned to Constantinople with the pretext that he was being removed from office so that no rumors of preparation would reach the Vandals.

DISAGREEMENTS OVER THE WAR

When Justinian presented his advisers with his thoughts on gathering an army to attack Gelimer and conquer the Vandal kingdom, they immediately opposed it, reminding him of the disastrous results of all previous attacks on North Africa, such as the great expedition of General Basiliscus of 468.

The main opponent was the praetorian prefect, John the Cappadocian, who was responsible for the collection of taxes. The expedition would need massive funding, which could only be provided by increasing taxation. Such measures would make John greatly unpopular with the population, and failure to bring in the required amounts would mean severe punishment by the emperor. John opposed the emperor, citing the troubles of coordinating the expedition over such a long distance, and the difficulty of retaining North Africa while the Ostrogoths held Sicily and Italy. If the army or fleet was defeated, there was no place to retreat to. Furthermore, it was also difficult to supply the expedition once it reached North Africa, particularly when the powerful Vandal fleet patrolled the sea. If the expedition failed, the old treaty with the Vandals had been broken, and they would resume their piratical raids and disrupt the trade in the Mediterranean.

Some of the generals were also against the expedition, because they were reluctant to attempt a sea invasion, and to fight the Vandal fleet and the Vandal army with only their ships as a base. They were supported by the troops, who had only just returned from the Persian War and had had no time to rest, and so did not favor the idea of now going to the far west. The common soldiers were also afraid of a sea battle, as they were not used to such fighting. This reluctance in the Roman army against sea battles is confirmed by Malchus the rhetorician, who reports that by the reign of Emperor Zeno in the late fifth century, Germanic federate units of the Eastern army were agreeing to serve only on condition that they were not sent to North Africa against the Vandals. The rest, as Procopius relates, mainly preferred to be spectators of new adventures, while others faced the dangers.

The words of the praetorian prefect and the imperial advisers moved the emperor, but the Catholic Church supported the invasion, which might return one of the most Orthodox populations of Europe—Catholics who had been severely persecuted by their Arian overlords—to the empire. According to Procopius, a bishop approached the emperor and told him of a dream in which God had visited him and told him to go to the emperor and rebuke him for not going to help the Catholics in North Africa, who were being persecuted by the Arian Vandals. The bishop furthermore related that God had told him that He would join in the war and make Justinian master of Africa.

While religious motives were some of the official reasons for the campaign, there were more-practical grounds. The Syrian chronicler Zacharias the Rhetor, a contemporary of

Justinian's, recorded the major role that exiled Roman nobles from North Africa played in the emperor's decision to send an expeditionary force:

> There was then in Constantinople certain African nobles, who because of a quarrel that they had with a prince of that land [Gelimer], had quit their land and sought refuge with the emperor, and they had given him information about this country and urged him to act, saying that this country was extremely vast and very peaceful, and it was dreamt of a war with the Romans, but was locked in a war with the Moors, a people established in the desert and living like the Arabs on brigandage and raids. They emphasized in front of the emperor that this land had been snatched and stolen from the Roman Empire in the time of Geiseric, who had also taken Rome, carried off the objects of value in gold and silver, and retired to Carthage in Africa. A fine city which he had seized and occupied.

THE ROMANS SEEK THE AID OF THE OSTROGOTHS

The emperor was, of course, aware of the difficulties of the expedition, but the situation was still favorable to his plans. One of the main factors was that since the rebellion of Amalafrida, widow of Thrasamund, and her subsequent execution, relations between the Ostrogoths and Vandals had been ice cold. Theodoric the Great's daughter Amalasuntha, the mother of the boy king, Athalaric, and the de facto ruler of the Ostrogothic kingdom of Italy, had also refused to recognize Gelimer's rule. Justinian used the animosity between the two kingdoms and asked Amalasuntha if a market with provisions and horses could be made ready in Sicily to supply the Roman army on the expedition. Amalasuntha agreed and thus got her revenge for the death of Queen Amalafrida.

Sicily was of great importance, as North Africa could not be attacked without a secure base from which to resupply the army and get replacement horses for the cavalry before the invasion, both of which were essential for a Roman success. Sicily was also needed to function as a resupply point for the Roman fleet, which could ferry supplies across to North Africa. Otherwise, supplies would have to be sent from the nearest other ports, which were in Greece.

Revolts of Pudentius and Godas

Two other events turned out to fit perfectly with Justinian's plans. Pudentius, a Roman noble from Tripolitania, rebelled from the oppressive rule of the Vandals and asked for troops to help him. Accordingly, General Tattimuth was dispatched with a small force ahead of the main invasion force. With these forces, Pudentius managed to recapture the whole of Tripolitania, which did not contain any Vandal troops. Here again, we see how difficult it was for the few Vandals to secure such a vast region as Roman North Africa.

Furthermore, Godas, a Goth in Vandal service who ruled Sardinia for Gelimer, heard of the Roman displeasure with the Vandals and sent a letter to Justinian asking for troops and then rebelled, setting himself up as king of Sardinia. The letter pleased Justinian, and he sent Eulogius as ambassador to Sardinia with a letter promising alliance, soldiers, and a general who would guard Sardinia for him. That was more than Godas had bargained for, and he responded to the emperor that he was asking for troops and not for a commander, as he was well capable of that task himself. But the emperor had already made ready four hundred soldiers with Cyril as commander to assist Godas, and they traveled with the great expedition to Sicily before sailing for Sardinia.

These two rebellions came at the most inopportune time for the Vandal kingdom. The situation was further aggravated because Gelimer did not expect a serious Roman response to the removal of Hilderic so quickly.

Weighing the pros and cons, Justinian finally rejected the opposition of his advisers and began to collect provisions and troops. Belisarius was named general of the expedition, and preparations were made for it to sail in June 533. The combination of fortunate circumstances—peace with Persia, no immediate threats from the barbarians north of the Danube, the issue of the usurpation of Hilderic, the two revolts, and the availability of Sicily as a friendly base—could not be expected to be repeated.

COMPOSITION OF THE ROMAN EXPEDITION

Fortunately, Procopius describes the composition of the expedition in detail, giving us a unique insight into the Roman preparations. It was a moderately large army of fifteen thousand regular and auxiliary troops and one thousand barbarian allies, with the core of the army made up of Belisarius's veteran bodyguard, who probably numbered some thousands. Of the fifteen thousand regular and auxiliary troops, five thousand were cavalry and the rest infantry.

The force was carried by a fleet of five hundred transports, able to carry weights from 74 to 1,040 tons, manned by thirty thousand sailors from Egypt, Ionia, and Cilicia, and escorted by ninety-two small warships—the so-called *dromones* (Greek for "runners"), fast ships with one bank of oars—whose complement of marines totaled two thousand. The marines were not to fight on land, but to fight against the Vandal fleet if it came to an engagement at sea. The eunuch Solomon, and Dorotheus, general of the troops in Armenia, commanded the auxiliaries. Rufinus, Aigan the Hun, Barbatus, and Pappus commanded the regular cavalry, and John was in overall command of the infantry. The army was supported by a number of barbarian troops. King Pharas commanded four hundred lightly armed Heruli, and Sinnion and Balas commanded six hundred Hunnish horse archers. Admiral Calonymus commanded the fleet. To avoid a lengthy chain of command, Belisarius was given full powers to conduct the war in the name of the emperor.

THE SEA JOURNEY

Around the first half of June 533, the great fleet anchored off the emperor's palace in Constantinople. After the customary blessings by the patriarch of Constantinople, it sailed off. The fleet sailed along the coast of Greece but suffered from poor supplies, resulting in the deaths of five hundred soldiers. From the island of Zakynthos the fleet sailed to Sicily, where the army landed at a deserted place close to Mount Aetna. The voyage from Constantinople to Sicily took about two months.

THE LANDING IN NORTH AFRICA

Unfortunately, we have no Vandal sources on the campaign and so must observe it through the Roman eyes of Procopius. The long, troublesome journey had demoralized the army, which also feared a naval battle with the Vandal fleet. Procopius relates that the troops said that if they were put on land, they would fight to the best of their ability, but if engaged at sea, they would flee the Vandals. No doubt these thoughts were found among the army, whereas the marines and sailors, being more experienced in naval matters, probably did not fear the Vandal fleet as much. However, it must be remembered that apart from skirmishes with pirates, no fleet around the Mediterranean was experienced in actual combat at sea, as there had been no naval battles for more than two generations.

Much of the fear of the army was based on lack of knowledge of its enemy. Accordingly, Belisarius needed to know more about the Vandals: how many soldiers they had, how they fought, what their dispositions were, and the like. So Procopius, his adviser, was sent to Syracusa (Syracuse in modern-day Sicily) to get information about the Vandals. Meanwhile, the fleet would wait at a place called Caucana while the army rested after the journey. Provisions and horses were bought at local markets in Sicily.

According to Procopius, the Vandals were not even aware that the Roman expedition had left Constantinople. Procopius also found out that Gelimer was distracted by Pudentius's revolt in Tripolitania and the revolt of Godas in

Sardinia. Gelimer had sent five thousand warriors and one hundred twenty warships under his brother Tzazon to subdue Godas. Gelimer himself was with the royal army at Hermione, four days away from the coast, conducting a campaign against the Moors. It seems unlikely that Gelimer did not know of the Roman preparations for war, since Carthage was a great trading port where merchants from the whole Mediterranean shared information. However, he probably did not expect them to strike so soon in the hot season, but rather, at the earliest, during the later cooler season.

It appears that the one hundred twenty warships sent to Sardinia constituted the whole of the Vandal fleet, as no warships are heard of apart from these. Probably, Gelimer's strategy was to have Tzazon quickly suppress Godas's revolt while Gelimer himself attacked the Moors who had been running wild over the Vandal lands since the defeat of Hilderic in 528 or 529. With these two threats gone, Gelimer would be ready for the main war against the Romans. (The revolt of Pudentius was not an immediate threat and could be dealt with later.) The plan was sound, and it shows Gelimer's strategic ability, but the Romans were already on their way.

The Roman fleet sailed soon after receiving the heartening news that the Vandal fleet was occupied elsewhere and that the Vandals were not prepared for the invasion, and it arrived unopposed at Caput Vada (Chebba in modern-day Tunisia), about one hundred thirty miles southeast of Carthage, around August 31, 533. Altogether about three months had passed since the fleet left Constantinople.

Before disembarking, a council of war was held. Archelaus suggested moving straight to Carthage with the fleet and taking the city. They would thereby avoid the problems of water supply and have a good harbor to anchor the fleet, as they were afraid of storms. Furthermore, the Vandals would have to engage in a siege to defeat the Romans—a type of warfare in which they were not experienced. But Belisarius preferred to land the army and have it move against Carthage, with the fleet following the army in support. The aim was to take

Carthage before Gelimer could return from the campaign against the Moors and avoid having the whole expedition ruined by a storm at sea on the way to Carthage. If the Roman army could gain control of Carthage, it would have a secure base of operations from which to fight the Vandals and an excellent harbor for supplies. Probably, Belisarius also feared a naval engagement with the Vandal fleet, which could ruin the whole expedition in one blow, whereas the army could carry on the war if it had already landed. Accordingly, the army quickly established a fortified camp on the coast. The warships were arranged in a semicircle around the transports, to protect against a surprise attack by the Vandal fleet.

Belisarius revived the old custom of making a fortified camp at the end of each day's march, as the Vandals were horsemen with little knowledge of missile weapons and were not accustomed to dismount and fight as infantry. It would therefore be best to fight them from a fortification, to which it would be possible to retreat if they were attacked. Otherwise a rout would result in a total disaster for the Romans, of which two-thirds were infantry.

A propaganda war was also immediately initiated: it was proclaimed that the Romans had come to remove the usurper Gelimer and restore the rightful king, Hilderic. They had not come to fight the Libyans (as they called the local Romans), but Gelimer's men. The troops were given strict orders not to plunder the local inhabitants but to pay for the things they needed. A few soldiers who took fruit from local plantations were severely punished. In this way the Romans hoped to keep the confidence and support of the local inhabitants, which would make the campaign much easier. It was probably the Catholic Church and the Roman nobility that mainly welcomed the return of the Romans, whereas the lower classes might not have cared much.

The capture of Sullectum

The Romans were not entirely convinced of the local inhabitants' support for the imperial forces. We see an example of this the next day, when the army began to move along the coast road toward Carthage. About one day's march away was the city of Sullectum. As elsewhere, the Vandals had torn down the city walls, but the constant raids of the Moors had forced the inhabitants to make a barrier around the city using house walls and other obstructions. Some soldiers were sent in secret to the city, arrived at dusk, and passed the night hidden in a ravine. At early morning, they entered the city with the morning traffic and captured it with no resistance. The local bishop and the other notables of the city were called together, and it was announced that Sullectum was now a city of the empire. The Roman forces received the keys to the gates of the city, which they sent to Belisarius.

On the same day, the overseer of the public post of the kingdom deserted to the Romans, taking all the post horses. The Romans captured a royal messenger, whom they paid to bring a public letter from Justinian to the Vandals in Carthage. The letter stated that the Romans had not come to make war on the Vandals or to break the old treaty with Geiseric, but to remove the usurper Gelimer, who had deposed the rightful King Hilderic. The letter went on to ask the Vandals to rise up against Gelimer. But the messenger was so scared of bringing the letter to Carthage that he only showed it to some of his friends.

Marching on from Sullectum, Belisarius sent ahead a vanguard of three hundred men commanded by John the Armenian, and the allied Huns were sent to screen the left flank and scout ahead. The fleet sailed along the coast and guarded the right flank. The main force moved slowly along the coast road, passing through Leptis and Hadrumentum (since the reign of Huneric, it had been named Huniricopolis, and it would briefly be renamed Justinianopolis after the war with the Vandals). Belisarius stayed with the main force, as he expected Gelimer to assault them during the march. Probably because of the heat, they marched about ten and a half miles each day. If they did not stay in a city, they made a marching camp to protect against surprise Vandal attacks.

After moving through Leptis and Hadrumentum, the army reached the royal estate at Grasse (Sidi Khalifa), some ninety-three miles from Caput Vada and forty-six miles from Carthage. Here the troops were allowed to eat their fill from the fruit plantations of the Vandal king.

Murder of Hilderic

On hearing of the Roman landing, Gelimer sent word to his brother Ammatas, who was holding Carthage with a strong garrison, to kill Hilderic, Hoageis, and the Romans imprisoned with them, and to take prisoner the Roman merchants present in Carthage and keep them in custody. Hoamer had already died in prison before 533.

That Gelimer took the situation extremely seriously is reflected in the fact he had the royal treasure placed on a fast ship with orders to sail to Visigothic Spain if the war was lost. He would then try to get there himself. And Gelimer had not been idle in Hermione. Shortly before the Roman army landed, he had sent ambassadors to the court of Theudis, the Visigothic king in Spain, asking for support. We may wonder somewhat why he hoped for support from the Visigoths in this matter. The Visigoths were on close terms with the Ostrogoths and did not otherwise seem to be allied to the Vandals. Possibly he was offering great sums of money to gain their help.

To defeat the Romans, Gelimer had formed a cunning plan. He would move quickly with the main army and follow Belisarius, while Ammatas would move with his troops in Carthage to prepare an ambush in the suburb of Ad Decimum Miliare (At the Tenth Milestone), a little more than nine miles outside Carthage. Here they would trap Belisarius between their troops and a detachment of two thousand Vandals under Gelimer's nephew Gibamund, who was moving parallel with the Roman main force.

The spot was carefully chosen. Here, hills would mask the advance of the Vandal army, and after the Roman army left Grasse, the Roman fleet would not be able to support the army, as it had to round a great peninsula, the Promontorium Mercurii. Gelimer believed in his plan so much that a grand victory feast was prepared in Carthage on the day of the battle.

BATTLE OF AD DECIMUM

While the Roman army camped at Grasse, a nightly skirmish between scouts ensued. The Romans did not know how many Vandals there were or how close they were, but they now knew that they were shadowing the Roman army.

Gelimer had a good plan, and the situation could well have ended in disaster for the Romans if General Belisarius had not taken precautions. Even then, the Romans might have been defeated if not for Ammatas, who went to Decimum ahead of time with only a small part of his forces. The rest of the army in Carthage was ordered to come as soon as possible. Accordingly, around September 13, 533, Ammatas's small force clashed with the vanguard of John at Decimum. Ammatas fought bravely, single-handedly killing twelve Roman soldiers, but was killed himself and his troops routed. The remainder of Ammatas's army was coming along the road from Carthage in small bands of twenty and thirty warriors, and they were carried along in the rout. John and his forces pursued the fleeing barbarians and slaughtered them in great numbers.

At the same time, Gibamund, with his two thousand Vandals, had reached the village of Pedion Halon, about four and a half miles from Decimum. The elite Hunnish cavalry caught his forces there and destroyed them all. The Vandal light cavalry—with little or no armor and no missile weapons—had no response to horse archers, and so the Huns suffered no casualties.

Meanwhile, Belisarius left his infantry in a fortified camp about four miles from Decimum and sent his cavalry ahead with the intention of first skirmishing with the Vandal army to ascertain its strengths and then engaging it with his full forces. His vanguard reached Decimum and saw the battle-

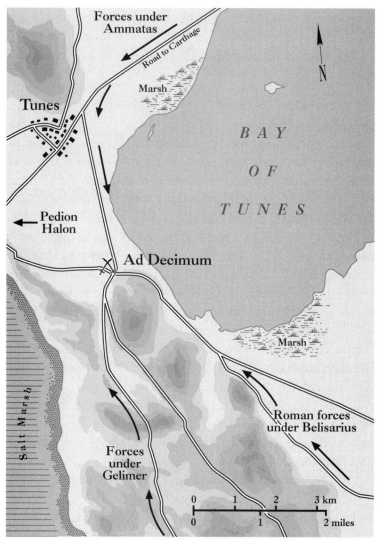

Battle of Ad Decimum, September 13, 533.

field where Ammatas was lying dead. At the same time, Gelimer came up with his army, and a fight erupted. The Roman vanguard was routed and fled down the coastal road toward Belisarius. On the way, they met Belisarius's bodyguard Uliaris with eight hundred guardsmen but they were pulled along in the flight, which only stopped when they met the main force under Belisarius. Gelimer still had victory within his reach if he had moved against Belisarius or John's detachment, which had been disorganized by the pursuit of Ammatas's troops. However, when seeing his brother lying among the fallen, Gelimer broke down weeping and insisted on taking care of his burial arrangements on the spot.

Belisarius quickly received his fleeing vanguard and, after organizing it, marched immediately against the Vandal army at Decimum. Unprepared and in disorder, the Vandals were quickly put to flight by Belisarius's cavalry, and on the evening of September 13, he could rest his weary but victorious army on the battlefield at Decimum. As for Gelimer and his army, they were fleeing toward Numidia and the plain of Boulla. It may seem surprising that Gelimer did not retreat to Carthage, but he considered that the city walls were in such disrepair that the city could not be held. Also, the civilian population strongly favored the Roman cause, and the Vandal army was best employed in open areas, favoring its cavalry. (Although the presence of Hunnish horse archers now eliminated some of that advantage.) The other Vandals in the cities surrendered or fled. The Romans had won the battle by luck and ability, but it could easily have ended otherwise.

On the day after the battle, the Roman infantry arrived at Decimum, and from there Belisarius cautiously moved toward Carthage and camped outside the city. On the second day, the Roman army entered the capital and was met by the jubilant inhabitants. They then found out that Hilderic had been killed on Gelimer's orders. This strengthened the official legitimacy of the campaign. Now the Romans would appear to be revenging the murder of the rightful Vandal king. However, it still did not appear that there was any Vandal opposition to the rule of Gelimer, or at least we do not hear about it, and we must assume that the pro-Roman Procopius would have mentioned it if it existed. The Roman fleet arrived at Carthage the same day, and the population removed the great chain from across the entrance to the harbor of Mandracium. The Romans were still wary of the

Vandal fleet, however, and were unsure if the whole Roman fleet could fit into the harbor, so it returned down the coast and anchored in the safer bay of Tunes (Tunis in modern-day Tunisia). Meanwhile, the jubilant inhabitants freed the Roman merchants.

Belisarius billeted his troops in Carthage as he would in any Roman city, and Procopius seems somewhat surprised that the troops moved orderly around in the city without taking advantage of the situation to plunder the inhabitants. Belisarius made the former residence of the Vandal kings on the Byrsa Hill his headquarters, and he sat on the throne of the Vandal king. Solomon was sent to Constantinople to announce the great victory to the emperor, and Justinian took the victory names of Africanus, Alanicus, and Vandalicus, first used on November 21, 533. This was the first and only time a Roman emperor would take the victory name Vandalicus.

The Vandal request for aid from the Visigoths in Spain was now rejected. The Visigoths sided with the Ostrogoths in their attitude toward the Vandals, and Belisarius's swift and decisive victory—news of which arrived in Spain before the Vandal envoys—probably also weighed strongly in the decision. Also as a result of the victory at Ad Decimum, most of the Moorish tribes in Mauretania, Numidia, and Byzacena offered their allegiance to the Roman Empire. Meanwhile, the Roman army was busy repairing the fortifications of Carthage, and a ditch was dug around the city walls and a palisade set up at the endangered parts. The Vandals who had sought sanctuary in the churches were given pledges of safety.

The Vandal kingdom was dissolving around Gelimer, and he had little choice other than to challenge the Roman army in battle. The king gathered his remaining warriors and some Moors who were still friendly to him. The attitudes of the Moorish tribes wavered as they awaited the outcome of the struggle. Officially they supported the Romans, but they sent no troops. Gelimer also sought to win the hearts and minds of the local peasant population by distributing money, and he won over many. These he commanded to kill any Romans who went into the country, and in return he would give them gold for each person killed. Accordingly, the peasants killed many from the Roman army, but mainly slaves and servants who were looking for plunder. The locals cut off their heads and received their reward from Gelimer, who thought they were all from Roman soldiers. This shows that at least parts of the lower classes did not support the return of the Roman emperor, and that groups among them were willing to support the Vandals in return for money. Belisarius also found a local citizen of Carthage guilty of treason and impaled him on a hill before the city to discourage others from aiding the Vandals.

Tzazon returns

Gelimer would also receive further support from his brother Tzazon. Tzazon had defeated Godas and his rebels in Sardinia, but received word from Africa of the serious situation there. He set sail with his army and landed on the coast of North Africa, probably at Thabraca on the border between Proconsularis and Numidia. From there he marched to the plain of Boulla, some four days from Carthage, where Gelimer was organizing his troops. We hear nothing further of the Vandal fleet, but probably it went to a safe harbor and was later captured by the Romans, as we hear nothing of it being burned. The reunion was an unhappy one, and Procopius relates how the two brothers embraced each other and remained locked in a long, silent embrace, neither able to speak for tears. When Cyril, the leader of the troops sent to support Godas in Sardinia, heard of the death of Godas, he sailed to Carthage and joined the Roman army there.

The Vandals hoped for treachery among the inhabitants of Carthage or among the Roman soldiers, many of whom were of Germanic origin and therefore Arians, and also entered into secret negotiations with the Roman Hunnish allies, and promised them great sums of money in return for supporting the Vandals. The Huns decided to support the victor in the coming battle, be it Roman or Vandal. Meanwhile, Gelimer moved close enough to Carthage to cut the aqueduct and block the roads. But Belisarius heard of the negotiations with the Huns from deserters from the Vandal army—probably Roman provincials—and was therefore prepared. Accordingly, he gave the Huns many gifts and invited them for banquets, and in this way persuaded them to tell him what Gelimer had been promising them. The Huns explained that they feared that if the Romans won the war, the Huns would never be allowed to go back to their native lands and the booty they had already captured would be taken from them. But Belisarius promised them that if the Vandals were defeated, they would be sent home as soon as possible, with all their plunder. Thus he regained the support of the Huns.

BATTLE OF TRICAMARUM, DECEMBER 15, 533

Belisarius, trusting in the open areas where his horse archers would be superior, sent his army against the Vandal king. His main cavalry force except five hundred soldiers under John the Armenian were sent ahead to scout toward the Vandal army. The following day, Belisarius moved out with the infantry and the remaining five hundred cavalry. No doubt the reason for the disposition of his forces was the same as during the march to Carthage and designed to counter the fast-moving cavalry force of the Vandals. If engaged, the Roman cavalry would retreat to the main infantry force, and he would engage with his whole army.

The Roman cavalry encountered the Vandal camp at Tricamarum, some nineteen miles west of Carthage (the actual site has not been identified), and camped on the other side of a small stream. After the usual speeches, in which he—according to Procopius—asked the Vandals not to shame the memory of Geiseric, Gelimer led out his forces at lunchtime, when the Romans were unprepared and busy at their meal. The Vandals deployed along the small stream, and the Romans hastily placed themselves on the other side. Belisarius moved to the center with five hundred cavalry, leaving the infantry behind advancing at a walk. The Huns were

**DEPLOYMENT AND FIRST PHASE
OF THE BATTLE**

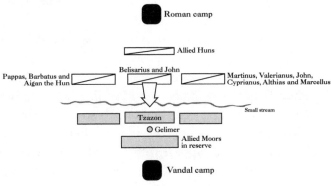

END PHASE

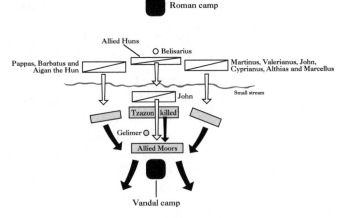

Battle of Tricamarum, December 15, 533.

stationed at the rear, as they disliked mingling with the rest of the Roman army. Furthermore, this position was particularly favorable to their plans to see who was winning before joining the fight. It is a wonder why the Vandals did not take the opportunity to attack immediately, when the Romans were in disarray. Perhaps, having interrupted their meal, they wanted to let the Romans tire from thirst, hunger, and the heat before attacking.

The Vandal wings were led by the chiliarchs—leaders of thousandship units—and the center was commanded by Tzazon, with the allied Moors in reserve. Gelimer himself moved around to urge on the troops where needed and gave the order not to use their spears or other weapons, but to close and only use swords. No doubt the destruction of Gibamund's detachment by the Hunnish horse archers had made him understand that the Vandals stood a chance only if they closed as soon as possible and used their abilities in close combat. The Vandals appear to have had a somewhat greater army than the Romans, possibly around fifteen thousand warriors, although there is no reason to believe Procopius when he states that they were ten times more than the Romans.

The armies stood waiting for a while, after which the Romans attacked the Vandal center with Belisarius's elite bodyguard. Belisarius probably knew that his troops would only weaken from lack of food and so had to force a decision before nightfall. The Vandals repulsed the Romans in the first two charges, but in the third, Tzazon was killed, and the Vandal center started to flee. With the rest of the Roman forces now crossing the stream, the Vandal warriors began to flee on both wings, and the undecided Huns joined the Roman army in the pursuit. The Vandals fled into their camp, while the Romans stripped the Vandal dead of their valuables. The Romans lost fewer than fifty dead, the Vandals around eight hundred.

In the late afternoon the same day, when the Roman infantry arrived, Belisarius moved to attack the Vandal camp. The camp was surrounded by a stockade such as the Vandals usually erected, but it was mainly intended to keep their horses safe inside and was not meant to be defended. At the sight of the advancing Roman army, Gelimer fled on the road to Hippo Regius with a small group of his kinsmen, leaving the rest of the Vandals to fend for themselves. With no leadership, the Vandal army disintegrated and fled. The camp was easily taken, and the Romans were astonished by the amount of treasure in it. The treasures from the sack of Rome in 455 were there, as were the spoils of the Vandals' raids on the Romans and Goths. This shows that the Vandal king probably always traveled with parts of the royal treasure. The Vandals' camp was captured three months after the Roman army had come to Carthage, on about December 15, 533.

On taking the camp and finding such plunder and the beautiful Vandal women, who had traveled with their husbands, the Roman army became completely disordered, and Belisarius was unable to check it until daybreak. Procopius states that if at this point the Vandal army had collected itself and attacked the Romans, they would all have been destroyed. In the morning, Belisarius managed to collect a few hundred of his guardsmen, and he sent John the Armenian with two hundred of them to ride day and night to catch Gelimer. Belisarius knew that capturing the Vandal king would end the war. The captured Vandals from the battle and elsewhere were collected in Carthage so they could be sent to Constantinople in the spring for enrollment in the Roman army—a common thing to do with defeated barbarians in this period. It was probably at this time that the Vandal fleet was captured. As we hear of no sizable Vandal forces coming from the fleet, we can assume that it was probably crewed by Roman provincials.

After five days and nights, John was catching up with Gelimer, but by accident John was shot with an arrow by a drunk soldier. The Romans stopped to care for the mortally wounded John, and Belisarius had to take over the pursuit, which was now seriously delayed. When he reached Hippo Regius, he learned that Gelimer had fled to a fortress on Mount Papua (unfortunately, the exact place of this mountain has not been located) and so could no longer be captured. The mountain could only be climbed on a difficult path, which was defended by the Moors dwelling there and Gelimer's Vandals. Belisarius needed to go back to Carthage to oversee the campaign, so a force of lightly equipped Heruli was set to besiege Gelimer, as it was too difficult to capture the place. Meanwhile, Belisarius brought many Vandals from Hippo Regius, as well as some of the Vandal nobility, to Carthage.

When news of the great victory at Tricamarum reached the emperor, he issued two edicts that set out the civil and military organization of the conquered provinces. A third praetorian prefecture was established for North Africa, and it included Sardinia, Corsica, and the Balearic Islands. Seven new provinces were created. The establishment and salary of every official, down to the lowest clerk, were described in detail. The praetorian prefect was to have a staff of 396 and an annual salary of one hundred pounds of gold. In the edicts, which were issued in 534, Justinian announced that Christ had decided that Africa should once again feel his generosity after 105 years of captivity by the Vandals, who were "at once enemies of souls and bodies," referring to their heretical beliefs.

Capture of the Vandal royal treasure

While staying in Hippo Regius, the Romans had an extraordinary piece of luck. Gelimer's scribe, Bonifacius, had been put in charge of part of the royal treasure at the start of the war. His orders were to board a fast sailing ship in Hippo Regius and head to Visigothic Spain with the treasure if the war was lost. After the defeat at Tricamarum, Bonifacius did as he had been ordered and set sail for Spain. But the wind was against the ship, and he was forced back into Hippo Regius. When he heard of the coming of the Roman army, he tried to make the sailors sail anywhere, but a storm had risen, and they refused to sail out of the harbor. With no other options, Bonifacius surrendered the treasure to Belisarius and in return was not harmed. Thus Belisarius took the rest of the Vandals' treasure. We do not know the size of the royal treasure, but the Ostrogothic Queen Amalasuntha was known to have had a treasure of 400 centenaria, or 2,880,000 solidi—around 13 tons of gold—at her disposal. When the Romans captured her treasure, it was not described with such superlatives as Procopius uses to describe the Vandal royal treasure,

Gelimer's silver bowl.
(*Bibliothèque nationale de
France, Cabinet des
Medailles, Paris*)

so we can surmise that the Vandal treasure was somewhat greater. A piece from the Vandal royal treasure still exists—a silver bowl with the inscription *Geilamir Rex Vandalorum et Alanorum* (Gelimer—King of Vandals and Alans).

When Belisarius returned to Carthage, he collected the captured Vandals from North Africa and prepared them to be transported to Constantinople when spring came. Meanwhile, troops were sent to occupy their outlying dominions, including Sardinia, Corsica, and the Balearic Islands, Minorca and Majorca, and even occupied Septem opposite Gibraltar. Cyril brought the head of Tzazon to the inhabitants of Sardinia, as they refused to believe that the Vandal kingdom had fallen. Caesarea in Mauretania Caesarensis was occupied by a garrison. Troops were also sent to Tripolitania, where Pudentius and Tattimuth were hard pressed by the Moors. There was no attempt to occupy the rest of the Mauretanian provinces, the southern part of Numidia, or the western part of Byzacena, which for the time being remained in the hands of the Moors.

The Moorish chieftains, who had awaited the outcome of the struggle, renewed their allegiance to the empire. Roman troops were also sent to the city of Lilybaeum in Sicily, which had been given to the Vandals as dowry of the Ostrogothic Princess Amalafrida when she married King Thrasamund.

But the Ostrogoths, who had already occupied the important city and its fortress, refused to surrender it to the Romans, claiming it was now their possession. The Romans sent an angry note to the Gothic commanders holding Lilybaeum, claiming that they had taken over a Roman possession that the Romans had gained by defeating the Vandals and the usurper Gelimer. If the city was not handed over to the Romans, there would be war. Of course the Ostrogoths were not about to give the Romans a stronghold in Sicily, and they refused. But they were willing to bring the matter before the emperor for arbitration. Emperor Justinian wanted to retake Italy, and by their actions, the Romans now had a *casus belli*— a justification for making war on the Ostrogothic kingdom. The coming war in Italy would have a great impact on the affairs in North Africa.

END OF THE VANDAL KINGDOM

Meanwhile, with the coldness of the winter season, the Heruli were becoming tired of keeping up the siege of Gelimer on Mount Papua. Accordingly, they tried to force the ascent. But the Moors and Vandals easily defeated the attempt, and they were thrown back, with 110 warriors killed. However, the Vandals on the mountain were pressed by hunger and not used to such deprivations, whereas the Moors were used to hard living and were not so much affected by the tight Roman blockade. With a direct assault impossible, Pharas, commander of the Heruli, turned to offering Gelimer terms if he would surrender. The offer from the emperor was to give him patrician rank, money, and lands in the Roman Empire to which he could retire. According to Procopius, Gelimer refused the offer and instead asked to have one loaf of bread, a sponge, and a lyre. He wanted the bread because he had not had baked bread since he came to the mountain, the sponge was for his eye, which had become infected, and the lyre was to play along with an ode relating to his great misfortune, as he was a skilled harpist. We may or may not choose to believe this portrait of Gelimer's personality.

After three more months, the winter was ending and so were Gelimer's spirits. His family was suffering from hunger, and when he saw two children fighting over a piece of bread, he finally gave up and informed Pharas that he would surrender if the original terms were met. After Pharas consulted with Belisarius in Carthage, the conditions were confirmed, and Gelimer, his family, and his followers on Mount Papua surrendered at the end of March or the start of April 534.

The Vandal kingdom was thereby ended. Ninety-five years after Geiseric's capture of Carthage, the Vandal kingdom had fallen, and Carthage and North Africa were once more Roman. Procopius estimated that there were about eighty thousand Vandal men in North Africa at the time of Belisarius and that almost all were killed in the war. While that is undoubtedly an exaggeration, it is certain that the Vandal nation was crushed and there would be no rebellions, as there were too few left to fight.

For the Roman Empire, the defeat of the Vandal kingdom was a victory of strategic importance. The campaign was swift, and in just a few months, North Africa had been taken without any damage to speak of and few losses. The enormous treasure of the Vandal kingdom was to be sent to Constantinople to finance the coming operations against the Ostrogoths. With North Africa secure, an assault on Sicily and the Ostrogothic kingdom of Italy was now possible. The threat of the Vandal fleet was gone, and the campaign in Italy could be supplied from North Africa and Sardinia without troubles.

The astounding victory also caused the Romans to change their tactics and field a different and more-efficient army. All the major battles had been won using the force of five thousand cavalry, with the infantry not even being present. The cavalry was therefore strengthened greatly. Particularly interesting tactically was the battle between the Hunnish horse archers and Gibamund's detachment of two thousand cavalry, in which the Vandals were destroyed with no loss to the Huns. Accordingly, the Roman cavalry was trained further in these tactics so as to be able to function as both shock cavalry and horse archers. For the Roman and barbarian world, the prestige of the victory was great. One Roman general and five thousand cavalry had defeated the fierce Vandal nation, once the terror of all the Mediterranean.

On April 13, 534, Justinian issued instructions for the civil and military organization of the reconquered provinces. Archelaus was appointed praetorian prefect of Africa, and Solomon was made master of the soldiers and was left with some forces. The Roman generals were instructed to recover the territory that the Vandals had lost to the Moors, to reestablish the old military border, and to build up regiments of *limitanei* to patrol it as soon as possible in order to relieve the strain on the field army.

Belisarius returned to Constantinople with the captured Gelimer and several thousand Vandal prisoners, who were enrolled in five regiments for use on the Eastern frontier. He also brought with him the enormous royal treasure of the Vandals.

On arriving at Constantinople, Belisarius was granted a triumph, a special honor awarded to particularly successful generals. This was the first triumph celebrated by a Roman subject since the reign of Augustus (31 BC–AD 14), as only emperors and their close relatives were permitted so great an honor. It would also be the final triumph celebrated in the history of the Roman Empire. The occasion was marked with much pomp, and Belisarius went from his house in the sub-urbs to the Hippodrome, where the victorious general and the defeated king of the Vandals bowed before the emperor. When the Vandal king came before the emperor's seat in the Hippodrome, his purple robe of kingship was stripped off and he was forced to fall prone on the ground to do obeisance to Justinian. According to Procopius, in despair of falling such a long way from being the king of a strong kingdom to being a prisoner, he did not weep, but kept on saying the words from the Bible, "Vanity of vanities, all is vanity" (Ecclesiastes 1:2). In this way the Vandal kingdom ended. For his victory, Belisarius was made consul on January 1, 535.

Drawing of the lost 36 solidi piece struck by Justinian to honor his victory over the Vandals in 534. The coin was stolen from the French Bibliothèque Nationale in 1830 and never recovered. (*Author*)

To commemorate the great victory over the Vandals, Justinian had a mosaic created on the ceiling of the Chalce, the gate to the Imperial Palace in Constantinople, showing the emperor and empress surrounded by the congratulating Senate, the victorious Belisarius, and the defeated King Gelimer, prostrating himself in front of the emperor and wearing the purple for the last time. The scene was even stitched into Justinian's funeral pall at his death in 565. A gold medallion of thirty-six solidi marking the occasion was also made. The obverse has the emperor's image and the reverse the emperor on horseback with the goddess of Victory walking in front of him.

Gelimer and his family were given lands in Galatia in Asia Minor and permitted to live there until they died. But he was not given patrician rank, because he refused to convert from Arianism. Hilderic's children, who were descended from Emperor Valentinian III, received large sums of money.

GELIMER'S CHARACTER

Gelimer has been harshly treated by the pro-Roman sources, and it is difficult to form a clear picture of this last king of the Vandals. He was known as an able warrior and general, and he appears so in the early stages of the war against the

Romans. He focused on subduing the troublesome Moors and struck at the rebellious Godas in Sardinia with great energy. The two battles against the Romans were well thought through and could easily have ended in disaster for the Romans. He appears to have been overcome by his feelings at Ammatas's death, but he is also seen as coolly planning his escape to Visigothic Spain. He flees after the defeat at Tricamarum, where a Geiseric would perhaps have decided to die fighting. The story of his self-pitying behavior—asking for bread, a sponge, and a lyre while besieged on Mount Papua—may have been invented by Procopius. The story does not entirely fit with some of his other actions—eagerly trying to engage the Romans in battle, even after the defeat at Decimum, and refusing to abandon his Arian beliefs—but it fits well with his feelings at the death of Ammatas. While Gelimer can appear cruel in dealing with Hilderic and Hoamer, this was probably not unusual behavior for someone in his position at the time, and his forefathers were no less cruel. He did not persecute the Catholics, but neither did he have the chance to do so in his short reign. In keeping to his Arian faith and thus precluding his being given a patriciate, he appears quite strong and determined.

EIGHT

Rise of Stotzas

"[He] ... moved the wavering hearts of our men with his cunning words. At one and the same time he predicted civil war and urged and exhorted them with various tricks to engage in it themselves. .... Compelled by terror, the men threw down their arms, swiftly ran to the tyrant's knees and greeted him with friendly words."—*Corippus on the Roman rebel General Stotzas, mid-sixth century*

We now turn to the events in North Africa after the fall of the Vandal kingdom, as the remaining Vandals played an important role in these until their extinction as a tribe. If the rebel Stotzas, a Germanic bodyguard in Roman service, had succeeded, a new Kingdom of Africa would have come into being.

The Moors had been awaiting the outcome between the Vandals and Romans. When the winds of war went against the Vandals, the Moors offered their allegiance to the Romans. But when they heard that Belisarius was boarding the ships in Carthage with his guardsmen and the captured Vandals, the Moors in Byzacena and Numidia rose in revolt and began to raid the Roman towns. The forts and towns on the border were not yet fully garrisoned and could not prevent the raids, in which many slaves and much plunder from the border regions was carried off. The revolt was reported to Belisarius just when he was about to set sail. He could not change his plans and was needed for the invasion of the Ostrogothic kingdom, so he entrusted Solomon with the greatest part of his elite bodyguards, which numbered perhaps around two thousand, along with the regular troops, altogether probably around thirteen thousand soldiers. His orders for Solomon were to move as quickly as possible against the Moors and defeat them. No doubt he was well aware of the weakness of the Roman forces in North Africa and realized the revolt would only expand if the Moors were not suppressed immediately.

Emperor Justinian sent out another army to protect the newly conquered provinces with Generals Theodorus the Cappadocian and Ildiger. The two administrators Tryphon and Eustratius were also sent to assess the taxes for the provinces, as Geiseric had destroyed the records for gathering the taxes when he conquered North Africa. For the Roman provincials, it was a rude awakening to the tax levels of the empire.

Solomon was much in doubt about how to handle the situation. He soon received information that the few troops in Byzacena and Numidia had been destroyed, including two officers commanding cavalry detachments in Byzacena. The Moors were overrunning the provinces, pillaging and plundering everywhere.

When the terrible news reached Carthage, Solomon prepared his troops for war against the Moors. He wrote to the Moorish chieftains asking them to abstain from further raids, as they should learn from what had happened to the Vandals, and he reminded them that they had given many of their children as hostages for the peace. The Moors refused the call for peace and replied to the threats against the hostages by saying, "And as for children, that will be your concern, who are not permitted to marry more than one wife; but with us, who have, it may be, fifty wives living with each of us, offspring of children can never fail."

BATTLES OF MAMMES AND MOUNT BOURGAON, 534

Solomon marched quickly to engage the four Moorish commanders, Coutzinas, Esdilasas, Iourphouthes, and Medisinissas, who were encamped at a place called Mammes on the borders of Mauretania. Here he constructed a fortified camp and prepared himself for battle. The Moors formed up in their traditional circle of camels about twelve animals deep, near the foothills of the mountains. They placed their women and children, whom they used during the campaigns for tending the horses and camels and other similar tasks, inside the circle of camels and took their stand on foot between the legs of the camels. They were armed in the usual Moorish fashion with shields and swords and small spears, which they used as javelins. Another smaller force was placed on the mountains. The Roman troops were apprehensive because of the recent defeats that the Romans had suffered in the campaign, but Solomon adressed them in a speech in which he reminded them that they had defeated the Vandals, and the Vandals had defeated the Moors. He also pointed out the poor equipment of the Moors.

The Romans then attacked this strong defensive deployment, but the smell of the camels threw the attack into disorder. However, Solomon led an attack by five hundred dismounted troops, who hacked into the circle of camels. With their circle broken, the Moors fled to the mountains with the Romans in pursuit. According to Procopius, some ten thousand Moors were killed, and all their women and children were taken as slaves. The numbers are probably exaggerated, but it was a great Roman victory. With the surviving camels in tow, the Roman forces returned to Carthage. After the battle of Mammes, the Moors in Byzacena began to overrun the country. When Solomon returned to Carthage, he received information of the Moorish assaults and the plundering of Byzacena.

To counter this new threat, Solomon immediately marched with the whole army against the enemy, which was encamped on Mount Bourgaon. Mount Bourgaon was for the

most part precipitous and, on the eastern side, extremely difficult to ascend, but on the west it was easily accessible and
with an even slope. Accordingly, Solomon made his camp
below the mountain and waited for the Moors to come down
on level ground. The Moors did not appear eager to fight on
ground that would favor the Romans, and so after some days,
Solomon marched the army out and prepared for battle. But
the Moors knew about the strength of the Roman cavalry and
refused to engage it, using the same tactics they had used
against the cavalry of the Vandals—that is, keeping to rough
or mountainous ground.

Solomon was eager to reach a conclusion by battle, as he
did not have the supplies to besiege the Moors in the desert.
Despite the recent victory over the Moors, the Roman soldiers were still uncomfortable about the great number of enemies, and Procopius relates that this Moorish army was
greater than the one defeated at Mammes. In a daring attack,
one thousand Roman troops were sent around the mountain
to scale it behind the Moors. Their orders were to remain
there until the next morning and at sunrise show the standards and begin to shoot at the enemy below. At dawn,
Solomon brought the rest of the army against the Moorish
camp. Everything went according to plan. The troops on the
mountain began their attack while the main forces assaulted
the camp. Surprised and attacked from front and back, the
Moors fled immediately, and most were slaughtered. No
Romans were wounded in the battle, but according to
Procopius, who used captured Moors as reference, fifty thousand Moors were killed. No doubt this number is once again
exaggerated, but it must be regarded as a great Roman victory.
All the Moorish chieftains escaped, apart from Esdilasas, who
surrendered to the Romans. So great was the number of
women and children taken as slaves that a Moorish boy was
sold at the slave market for the price of a sheep—an exceedingly low price.

After the victory, Solomon marched back to Carthage. The
remaining Moors in Byzacena were now too few to settle

there and so went into Numidia and submitted to the chieftain Iaudas, who ruled the Moors on Mount Aurasium. The only Moors remaining in Byzacena were the tribes led by Antalas, who had not joined the plundering.

Uprising of Iaudas

But this was not the end of the Moorish revolts. While Solomon was occupied in Byzacena, the chieftain Iaudas was plundering and enslaving the inhabitants of the province of Numidia. According to Procopius, his army consisted of more than thirty thousand warriors. Only the actions of the local count, Althias, who was guarding the forts on the border with a small force, caused them to temporarily withdraw. After delaying shortly in Carthage, Solomon marched his army to Mount Aurasium and the Moors of Iaudas. Solomon also cleverly made use of the animosities between the various Moorish tribes. Two Moorish chieftains, Massonas and Ortaïas, joined him with their forces. Massonas's father had been killed by Iaudas, and Ortaïas came because Iaudas and the ruler of the Moors in Mauretania, Mastinas, had tried to take over the regions he held.

Solomon and the allied Moors made their camp along the River Abigais, below Mount Aurasium. But like the other Moors, Iaudas had learned not to face the Romans in the plains, but on ground that favored his own forces. The ascent to Mount Aurasium was difficult, but when the top was reached, it opened up into a fertile plateau with water, fruit plantations, and fields. There were also some fortresses on the mountain, but they had been neglected, as there had been no threats to the Moors since they had taken the region from the Vandals. The city of Thamugadi (Timgad), which lay below the mountain on the eastern side, had been attacked so many times by the Moors that it had become depopulated, and the Moors finally razed it. The Moors on Aurasium also held the fertile lands west of the mountain. Beyond these lands were the tribes ruled by Ortaïas. The description of these lands comes to us from Procopius, who spoke to Ortaïas about them.

After Solomon paid large sums to his Moorish allies to keep their loyalty, the Roman army began the ascent of Mount Aurasium. Solomon had expected to do battle immediately and so brought little food and initially moved in battle formations. After moving over very difficult ground for some five and a half miles, the army made camp without having engaged the enemy. After marching around for more than a week while the Moors evaded the cumbersome Roman army, its provisions were dwindling. Solomon believed that the allied Moors had betrayed him, as they knew the difficulty of the ground and went out to scout the area every day but probably gave false reports so the Romans would eventually use up their supplies. Because his supplies were dwindling and winter was coming, Solomon moved back to the plains along the river Abigais with his allies, whom he suspected of treachery. He left part of the army in Numidia and sent the rest back to Carthage. He also went to Carthage, with plans to prepare for an expedition against Aurasium in the spring without his untrustworthy Moorish allies.

Procopius reports that while in Carthage, Solomon also sent out an expedition against the Moors in Sardinia, who were causing trouble for the local inhabitants. Many years earlier, the Vandals, after troubles with the Moors, had deported some of them and their wives to Sardinia. Since then they had multiplied and raided the island from their outposts on the mountains near Caralis. Now they numbered some three thousand and were plundering more openly because of their strength. They were known as Barbaricini, and it is believed that the mountainous region in the interior of Sardinia called Barbagia still preserves this name. However, no other sources mention the Moors in Sardinia, and Procopius's explanation of the origin of the barbarians there is not generally accepted.

The rebellion against Solomon

Despite the victories over the Moors, Solomon had not yet succeeded in striking down the revolts. Iaudas was still mounting raids from the plateau of Aurasium, and in these campaigns we may get a glimpse of the difficulties the Vandals would have faced had the kingdom not already fallen. But on Easter, March 23, 536, the situation changed for the worse when a universal mutiny broke out among the Roman troops in North Africa.

The dangerous mutiny was caused by four main factors. After the victory over the Vandals, many of the Roman soldiers had married Vandal widows and had counted on taking over the Vandal allotments that the widows inherited from their dead husbands. But that was not how the Roman administration decided it would be. The land and estates of the defeated Vandals were to go to the imperial treasury, and if the husband of a Vandal widow was cultivating them, it would be as a tenant under the burden of a land tax, no matter if he was civilian or soldier. This decision aggravated the passionate soldiers, whose newly won wives whispered in their ears about the great riches they would miss, and they were soon disaffected. Had they not conquered the land for the empire, they asked themselves, and did they therefore not have a right to the lands? But Solomon saw it in a different way, as Procopius writes:

> While it was not unreasonable that the slaves and all other things of value should go as booty to the soldiers, the land itself belonged to the emperor and the empire of the Romans, which had nourished them and caused them to be called soldiers and to be such, not in order to win for themselves such land as they should wrest from the barbarians who were trespassing on the Roman Empire, but that this land might come to the commonwealth, from which both they and all others secured their maintenance. This was the law of the empire, and Solomon steadfastly kept to it.

Another cause of the rebellion stemmed from the fact that most of the Roman soldiers were Germanic by birth and were therefore Arian, like the Vandals. Particularly one group of about one thousand Heruli barbarians steadfastly held onto their Arian beliefs. The remaining Arian priests preached that despite their victory over the Vandals, they were subject to suppression and persecution by the emperor because of their beliefs. In an effort to stamp out the heresy, the emperor had even proclaimed that no person could be baptized or baptize others if he did not hold the Orthodox faith. Easter was approaching, and the Arian soldiers knew that none of their children would be baptized and none of them would be able to participate in the celebrations without renouncing the faith of their forefathers.

A third problem was that the soldiers had not yet received their pay, which was months behind. The emperor had quickly sent tax gatherers and other officials to the reconquered provinces, but no money to pay the soldiers had yet arrived. For the soldiers, who had just captured and sent off to Constantinople the great royal treasure of the Vandals, it was a great insult.

A fourth element increased the tensions that led to the mutiny. The Vandals whom Belisarius had brought to Constantinople as prisoners of war had been formed into five cavalry regiments named the Vandals of Justinian and were ordered to the East to garrison the cities of Syria against the Persians. Most of them proceeded to their appointed cities and would serve the empire faithfully in their new lives. But during the voyage, after reaching Lesbos, four hundred of them forced the sailors to set the course for the Peloponnesus and then for Africa. When they reached the coast, the ships were set on shore, and the Vandals marched to a fortress on Mount Aurasium near Carthage. Here they corresponded with the mutinous soldiers at Carthage, and after exchanging oaths, they agreed to support the revolt. It does not appear that the Vandals intended to put one of their leaders on the throne again, but to make a new Arian or Germanic kingdom of North Africa. It appears that Iaudas and his Moors were not yet actively supporting the Vandals at this time.

At Easter 536, everything was ready for the rebellion. The preparations had been kept secret because most of the bodyguards and domestics of Solomon with an eager eye to the lands they might acquire had become associated in the rebellion. The signal for the revolt was to be the murder of Solomon in the great basilica of Carthage on Good Friday. But that attempt failed, as did another the next day, because the would-be assassins lacked the courage to go through with it. Believing that the plan was now generally known, the leaders of the mutiny left the city and started raiding the country districts, while many others stayed in Carthage and pretended not to have known about the plot.

When Solomon realized the danger he was in, he exhorted the remaining soldiers in Carthage to remain faithful to the empire and not support the mutiny. Initially, it appeared that the rebellion would not develop, but after five days the soldiers in Carthage saw that the mutinous soldiers in the country districts were ravaging without check. The disgruntled soldiers in Carthage gathered at the Hippodrome, and attempts to quiet them were unsuccessful. The popular officer Theodorus the Cappadocian was sent to calm them, but the soldiers instead chose him to lead their rebellion, as they believed he was secretly opposed to Solomon. But Theodorus remained loyal to the emperor and only humored them for a while to help Solomon escape. The rebels then went around the streets of Carthage killing everyone who was suspected of supporting Solomon or who had money to rob, among others another Theodorus, the commander of the guards (*comes excubitores*). When night came and the rebels were drunkenly asleep, Solomon and Martinus, his second in command, who had been lying low in the Governor's Palace all day, stealthily went to the house of Theodorus the Cappadocian, who then gave them food and helped them to a ship in the harbor.

The rebellion was now in full flame, and Solomon had no option but to flee to Sicily, with five of his officers and Procopius, who would later record the history of the events. After traveling some thirty-four miles, they reached Misuas, the shipyard of Carthage, and were for the moment safe. Martinus was sent to Numidia to Valerianus, who commanded the forces there, and was told to return the troops to the side of the emperor by whatever means necessary, including cash payments. Solomon also sent a letter to Theodorus the Cappadocian, ordering him to handle matters in Carthage as seemed best to him. From Misuas, Solomon and his little group traveled to Belisarius in Syracusa and related the events of the mutiny.

STOTZAS IS PROCLAIMED KING

Meanwhile, the insurgents had gathered on the plains of Boulla, a short distance southwest of Carthage. As Theodorus had refused to lead the rebels, they instead chose Stotzas, a bodyguard of Solomon's second in command, Martinus, and acclaimed him their leader. Stotzas learned that as many as eight thousand soldiers had joined his standards. Soon after, a thousand Vandals joined them—the recent fugitives from Constantinople and those Vandals who had hidden after the war ended in 534 and escaped the notice of the Romans. Furthermore, many slaves from the Roman estates in the region also joined them, and soon they had a sizable army.

The goal of the mutineers appears to have been to drive out the Romans and make themselves masters of North Africa. The rebels then marched to Carthage, which was still held by Theodorus and a few loyalist troops, and demanded their surrender, but without success. The initial lack of unity and a leader caused the mutiny to lose the opportunity of taking Carthage easily. If the rebels had stayed in Carthage and taken the city, the mutiny would surely have been a success.

BELISARIUS ARRIVES

Josephius, a clerk on Belisarius's staff who happened to be in Carthage, was sent to Stotzas as an envoy to persuade him to end the mutiny. But the mutineers quickly showed their unwillingness to compromise by brutally murdering him and initiating a siege of the city. The few loyal troops left in Carthage were soon despairing at the hopeless situation and were on the point of surrendering the city to the rebels.

The Romans were in a difficult situation. With the army almost ready to march against the Goths, they could ill afford to have an active and unchecked rebellion at their backs. At the same time, Belisarius could not jeopardize the Gothic campaign by bringing his entire army against the mutiny. After Solomon's report on the desperate state of things in North Africa, Belisarius chose instead to board a single ship with one hundred men picked from his bodyguard and set out with Solomon for Carthage.

When he arrived, the mutineers were encamped around the city, confident of taking it by surrender or assault the following day. But by dawn the next day, the news of Belisarius's arrival had filtered outside the city. In fear of the name of their old commander, the rebels broke up their camp and started a disorderly retreat that led them to the city of Membresa (Mejaz al-Bab in modern-day Tunisia) on the Bagradas River, about forty miles southwest of Carthage. Here they made camp, probably exhausted from the hasty and long retreat. But Belisarius was already hard on their heels, now with two thousand loyalist troops whom he had persuaded to return to the imperial cause with gifts and promises. Like almost all the North African cities, Membresa was not walled, and so neither army wanted to occupy it. Belisarius made camp at the river, and Stotzas and his army, which was still at least five times the size of Belisarius's force, pitched camp on a hill well suited for defensive operations.

The battle of Membresa, 536

Pressed for time because of the impending campaign against the Ostrogoths, Belisarius had to force the issue and quickly led his troops out to do battle. Both commanders harangued their troops in the customary manner before the battle. Belisarius declared that the mutineers had brought ruin upon themselves by their actions, and that the slaying of their loyalist comrades demanded vengeance. He ended the speech with extolling the virtues of a disciplined and brave army, which would win against armies much greater in size.

Procopius also quotes the speech of Stotzas. We may choose whether to believe that he made it up himself, but it must be expected that Procopius to some extent tried to make the speech realistic. In his speech, Stotzas expanded on the ingratitude shown to the soldiers after their great victory over the Vandals. After the freedom they had felt in the past few weeks, a return to slavery, as he termed service under the emperor, would be ten times more bitter than if they had never experienced liberty. Also, they could not expect pardon from the emperor after what they had done during the mutiny. They could but die once, so let them die, if need be, as free warriors on the battlefield. A victory over the pitiful band of loyalists would give them mastery over North Africa and their hearts' desires. To the mainly Germanic element in the rebel army, the words rang true. We may wonder about the fact that no word of Arianism is mentioned in the speech, but again, we don't know if Procopius, who recorded the events, made up the speech or got it from some of those who were there.

The battle was short. Belisarius had positioned his army so that a strong wind blew in the faces of the mutineers, hindering their use of missile weapons. When the rebels attempted a flanking movement to get windward of the enemy, Belisarius ordered his troops to assault at once while the mutineers were in disorder. The unexpected and sharp attack was a success, and the bulk of Stotzas's army fled in disorder. The rebels did not stop until they reached Numidia. For the Vandals who had joined Stotzas, this was a disastrous battle, as they seemed to be the only ones in the army who had listened to his speech. Most of them refused to flee and died on the field of battle. The camp of the rebels was plundered, and in it was found much treasure from Carthage as well as the Vandal wives of the soldiers, who were considered to be the original instigators of the revolt.

With Stotzas and the mutineers either killed or in flight, Belisarius thought the situation to be sufficiently in hand to let the local generals handle the mopping up and left quickly for Sicily. Ildiger and Theodorus of Cappadocia were left in charge of the troops in North Africa when Belisarius sailed away in April or May 536, to start the campaign against the Ostrogothic kingdom of Italy. The campaign went as planned, and Belisarius secured Sicily with little resistance from the Goths. But while the Romans were engaged in the Ostrogothic War, troubles were still brewing in North Africa.

BATTLE OF GADIAUFALA, 536

General Marcellus was in overall command in Numidia and had under him four other generals who commanded the barbarian auxiliaries, the cavalry, and the infantry. The five Roman generals quickly moved against the fleeing Stotzas and his small band of mutinous soldiers and caught up with them at Gadiaufala (Ksar-Sbehi in modern-day Tunisia), some two days' journey from Cirta (Ksantina). The battle seemed a sure victory, but at the start of it, Stotzas went alone among the imperial soldiers and addressed them in a short, vigorous speech, reminding them of the pay that had not been forthcoming for a long period and that they had been deprived of the spoils of the Vandal War, which he claimed the generals had taken for themselves. His words must have rung true, because in the end, the imperial soldiers abandoned their generals and switched sides to support the well-spoken Stotzas. The five generals fled and hid in a church, but were found and killed, after Stotzas lured them out by promising them their lives. Suddenly the tables had been turned, and the rebellion was again in full flame.

GERMANUS IS SENT TO AFRICA

The new development could seriously threaten the campaign in Italy against the Ostrogoths by robbing the Roman army of reinforcements and supplies. Emperor Justinian now took the dangerous situation much more seriously. He dispatched his popular and able nephew, Germanus, with enough money to pay the rebellious soldiers their wages, which had not been paid for many months. But Justinian could spare only a few soldiers. He instructed Germanus to try to reconcile with the rebels rather than fight them.

When Germanus arrived in Africa, he looked over the registers of soldiers and found that only a third of the Roman army was still loyal to the emperor while the rest—some ten thousand—had joined the rebels. Instead of immediately moving against Stotzas, Germanus sought to reconcile the soldiers and granted deserters amnesty. He soon persuaded most of Stotzas's army to end its mutiny and return its allegiance to the emperor. The deserters were even paid for the period they had been fighting for Stotzas.

Now it was Stotzas who was in trouble. Plagued with mass desertions, he sought to press for a decisive battle with Germanus and moved against Carthage with his remaining troops. The two armies met some four miles from Carthage and remained in position for a while opposite each other, but soon the rebels broke ranks and withdrew into Numidia, where their women and plunder were located, with Germanus in pursuit.

BATTLE OF SCALAE VETERES

Germanus caught up with the mutineers at Scalae Veteres in Numidia at the end of 536 or early in 537. The loyalists deployed their supply wagons in a line, with all the infantry under the leadership of Domnicus in front of them, so as to strengthen their morale by removing any threat to their rear. Germanus, with the best of the cavalry, placed himself on the left wing, and the rest of the cavalry was placed on the right wing in three divisions, led by Ildiger, Theodorus the Cappadocian, and John, the brother of Pappus.

The mutineers took their stand opposite the Roman army in a somewhat more scattered formation, in the manner of barbarians. The Moorish chieftain Iaudas, with thousands of his Moors, watched the struggle close to the battlefield.

Officially they were there to support Stotzas, but they had also promised their support to the loyalists. Here we see again the fluctuating loyalties of the Moors, as Iaudas recently had fought the Romans bitterly but now supported them.

After a tough fight, Germanus routed the rebels, Stotzas was forced into a disorderly retreat, and the loyalists were able to capture the rebels' camp. With the victory of the loyalists evident, the Moors launched themselves upon the fleeing rebels, and Stotzas, only with difficulty, managed to flee with a hundred Vandals. His retreat ended in Mauretania, where he later married the daughter of one of the local Moorish chieftains. The remaining rebels were either killed or joined the army of Germanus. The mutiny was over.

NINE

The Final Campaigns

"And Gontharis was intending to kill Areobindus, but, in order to avoid the appearance of aiming at sole power, he wished to do this secretly in battle, in order that it might seem that the plot had been made by others against the general, and that he had been compelled by the Roman army to assume command over Libya."—*Procopius, on the Roman rebel General Gontharis, mid-sixth century*

Stotzas was now in full flight, so Germanus was able to withdraw to Carthage and attend to the government of North Africa. But the troubles for North Africa were not over.

A large number of disgruntled soldiers had gathered around Maximinus, a bodyguard of Theodorus's, and were willing to join him in a rebellion. The plot was revealed to Germanus, but he was reluctant to upset the soldiers in any way. So instead of punishing Maximinus, he tried to regain his loyalty by promoting him to his personal bodyguard. Maximinus happily accepted, but he saw the promotion as a way to effect his plot more easily now that he was close to Germanus.

On the day of the uprising, Maximinus's followers went to the palace in Carthage, where Germanus was entertaining friends for lunch. Maximinus stood with the other body-guards behind the dining couches when a messenger entered and announced that a large group of soldiers had come to the palace to complain that the emperor owed them pay for a long period. Because Germanus knew of the conspiracy, he ordered some of his loyal troops to watch Maximinus so he could not leave the palace while Germanus went to see the mutinous soldiers. As had been planned, the rebellious troops went to the Hippodrome, where they were to meet the rest of the rebels and Maximinus, who did not show up. While the rebels were in confusion without their leader, Germanus sent a force of trusted soldiers to the Hippodrome, where the rebels were killed or surrendered. Maximinus was impaled before the walls of Carthage as a signal to others who would think of rebellion.

The unrest in North Africa now seemed quelled, and Germanus returned to Constantinople. In 539, Solomon was again sent out to govern North Africa. Martinus and Valerianus were also recalled, and reinforcements were sent under Rufinus, Leontius, and John, the son of Sisiniolus. Solomon sent away rebellious elements among the troops, and new ones were enrolled. The remaining Vandals, and par-ticularly all the Vandal women, who were considered instiga-tors of the revolt of Stotzas, were sent elsewhere in the empire and passed from recorded history.

CAMPAIGN AGAINST THE MOORS

Some Moorish tribes were still in rebellion. To defeat them, Solomon sent one of his bodyguards, Gontharis, with a force against the troublesome Iaudas and his Moors on Mount Aurasium. But Gontharis was defeated at the Abigais River and had to be rescued by Solomon, who brought the whole army with him. Solomon and his army could not stay, howev-er, as they were needed to protect Byzacena, so Gontharis was still hard-pressed in his camp after Solomon left. Only the timely return of Solomon saved Gontharis, and the Moors were defeated decisively in a battle near Mount Aurasium.

Chastened by the defeat, the Moors no longer wanted to confront the whole Roman army in regular battle, but instead sought to avoid defeat by retreating to the difficult terrain around Aurasium. They expected that the Romans soon would retreat because of lack of water and provisions. Accordingly, Iaudas sent most of his warriors home to Mauretania and the regions south of Mount Aurasium, and he remained in the forts on the mountain with only a small army.

But Solomon was determined to reach a conclusion and remove the Moorish threat, so he destroyed the fields on Aurasium and began to besiege the Moorish forts there. Despite serious deprivations, the Romans defeated the Moors in several skirmishes and sieges, and even wounded Iaudas, who had to flee to Mauretania. After capturing Iaudas's treasure and household, Solomon garrisoned the forts on Mount Aurasium and returned to Carthage. With the Moors retreated from Numidia, the province of Mauretania Primus was liberated. The Moors still held Mauretania Caesarea, but the Romans held the port of Caesarea. Finally, in 539, North Africa was at peace. But it was a peace that would last only four years.

REFORTIFICATION OF THE ROMAN CITIES IN NORTH AFRICA

In 539, Solomon began a program of restoring the city walls destroyed so many years earlier by the Vandals, using, among other resources, the great treasure of Iaudas. North Africa had a respite to regain its once-prosperous state.

After the Vandal War and the defeat of the Moorish uprising, Solomon reused the military principles of Diocletian with the deep frontier defense. He strongly fortified the harbors Rusguniae (Lapérouse), Caesarea, and others, as well as the cities inside the country, such as Thubunae (Tobna), Lambaesis (Lambése), Mascula (Khenchela), and Thamugadi. Excavations in the middle of the twentieth century further examined the fortifications of Sitifis, Theveste

(Tebessa), Ammaedara (Haidra), and Limisa (Ksar Lemsa), where the walls appear to have been made very close around the city, often in a smaller ring than before. Many archaeologists believe this implies a reduction in the population. However, it could also be that Solomon was merely following the fortification standards of the period, in which the fortresses were made so that the needed number of soldiers to defend them was reduced as much as possible. Some of the fortifications erected in North Africa during Justinian's reign can still be seen today.

AFFAIRS IN ITALY AND IN THE EAST

North Africa was not the only region in which the Romans were challenged. In Italy, the Romans were fighting a successful war against the Ostrogoths, and Rome was taken in 536. The Ostrogoths besieged Rome for a year before being forced to retreat to Ravenna, after taking huge losses. Fighting had again erupted on the eastern border of the empire, which was seriously pressed by Persian invasions in 540, 541, and 542. In 543 and 544, sporadic fighting continued, but by this time the war had ceased to bring quick profits to the Persians, and in 545, King Chosroes agreed, in return for a payment of five thousand pounds of gold, to sign a truce for five years. The wars in Italy and on the eastern border were a serious drain on the finances and manpower of the Roman Empire.

MOORISH UPRISINGS

In 543, the Emperor Justinian sent Cyrus and Sergius, nephews of Solomon the eunuch, to North Africa to govern Pentapolis in Cyrenaica, and Tripolitania. The local Leuathae Moors came with a great army to Sergius at Leptis Magna (Al Khums in modern-day Libya), to see if he might give them the gifts and insignias of office that their rulers customarily received from the Roman emperor. On the advice of Pudentius, who had played the main role in the revolt of Tripolitania against the Vandals ten years earlier, eighty of the Moors were received into the city. At the conference disagreements over the Moorish demands soon turned into a full-scale fight, and all the Moors were killed by Sergius's bodyguards.

When the Moorish army outside the city heard of the incident, it attacked Sergius, who came out to meet it with Pudentius. In front of Leptis Magna, the Romans defeated the Moors, but Pudentius was killed during the battle. Later, the Moors went against the province of Byzacena with an even greater army, so Solomon had to collect the whole Roman army and summoned Sergius and Cyrus with their troops. The otherwise pro-Roman Moorish chieftain Antalas also went into rebellion at this time in 543, allegedly because of some acts of ill faith by the Romans.

The armies met at the city of Tebesta, where Solomon again defeated the Moors and captured their plunder. However, the Roman soldiers complained after the battle that the booty was not being distributed, and they were not satisfied when Solomon explained that he was awaiting the outcome of the whole campaign, after which the booty could be distributed more fairly. Accordingly, when the Moors again offered battle at Colonia Cillitana, some Roman soldiers did not enter the fight, and the others fought without enthusiasm. As a result, the large Moorish force soon routed the Romans. During the rout, Solomon's horse stumbled in a ravine, and Solomon was caught by the pursuing barbarians, who killed him.

SERGIUS APPOINTED GOVERNOR

In his stead, Solomon's nephew Sergius was appointed to govern North Africa. Sergius was known for his avarice and was an arrogant and incompetent governor and general. He soon brought the province to its knees through misadministration and inability to handle the war with the Moors. Most of the generals in North Africa, in particular John, the son of Sisiniolus, disliked him greatly because of his character and were therefore reluctant to support him against the raiding barbarians. Justinian was aware that Sergius was an incompetent governor, but he was not willing to remove him from office, out of respect for the dead Solomon.

Meanwhile, the Moorish rebellion continued, and Antalas now summoned the old nemesis of the Romans in North Africa, Stotzas, who came from Mauretania with his remaining Vandals. Antalas and Stotzas soon gathered a large army and were raiding Byzacena unhindered. Stotzas's name was still a great magnet to the disaffected Roman soldiers, and some of the Roman soldiers he captured joined his standards. Finally, John was stirred by the entreaties of the provincials and moved his army against the Moors. On his way, he sent a letter to General Himerius, who was commanding the Roman troops in Byzacena, ordering him to bring his troops to the city of Menephesse, where the armies would combine. Later John was informed that the enemy was already at Menephesse, so he sent a message to Himerius directing him to meet him somewhere else. But the message did not reach Himerius, who marched straight into the Moorish army. Most of the troops joined Stotzas, and Himerius was captured. The revolt was again growing.

THE CAPTURE OF HADRUMENTUM

Antalas and Stotzas then thought of a stratagem to take the important city of Hadrumentum. The captured Himerius was forced to approach the city walls with some of Stotzas's troops and some Moors in chains and say to the guards that John had won a great victory over the barbarians and would arrive soon. The guards should therefore open the gates for the small party of Roman soldiers. Deceived by the ploy, the guards allowed them all to enter the city. The rebels managed to keep the gates open and let the waiting Moorish army enter. Hadrumentum was sacked and a small garrison placed there. A short time later, however, loyalists retook the city with the help of the local provincials. Despite the minor victory, the Moors and Stotzas still roamed unchallenged throughout the North African provinces, plundering the local inhabitants. Because of his hostility toward Sergius, John remained quiet and did not seek to engage the rebels, whose numbers had grown even stronger from deserters.

With the Moorish rebellion running completely out of control, in 545, Justinian finally sent more soldiers and better generals to regain the initiative. Among the generals was the energetic Areobindus, who was married to Justinian's niece. Their orders were to end the rebellion as soon as possible. The emperor still did not recall Sergius, but instead divided the provinces between the two generals. Sergius was to carry on the war in Numidia while Areobindus would command in Byzacena. When Areobindus learned that Antalas and Stotzas were encamped about one hundred miles southwest of Carthage at the city of Sicca Venerea (El Kef in modern-day Tunisia), he summoned Sergius and John to join forces with him and engage the Moors in battle. Sergius ignored the request, so only John, with a small army, joined Areobindus. The little Roman army met Antalas and Stotzas outside the city.

Battle of Sicca Venerea and the end of Stotzas

Stotzas and John were mortal enemies and had been trying to kill each other for years. At the start of the battle, they rode between the two armies to fight each other in single combat. As they rode against each other, John mortally wounded Stotzas with an arrow in the groin. He fell from his horse, but the rebels and their allies attacked the small imperial army and swept it away. John was killed when his horse stumbled down a steep incline. After the battle, Stotzas was found dying under a tree. The death of the energetic and magnetic Stotzas marked the end of Vandal self-determination; they were never to establish even a small principality again.

The end of the rebellion

With such a disastrous outcome of the battle, Justinian realized that Sergius had to be removed, so he was sent to Italy and the Gothic War. In his place Justinian appointed Areobindus governor in 545, and sent him some Armenian troops under Artabanes and John. Soon, however, Areobindus was treacherously slain by Gontharis, the Roman general in Numidia who had promised the soldiers that he personally would advance them whatever they were owed in pay. Gontharis has sometimes been seen as having Vandal origins because of the similarity of his name to other Vandal names. But there is no indication that he was trying to reestablish the Vandal kingdom. Among his supporters were the remaining one thousand troops of Stotzas—500 Romans, 80 Huns, and 420 Vandals—as well as the Moors of Antalas.

Although Gontharis did send the head of Areobindus to the Moorish chief Antalas, he decided to break the alliance with the Moors and gain the command of Stotzas's soldiers. Antalas was disgusted at the deceit and so decided to submit again to Emperor Justinian. He contacted the Roman general commanding the troops in Byzacena, who had fled to an island off the coast of North Africa, and gave pledges of loyalty. Stotzas's remaining troops perceived the change of heart in Antalas and marched in great haste to join forces with Gontharis in Carthage. Artabanes, too, promised himself and his Armenians to Gontharis, but secretly thought of how he could assassinate him. Gontharis now forced Areobindus's wife, Praeiecta, to write to her uncle, the emperor, that Gontharis was honoring Areobindus's wife and sister and that Gontharis had no part in the murder of her husband. He did this in the hope that the emperor would accept his marriage to Praeiecta.

Meanwhile, Gontharis commanded Artabanes to take the army against Antalas and the Moors in Byzacena. In this he was supported by the Moorish chieftain Coutzinas, who had fallen out with Antalas and had now allied himself with Gontharis. The army met Antalas in battle close to Hadrumentum. Antalas was defeated, but Artabanes did not pursue him, explaining that he was afraid that the loyalists in Hadrumentum would assault him from the back. Artabanes was now thinking of joining the loyalists in Hadrumentum, but instead decided to kill Gontharis and end his tyranny. He returned to Carthage claiming that he needed a larger army to defeat the Moors of Antalas.

Gontharis accepted the plea but decided to march out himself with the army and only leave a few troops in Carthage. To celebrate the expedition, he held a banquet. At the banquet, he entertained the generals, as well as the first and noblest of the Vandals. Artabanes arranged to have Gontharis, his friends, and the leading Vandals killed at the banquet. This was the start of a loyalist uprising in Carthage, in which the mutineers were killed. John, the leader of Stotzas's troops, fled with some Vandals to a sanctuary. Artabanes gave them pledges of safety, and they were sent to Constantinople.

Surrender of the remaining Vandals

So after thirty-six days of tyranny, Gontharis was killed. Afterwards, some of Stotzas's Vandals were killed, and the rest surrendered to Artabanes. This was the end of the remaining Vandals in North Africa, and they disappear from history. The wife of Areobindus rewarded the entrepid Artabanes with large sums of money, and Justinian appointed him general of Africa.

The chaotic period for North Africa finally ended in 546, when John, the brother of Pappus, was appointed master of the soldiers and governor of North Africa, and the Moors were suppressed. After years of devastations, Moorish raids, and the pillaging of the rebels, North Africa enjoyed peace for the rest of Justinian's reign, except for one Moorish rebellion in 563, which was quickly put down. But the provinces never recovered completely despite having been conquered intact by the Romans.

TEN

Aftermath

"Now as for those Vandals who remained in their native land [North of the Danube], neither remembrance nor any name of them has been preserved to my time. For since, I suppose, they were a small number, they were either overpowered by the neighboring barbarians or they were mingled with them not at all unwillingly and their name gave way to that of their conquerors. Indeed, when the Vandals were conquered at that time by Belisarius, no thought occurred to them to go from there to their ancestral homes."—*Procopius, mid-sixth century*

After 546, only scattered individual Vandals were left in North Africa. The regiments sent to the East appear to have fought faithfully for the Romans, but there are no traces of them in the sources.

Nothing is known for certain of the Vandals who remained north of the Danube. Procopius tells us that at the time of Geiseric, they sent a delegation to the Vandal kingdom asking that he give them their lands. We do not know what year that happened, but it was probably after the peace of 442, or possibly after the battle of Nedao in 454, when the Germanic tribes under Hun overlordship rose up and gained their freedom. There is no doubt that if Vandals still existed north of the Danube, they were under the Hunnish yoke like their neighboring tribes, such as the Gepids. The Danubian Vandals may have been absorbed by the Gepids after the victory at Nedao. Procopius tells us that their name was no longer "preserved" in his time, in the first half of the sixth century. While the story seems incredible, it is not without parallel, as we have similar examples from the Heruli and Langobards that emmigrants kept in touch with those who stayed behind. If any Vandal remnants were left in Silesia, they would be absorbed by the Slavonic invasions of that region around the sixth century.

So the Vandal tribes went the way of many other tribes of the great migrations, into obscurity, when the few remnants were absorbed by the Roman Empire and other tribes.

The fate of Arianism

Religiously, the Vandal War caused the destruction of the most aggressive Arian kingdom, and the later destruction of the Ostrogothic kingdom of Italy sealed the fate of Arianism: it would survive several more centuries, but it would never be more than an antiquated heresy. The third great Arian nation, the Visigoths, converted to Catholicism in 589, when King Reccared announced their allegiance to the Orthodox faith at the Third Council of Toledo. Other lesser tribes, such as the Lombards and Heruli, continued in their Arian beliefs, but by the early eighth century, no Arian nations existed.

In the wars of Justinian, it was only against the Vandal kingdom that religion played any great role. However, Justinian does not appear to have continued to treat the Arians harshly after suppressing the rebellion. And while he took great care to protect the Christianity of his subjects, religion does not appear to have been even remotely important in the later war against the Ostrogoths, who were also Arians. We may well suspect that religious issues were more of a pretext than a true motive in that war. During the war in Italy, he appealed to the Orthodox Franks by referring to their common faith, but this had no effect.

Reasons for the Vandal kingdom's demise

It might be said that the Vandal kingdom had outlived its time. While the Vandals had had great enough numbers and skill to defeat the Roman forces in North Africa during a long period of great instability, they succeeded in conquering a far greater kingdom than their limited numbers could control and rule. The massed forces of perhaps twenty thousand or thirty thousand battle-hardened Vandal cavalry could win in battle; however, a people of perhaps one hundred thousand individuals was much too insignificant compared to the several million Romans living in the kingdom. It has been said that a great army makes but a small nation, and while the Ostrogoths were forced to concentrate in a few cities of Italy—they were probably only the majority in Ravenna, Ticinum, and Verona—the Vandals faced a problem just as great if not greater. The Vandals appear to have formed only a warrior aristocracy to govern the Roman population, which was generally unarmed and so could more easily be controlled by a small number of conquerors. Despite this, and even after almost one hundred years of rule, the Vandals still faced uprisings in parts of their kingdom, such as Tripolitania and Sardinia.

The only chance for the Vandals to succeed in the long term was to merge with the Roman population in the same way as the Franks and as the Ostrogoths of Theodoric the Great attempted. However, the Vandals had the odds against them. They were heretics and went through a number of harsh persecutions, which must have alienated them from parts of the population. By concentrating themselves in the rich inner regions, they did not provide security for the great number of provincials living outside the Vandal Allotments, who had to suffer the invasions of the Moors with no military support and no city walls. Moreover, the Vandals never had a great administrator like Theodoric, but after the death of their great warrior king, Geiseric, only a succession of kings who appear to have fought their own people as much as the enemies of the kingdom. We see a movement toward reconciliation with the provincials and a turn toward the Romans in the later period of the kingdom, and given time and quiet conditions, they might have succeeded in creating a lasting kingdom. But such conditions were unlikely, and the Vandal kingdom at the time of Hilderic was inviting disaster. The Moors were encroaching on the borders of the kingdom, and the Vandal armies could not afford to suffer great losses because of the shortage of replacements and because each loss made the Vandal hold on power less secure. If the Romans had not invaded North Africa, the Ostrogoths might have. Or the Moors might have chipped away at the structure of the kingdom until the Vandals no longer could impose their power on their many subjects.

The lethargy after Geiseric that some authors, both ancient and modern, have ascribed to the Vandals is probably not quite correct. However, it appears that apart from the coinage system, they did nothing new or created anything. Instead of combining the best elements of the Vandals and Romans, they adapted to the late Roman lifestyle. When the Romans returned to North Africa, they faced a society that was little different from how they had left it. Despite the dramatic political changes in North Africa in the fifth and sixth centuries, there was a strong pattern of continuity because the Vandals and Moors defined their political life in reference to the Roman model. The Vandals left no trace of themselves after their destruction, not even for a short period. They were an important part of late antiquity mainly because they sat on the grain and oil supply of Europe, they were fierce Arians, and they were masters of a region considered to be one of the greatest intellectual centers of the Roman world.

It may be said that Geiseric came close to his goal when he married his family into the imperial family and later put Olybrius on the Western throne. But in the context of the disintegrating Western Empire, it was too little, too late. The connection to the imperial family did not change anything, and while the Vandals used the presence of the imperial hostages Empress Eudoxia and her two daughters for their political advantage, they never gained much recognition from it. The Visigoths had learned this lesson before the Vandals during a somewhat more stable period of the Western Empire. And Olybrius would not be able to recover the fortunes of the fragmenting Western Empire.

Still, the aim of the great migration from the lands north of the Danube was attained. After thirty-nine years of traveling, the Vandals found a new homeland, one that would provide food and security for almost another century. The Vandals survived the chaos of the migrations of the fifth century, but they were not able to maintain their security during the sixth.

THE IMPORTANCE OF THE FALL OF THE VANDAL KINGDOM TO THE ROMAN WORLD

For the Roman Empire, the victory over the Vandals was one of the great moments of late antiquity, and it was celebrated in various ways. For Emperor Justinian, the glory of the victory would last until his death in 565. The court poet Corippus describes the magnificent piece of needlework that was the decorated pall under which the body of the dead emperor was carried as being

> stitched with precious purple, where the whole vista of Justinian's achievements was picked out in woven gold and glittered with gems. On one side the artist had skillfully represented with his sharp needle barbarian phalanxes bending their necks, slaughtered kings and subject peoples in order. And he made the yellow gold stand out from the colors, so everyone looking at it thought that they were real bodies. The faces were in gold, the blood in purple. And Justinian himself he had depicted as a victor amongst his courtiers, trampling on the brazen neck of the Vandal king, and Libya, applauding, bearing fruit and laurel.

Procopius also describes the mosaic in the great bronze gate named the Chalce, which formed the entrance to the

Imperial Palace, where, amid depictions of Justinian's victories achieved by General Belisarius, stood the emperor and his empress, Theodora, receiving from the Senate "honors equal to God."

After the conquest of North Africa, Justinian continued his campaigns to regain the lands of the Western Empire and greatly increased it by recovering Dalmatia, Italy, Sicily, and most of Spain south of the Baetis River. However, these conquests probably weakened the empire rather than strengthening it. Justinian's aggressive wars in the West—particularly the war against the Ostrogoths in Italy—may have seriously exhausted the empire's finances and manpower. And instead of adding to the treasury, the retaken provinces of the West may have been a burden, requiring Eastern troops to garrison them and yielding insufficient revenue to pay even for their defense. While the Ostrogothic War was the hardest, the pacification of North Africa required an additional twelve years of warfare. On the other hand, capturing the royal treasure of the Vandals not only financed the reconstruction of fortifications in North Africa, but also went a long way to finance the war against the Ostrogoths and Justinian's great building program.

The prolonged troubles in North Africa were due as much to mutinies of the Roman troops as to the revolts of the Moors, and the remaining Vandals only played a small part in them. The diversion of the empire's resources in manpower and money to the West inevitably weakened the Danubian and Eastern borders. As a result, the Roman armies were rarely able to meet the barbarian invaders elsewhere in the field, and the regions from the Adriatic to the Black Sea as far south as Dyrrhachium and Thessalonica and Constantinople itself were subject to perennial devastation.

We get a picture of conditions from a letter of 556 in which Pope Pelagius tells the bishop of Arelate that the estates of the Roman see were so desolated that no one could rehabilitate them. And in a letter to the praetorian prefect of Africa, he says that "after the continuous devastations of war which have been inflicted on the regions of Italy for twenty-five years and more and have scarcely yet ceased, it is only from the islands and places overseas that the Roman church receives some little revenue, however insufficient, for the clergy and the poor." When speaking of islands, he probably means the former Vandal islands of Sardinia and Corsica.

The war against the Vandals showed the Romans that more cavalry was needed against the Germanic tribes of the West. Fifteen thousand men were sent to North Africa, only five thousand of which were cavalry, but the infantry played no part in the battles. In response, the Romans made great changes in their equipment and tactics. Years later, the Roman forces in the war against the Ostrogoths consisted of the versatile armored horse archers, with the infantry of little importance.

The defeat of the Vandal fleet was also an important development for the Roman Empire. The Roman fleet now controlled the entire Mediterranean, and only the Ostrogoths succeeded in challenging them for a short while. This meant that the Romans could freely transport troops and supplies in the Mediterranean and dominate trade in the whole region.

THE FATE OF NORTH AFRICA

While North Africa survived in a rather better state than Italy, it was still greatly affected for some years. According to Procopius, the damages were enormous: "Libya, for instance, in spite of its enormous size, has been laid to utter waste that however far one went in it would be a remarkable achievement to find a single person there." His statement cannot be taken at face value, however, because he wanted to present the damages caused by what he saw as the misadministration of Justinian. Still, we do see evidence of a more insecure life for the provincials in North Africa. Byzacena, for example, contains a great number of forts constructed during the reign of Justinian, and in many cities, forts were constructed in disused public buildings such as forums, baths, amphitheaters, theaters, and pagan temples. A number of cities were also refortified with smaller, more-defendable city walls.

The Roman government never recovered the large areas the Moors occupied in the last years of the Vandal kingdom, and even within the area effectively under Roman administration, the many fortifications erected by Solomon and his successors suggest that prosperity was greatly reduced and conditions highly insecure. Even in the northern parts of Numidia and Byzacena, and in Africa Proconsularis itself, every town was fortified; in most the length of the walls was drastically reduced, and in many the forum was converted into a stronghold. Only Sicily and Sardinia had peace and enjoyed some prosperity.

Financially, North Africa can hardly have paid its way during this period, and it certainly cannot have contributed much toward the general expenses of the empire. Nevertheless, grain, oil, and other supplies could be delivered to Italy, while exports increased somewhat, particularly red slip ware. Italy was depopulated by the war and was undoubtedly a drain on the manpower resources of the Eastern parts. North Africa could contribute somewhat in this area. Not only were a substantial number of Vandals transported to the Eastern parts of the empire, but Moors were also recruited for service overseas, and some African regiments were raised—two, for example, are later found in Egypt. But these cannot have compensated fully for the large number of Eastern troops required for the garrison of North Africa.

THE END OF ROMAN AFRICA

Justinian's conquests did not endure long after his death in 565. Within four years, Roman Spain was attacked by the neighboring Visigoths, North Africa by the Moors, and Italy by the Lombards. The Lombards, who invaded in 568, had the greatest success, taking north Italy and most of the interior of the Italian Peninsula by 572. The early seventh century brought even more desperate conditions to the exhausted empire. Avars, Bulgars, Slavs, Persians, and others reduced it to little more than Anatolia, North Africa, and Egypt, along with small parts of Thrace, Greece, and Italy.

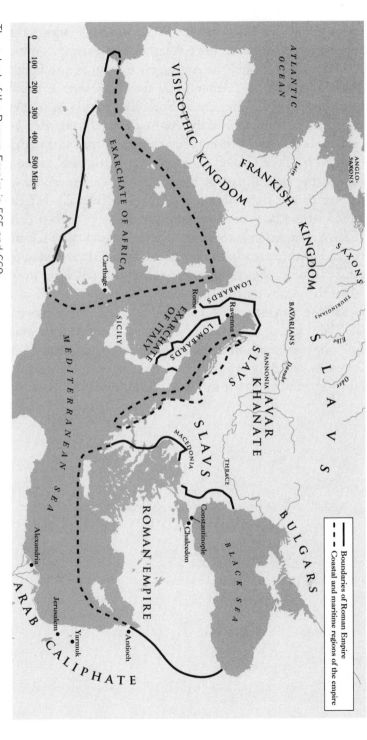

The extent of the Roman Empire in 565 and 660.

Emperor Heraclius (610–641) did win back large parts of the lost territory, but in the 630s, the Arabs, newly converted to Islam, erupted, and the empire once again had to fight for its life. In 647, an Arab raiding force defeated and killed Byzantine Exarch Gregory at Sufutela (Sbeitla in modern-day Tunisia). In the 660s, the Arabs attacked from their base in Tripolitania and began a long campaign for North Africa. Around 670, their chieftain, Uqba ibn Nāf'i, established his base in the central part of Byzantine Africa. He would lead his campaigns from his camp Qayrawān (literally, caravan), which would later be the capital of the new Arab province Ifrīqiya. The struggle to secure North Africa would last until the end of the seventh century. Carthage was captured in 695, retaken quickly by the Byzantine fleet, but fell again in 698, when the Arabs destroyed the city. This was the end of the Byzantine province of Africa. Soon after, the Arabs moved to the West, taking the remaining parts of North Africa, and in 711 they crossed into Spain. In 720 they crossed the Pyrenees, and only in 732 were they stopped, by the Frankish King Charles Martel at the Battle of Poitiers.

Aspects of the Vandal Kingdom in Africa

"So I, bending my neck in obedience to the person giving the order, shall attempt to reveal, in summary and brief fashion, the things which occurred in the regions of Africa as the Vandals raged. Like a rural laborer, with weary arms I shall collect gold from hidden caves, but I shall not hesitate to hand over something which still looks unrefined and disordered for it to be tested in the fire by the judgement of a craftsman who may be able to mint gold coins from it."—*Victor of Vita, introduction to his* History of the Vandal Persecution, *AD 484*

The Vandal kingdom of North Africa consisted of a number of peoples, if such a term can be used, who had different standings in the society. The Vandals were, of course, the most important part. These were the Hasding Vandals and the remnants of the Siling Vandals, who had been defeated in Spain by the Visigoths. No doubt many Roman slaves had also joined the Vandals during their migration and called themselves Vandals. Second came the Alans, who had a special position as seen from the title of the Vandal king—King of Vandals and Alans—and had before their defeat in Spain probably been the more powerful of the two tribes. Third came the Goths, Sueves, and other tribal splinters picked up during the migration who hoped for a better future in the Vandal confederation. The fourth and by far the most numerous part of the population was the Roman subjects. Outside this system were the allied Moorish tribes.

ETHNICITY

According to a modern sociological theory, ethnicity is a social construction rather than something that exists independently of human action. An ethnic group is not defined by the objective biological kinship of its members, by shared language, or by similarities in physical appearance, as has often been believed. Instead it can be seen as the acknowledgement of a group of similarities and differences that create ethnic identity. If the members of a group have a sense of their own unity, and if outside observers are aware of this, they could be said to have an ethnic identity. The groups could then use, consciously or otherwise, signs to mark this difference in ethnicity, for example, through physical attributes, language, or cultural choices such as religion. But it is the ideology of the group that defines its ethnic unity, and not its visible symbols in themselves. It is also believed that ethnicity was—and still is—a fluid thing. Ethnic identity could emerge, develop, and fade in response to political and economic changes. The symbols by which the cohesion of a group is expressed also fluctuate, and the affiliation of a given individual can change according to circumstances. Therefore, we see Romans taking Germanic names and wearing Germanic clothing, and the other way around.

This explains the difficulty in tracing ethnicity in names. The name Maioricus, for example, is a combination of the familiar Latin prefix *maior* with the Germanic suffix *rikus* (powerful). The name of the Vandal Arian Patriarch Cyrila also appears to be a hybrid of sorts, combining the Greek Cyril with a common Germanic suffix. Following the most recent studies, we have only ninety-nine names from the North African epigraphy and literary sources who are probably Vandal people. Names were often signs of ethnic identity, but we need to be careful when we attempt to interpret them too literally. Likewise, while the majority of Vandals in North Africa could probably speak Latin, they preferred Germanic, as their language provided a strong bond of association. As an example of this, we learn that Cyrila attempted to debate with the Nicene bishops in Vandalic, but his opponents rejected this, arguing that his Latin was perfectly adequate to be understood.

With regards to physical symbols, Victor of Vita mentions that if a man or a woman who looked like a Vandal entered a Catholic church, their long hair would be pulled out as punishment, thereby signifying that long hair was a typical Vandal appearance in the period. From Victor we also learn that the Vandals wore shirts and close-fitting trousers, and that Romans at court dressed in Vandal clothes.

By the time of Huneric, the Vandals had been strongly affected by Roman culture, but they continued to adhere to their own dress and hairstyles. The importance of dress might not appear to be so great now, but in ancient times the wearing of certain items was a symbol of support or allegiance, or a lack thereof. For example, in 397, Emperor Honorius issued a law forbidding the wearing of trousers and also of a type of Germanic footwear called *tzangae* within the city of Rome, because it was considered "un-Roman." The stipulated penalties were exile and confiscation of property. This law was reissued in 399 and again in 416. In the law of 416, the wearing of long hair, another barbarian trait, was added to the list of offenses. A mosaic found at Carthage, now in the British Museum, had been seen by many as picturing a Vandal horseman in closely fitting trousers during the hunt. However, this interpretation has recently been challenged because many Romans wore such Germanic clothing during late antiquity. Despite the fact that the mosaic might depict a Roman, the Vandals would have dressed similarly.

The question of ethnic identity in the Vandal kingdom is also difficult to answer because we know from Procopius that the Vandals soon took over the manners of the Roman upper class and spent their time hunting, dining, or even reciting poetry. Unfortunately, we know almost nothing of the social interaction of the Vandals and Romans. Could a Roman declare himself a Vandal? We know a case of a Roman who, for example, "became a Hun," as the Roman diplomat Priscus relates in the fifth century, which would appear to be much more difficult than to join the Vandals, as the Huns were more culturally different. The difficulty of determining what symbols the Vandals and Romans used to distinguish themselves from each other is compounded by our lack of knowledge of how the Alans and the other Germanic elements showed their own ethnic affiliations. However, when Procopius described the Roman invasion of Africa, he was clear that a visible distinction existed between Vandals and Libyans, as he termed the Roman inhabitants of the kingdom.

Despite the Vandals "becoming more Roman" in their manners and dress, they never doubted that they were Vandals. Possibly their identity was more tied in with common ancestry, following different laws and other such means of differentiating themselves from the Roman population.

THE ALANS

It has generally been assumed that the Iranian Alans were completely assimilated by the Vandals. However, the sources indicate that they remained an identifiable part of the tribal confederation. Bishop Possidius of Calama, who was present in Hippo Regius at the Vandal siege in 430, distinguishes between Vandals and Alans, as well as mentioning that there were also Goths in the confederation. In the late fifth century, the poet Blossius Aemilius Dracontius also distinguishes between Vandals and Alans. Dracontius was poet at the court of King Gunthamund and made a poem listing a number of tribes in a pejorative fashion. One of the tribes mentioned is the Alans. We can be surprised that the Vandal king finds it acceptable to speak in a negative fashion of the Alans, but it is clear that people still considered the Alans as a separate tribe. Later, during the Roman invasion, Procopius clearly indicates that the Vandal kingdom also included Alans, but he does not otherwise mention them as distinct from the Vandals. He even states that the name Vandal was applied to all non-Moorish barbarians in North Africa. Justinian took the victory name of Alanicus after defeating the Vandals, which also might indicate that the Alans were still a recognized ethnic part of the Vandal kingdom.

Nothing is known of how long the Alans kept their ethnic identity and language, of which no trace has survived. Neither is it known if they continued to be pagan or became Arians, but they were pagans while settled in Spain. We might favorably compare the status of the Alans with that of the Rugians in the Ostrogothic confederation. When Theodoric the Great invaded Italy in 489, a part of the Rugian people under their king, Fredericus, followed Theodoric's Ostrogoths and shared in his victory over Odoacer. The Rugians remained part of the Gothic tribal confederacy but always kept to themselves and maintained a separate "nationality," marrying only the women of their own tribe and probably having justice administered by their own chieftains and their own laws. In 541, when the Ostrogoths were hard pressed by the Romans, the Rugians even managed to put a king on the Ostrogothic throne.

THE OTHER GERMANIC ELEMENTS

We know that Goths are mentioned as part of the Vandal tribal confederation. The Goths were probably mainly remnants of the Visigoths of King Wallia, who stayed behind when he left Spain for Gaul. Furthermore, we know that Count Bonifacius used Gothic troops, and some of these might also have deserted to the Vandals during the invasion of North Africa.

In 1951, an epitaph was discovered in the Grand Basilica in Hippo that might indicate the existence of other Germanic sub-groups within the Vandal confederation. The inscription is dated to 474, when it was erected by one Ingomar to commemorate his wife, Ermengon, who had died. The inscription tells us that his wife was thirty-five when she died, and she was regarded by her husband as *Suava*—that is, Sueve. If we assume they were Vandal subjects, the inscription indicates that despite her being born around the time of the fall of Carthage, she was still considered a Sueve throughout her life. It is not surprising that some Sueves might have joined the Vandals during their long shared migration across Western Europe.

The members of the other Germanic groups were probably primarily warriors in the Vandal army, but we do not know their exact status. Did they intermarry with the other tribes? How were their laws administered? It may be that they were eventually assimilated into the Vandal thousandships and so no longer constitute separate tribes. At least in the final period of the Vandal kingdom, we may assume that the other Germanic elements were probably fully integrated as Vandals, particularly when following the statement of Procopius that by 533, all non-Moorish barbarians in the Vandal kingdom were called Vandals.

THE ROMANS

The Roman population of the kingdom was far greater than that of the Vandals, who never constituted more than perhaps 10 percent of the population in North Africa, and perhaps as little as 2 percent. The Romans were treated as a subject population and did not have the same rights as the Vandals. The harsh persecutions of the Catholic Church and the Roman nobility continued to keep the Vandals and Romans apart. They may not have intermarried, not least of all for religious reasons.

Despite the Romans' lower position, the administration of the kingdom appears mainly to have been in their hands. No doubt this is because the Vandals had no experience in such matters and focused on warfare and practicing for war. Furthermore, the administration mainly existed to deal with the Roman population and their taxes and laws, and so was best staffed by Romans, who had the right education. A kingdom the size of the Vandals' could not be ruled without a functioning administration. The same continuation of the Roman administration is seen in the other Germanic kingdoms on Roman soil.

In general, it appears that Roman class distinctions changed little under the Vandals. We hear of such classes as *illustres* (illustrious), *spectabiles* (admirables), *senatores* (senators), *possessors* (small and middle-size landowners), *negotiators* (tradesmen), and *plebes* (common people). Under the Vandals, the *illustres*, *spectabiles*, and *clarissimi* (highly regarded)—mentioned in a law of Huneric's dated February 25, 484—continued to maintain old prerogatives and discharge old functions.

The society of the Vandal kingdom has at times been viewed as a warrior aristocracy and professional army consisting of Vandals, with the Roman population working the fields, industries, and other professions outside the military. But Romans did hold influential positions in society. Fourteen names of higher officials are known, and of these, four are Vandal—or rather, Germanic—and ten Roman. In the early 480s, for instance, one Victorianus of Hadrumentum was *proconsul Carthaginis*. However, the highest positions appear to have been occupied solely by Vandals, just as it appears that only Vandals were allowed in the army. Between the free Romans and the slaves was the class of *coloni*—tenant farmers whose everyday rural life was probably little affected by the change of rule in Carthage, apart from the lessened security from Moorish raids in the later period of the kingdom.

The slave population of North Africa was already large by the time of the invasion and most likely continued to be a large number under the Vandals. Many provincials must have been enslaved during the Vandal invasion, and the later raids also carried slaves back to Africa from other parts of the Mediterranean. Many of the Roman slaves held high position, such as the slave Maxima, mentioned by Victor of Vita, who was in charge of the household of a chiliarch, leader of a thousandship unit. Most of the slaves worked in the fields, plantations, and mines doing manual labor. But the opportunity for Roman-style social mobility continued as demonstrated in the life of Godas, a former slave of Gelimer's who rose to be governor of Sardinia.

Indeed, for many Romans, the new Vandal lords were seen as offering a chance for social mobility, as Salvian relates by the time of their settlement in Spain. The exiled bishop of Carthage, Quodvultdeus, laments in his letters from Italy the eagerness with which some of his countrymen supported the Vandals. Later, Victor of Vita condemned the Romans who looked past the barbarism of the Vandals, as he termed it, to the opportunities for social and political advancement:

> Those of you, who love barbarians and sometimes praise them, in a way worthy of condemnation, give thought to their name and understand their ways. Surely there is no other name by which they could be called other than "barbarian," a fitting word connoting savageness, cruelty and terror? However many may be the gifts with which you befriend them and however many the acts of compliance with which you placate them, they can think of nothing other than looking on the Romans with envy, and, to the extent that things turn out in accordance to their will, it is their constant desire to darken the nobility and brightness of the Roman name.

And to a large extent, it appears that the Vandals rewarded their Roman supporters. Even during the early period of the kingdom, Romans could reach high positions within the Vandal administration. Neither does it appear that Romans were particularly singled out for victimization, despite the words of Victor. At least at court, the Vandal kings made life dangerous for Romans *and* Vandals, who could be exiled or killed.

But while some supported the Vandals, others were more or less actively against them, such as the provincial aristocracy and the church. Most of the wealthy Roman landowners, who had dominated the municipal governments, lost their lands and wealth on the arrival of the Vandals. Some of them chose or suffered exile and fled to other parts of North Africa, Italy, or the East. No doubt their wealth and power also made them a target for the Vandal kings, who needed to stabilize their kingdom and suppress or remove any major threats to their power. The Roman aristocrats would not forget their losses, and they played a significant part in convincing Justinian to attack North Africa.

For the Catholic Church, it was a religious matter—the question of the primacy of Catholicism in North Africa—but also a question of power. Naturally, the Catholic sources focus almost entirely on the religious principles, but the church in North Africa was rich and powerful and stood to lose everything by the hand of the Vandal kings—and indeed came quite close to losing all. From initially seeing the pope in Rome as simply a bishop among other bishops, in the end the North African Catholic Church had lost so much strength that it had to recognize his primacy. The bishop of Carthage was also close to losing his status, and his position was challenged seriously in the time of King Hilderic. It comes as no surprise that the exiled nobles and members of the Catholic Church also did what they could to convince Emperor Justinian that the Vandal kingdom should be destroyed.

THE MOORS

The Moors had a special position in relation to the Vandal kingdom. They were not part of the Vandal confederation but rather their allies, and sometimes their enemies. They may have initially seen in the Vandals a continuation of the Roman rule of North Africa. Supporting this notion is a statement by Procopius, who relates that there was a law among the Moors that no one should rule over them, even if he was hostile to the Romans, until the emperor of the Romans gave him the tokens of office: a silver staff covered with gold, a crownlike cap, a white cloak with a golden brooch, a white tunic with embroidery, and gilded boots. And though the Moors had received their tokens of office from the Vandals during the period of their rule, they did not consider the Vandal rule secure, and so they asked the same from Belisarius when the Romans returned. It may seem surprising that the Romans would give tokens of office to an enemy chieftain, but it is important to understand that the Moors never questioned the superiority of the Roman Empire, even when at war with them.

The Moorish wars were mainly raids for plunder and not an attempt to defeat the Roman Empire and take the North African provinces. The Moorish tribes and their rulers were well aware that they could not defeat the Romans. For the Romans, it was important to maintain this superiority by showing that they did not mind appointing a new chieftain even if he were hostile to them— although we must suppose that they would probably not remain so for very long—it was a way of saying that they did not care if some insignificant tribes were at war with them or not. When the Vandals first arrived in North Africa, the Moors appear to have kept quiet, possibly because they had recently been defeated by the Romans, but eventually they joined the Vandals as allies.

Geiseric appears to have managed the tribes well. Some troublesome elements were deported to the island of Sardinia, but some other exiles from the Vandal kingdom were sent to the Moorish desert regions. That appears to have been a common punishment for unruly clergy during the persecutions. Geiseric brought Moors along in the Vandal raids and gave them a share of the booty. This was a clever move, because they also functioned as a form of hostages, and it satisfied the Moors' hunger for plunder while lessening the need to guard the desert border. It was particularly important to the Vandals to have their backs free in the initial period of the kingdom, when they were the most vulnerable. Furthermore, the Moors provided light infantry to complement the Vandal cavalry and could absorb losses during the Vandal raids.

After Geiseric died, however, the Moorish tribes began to encroach on Vandal territory. They might eventually have greatly reduced the size of the kingdom, but it fell to the Romans before that happened. During the reign of Gunthamund, Moorish tribes erupted in southern Byzacena and southern Numidia. The region of Theveste and Capsa was raided, and possibly also Thelepte and Sufetela. Despite uneven success, from then on, an increasing number of Moorish tribes would be active in the outer parts of the kingdom. Their raids and invasions greatly damaged the prosperity of the provinces, which were under constant threat of attacks in the final years of the kingdom. When the Romans returned, some Moors initially kept quiet and watched the outcome of the struggle, but soon after they erupted against the Romans and were suppressed only with difficulty. Other Moors continued to support the

Vandals, and the last organized Vandals under Stotzas lived among them in Mauretania.

The Moorish states

There was no united Moorish kingdom, but rather the area outside Vandal control was divided into a number of small states, each with its own leader. Sometimes these groups were allied, and sometimes they fought each other.

That the Moors became restless after Geiseric died was no coincidence. Reduced control of the outer parts of the Vandal kingdom and removal of the Roman border garrisons led the Moorish tribes to coalesce into more powerful groups. In some cases they took over responsibility for local security that the Roman army had held in the border regions. A Latin inscription found in the middle of the Aures Mountains casts some light upon the changing political circumstances of the late 470s and 480s. The text is in honor of the Moorish leader Masties, ruler of the Hodna region, and is dated to the late fifth century:

> "I, Masties, duke [*dux*] for 67 years and emperor [*impera-tor*] for 10 years, never perjured myself nor broke faith with either the Romans or the Moors, and was prepared in both war and in peace, and my deeds were such that God supported me well."

Possibly he was made *dux* before the Vandal invasion and so had held out independently without orders from the imperial adminis-tration in Italy. As *dux* he would also have commanded a number of troops to police the border. That military leaders could be iso-lated by barbarian invasions and continue their functions for decades after is seen in many places, such as in Gaul. The Vandals did not have the military power to control the kingdom fully, nor probably the inclination to enforce their power over some remote region. They had their hands full in the more densely settled and rich regions of Proconsularis.

A later dedication was erected in 508 in Altava, in the far west of North Africa, commemorating the construction of a fort in the kingdom of Masuna, *Rex Maurorum et Romanorum* (king of the Moors and Romans). By 508, King Masuna was ruling the region of the towns of Safar, Altava, and Castra Severiana, and he used Latin to state his position. It is significant that so many years after

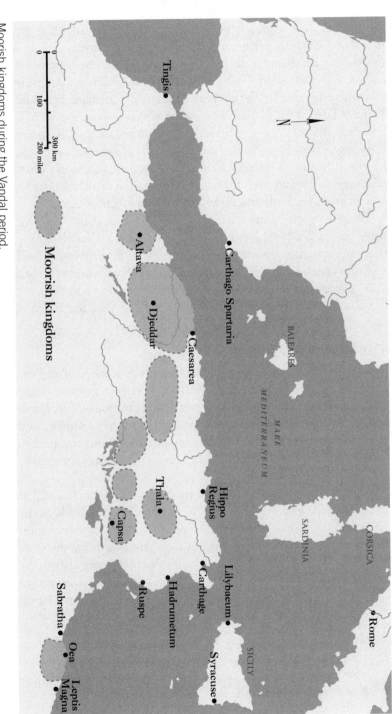

Moorish kingdoms during the Vandal period.

the Vandal occupation, a Moorish ruler still found it natural to set up a dedication in the Roman manner and using Latin.

About 510, the tribes around the Tunisian middle mountains between Theveste and Thelepte became restless. They raided the Roman territories led by a chieftain named Guenfan. His son, Antalas, later began raiding the cities on the Tunisian eastern coast and would cause great troubles for the Vandals and Romans. Thamugadi and Bagai to the west were also plundered and taken by the tribes of the Aures Mountains. By 525, or shortly after, Mauretania Caesarensis, apart from the capital, was lost, and so was Mauretania Sitifensis, as well as southern Numidia.

Despite all the battles between the Moors and the Vandals, there were still Moorish tribes that supported the Vandals during the last campaign against the Roman return. Perhaps we should view the general struggle between the Vandals and Moors not as a change from the same conflicts between the Romans and Moors, but that the Vandals simply took over the role that the Romans had, and were less successful militarily.

The Vandal population

Vandal society consisted roughly of four groups: the king and the royal family, the nobility, the common warriors, and the Arian Church. Vandal women held an important position in Germanic society, but unfortunately we hear little of them in the sources, and apart from three instances, we do not even hear about the queens. Only in the case of the rebellion of 536 do we get an idea of their influence.

Vandal society was divided into thousandship groups created at the time of the invasion of North Africa, which had possibly developed from the lesser tribes in the confederation. Before we examine these groups closely, we must answer one overriding question about the Vandal kingdom: how many Vandals were there? We have a number of statements from the ancient sources. Victor of Vita explains about the crossing of the Vandals into North Africa:

> A large number made the crossing, and in his cunning duke Geiseric, intending to make the reputation of his people a source of dread, ordered then and there that the entire crowd was to be counted, even those who had come from the womb into the light that very day. Including old

men, young men and children, slaves and masters, there was found to be a total of 80,000. News of this has spread widely, until today those ignorant of the matter think that this is the number of their armed men, although now their number is small and feeble.

Compared with this is the testament of Procopius, who also speaks of the crossing of the Vandals into North Africa:

> He [Geiseric] arranged the Vandals and Alans into regiments, over whom he set no fewer than eighty military leaders, whom he called Chiliarchs, so creating the belief that his forces amounted to 80,000 men. Nevertheless the number of the Vandals and Alans was said in the previous time before the invasion of Africa, not to amount to more than 50,000. But the natural increase of the population together with their practice of admitting other barbarians into their confederation, had enormously added to their numbers. The names, however, of the Alans and of every other barbarous tribe in the confederacy except the Moors, were all merged in the one designation of Vandals.

So both sources agree that the Vandals were counted and that the official number reached was eighty thousand—possibly based on an unknown common source. But here the similarities end. Victor believes that all ages as well as slaves were counted, whereas Procopius believes that only warriors were counted, and that the whole counting was a ruse anyway to hide the fact that they were only around fifty thousand. It appears from both that women were not counted. In Procopius it seems that the ruse was not in counting everybody, but in making more thousandships than could be filled up. Both statements have the usual problems with population figures in the ancient world. At what age was a man regarded as a warrior? What was the percentage of women to men? How many slaves did they bring? The percentage of warriors was high, as no doubt the old and infirm had died during the migrations through Gaul and Spain. Victor was concerned with emphasizing the low number of the Vandals, and so his estimate can hardly be taken to be too high. On the other hand, Procopius, who wanted to praise Belisarius, who destroyed the Vandal kingdom, had a point in making them appear great.

In the context of so many fantastic numerical estimates of contemporary chroniclers, it seems plausible that, excluding slaves, there were around fifty thousand Vandal, Alan, and other Germanic tribesmen of all ages. We can compare this with other statements from antiquity. Jerome says there were eighty thousand Burgundians, though that was probably not based on an actual census. There were supposed to be around two hundred thousand Goths on the Danube in 376, of which perhaps forty thousand to fifty thousand were warriors. There were around twenty thousand Visigoth warriors at the battle of Frigidus in 394. On the other hand, we see that even decisive battles in this period sometimes involved only five thousand to twenty thousand men. The strength of the Roman troops in North Africa at the time of the invasion may be calculated at about twenty-five thousand men, and it is unlikely that the number of Vandal warriors was lower than this. Hydatius also emphasizes that the Vandals went to Africa with their families and followers, making a total of fifty thousand men of all ages seem not too exaggerated. To this would be added perhaps twenty thousand to thirty thousand women, making a total of around seventy thousand to eighty thousand people in the Vandal tribal confederation at the time of the invasion of Africa. Perhaps two-thirds of the population were Vandals, and the rest Alans and other Germanic tribes. To this number should be added slaves. But this is no more than an educated guess.

Developments in their numbers

From their numbers at the time of the invasion of North Africa in 429, we can try to deduce their numbers at the time of the Roman invasion of 533. Victor appears to believe that the Vandals had become fewer by the time of his writing in 484, whereas Procopius, who writes three generations later, believes their number had increased. The explanations that Procopius offers appear to ring true to some extent. The three generations after Victor of Vita wrote were peaceful and would have meant an increase in the population. Victor, on the other hand, wrote after the long and exhausting wars with the Romans.

During the campaign to take North Africa, Geiseric must have lost many troops and noncombatants, particularly in the hardships of traveling across the desert and the siege of Hippo Regius. Furthermore, in 442, when Geiseric discovered the conspiracy of the nobles against him, many were killed, according to the chronicle of Prosper, but we might assume that they were mainly nobles and their followers. On the other hand, Procopius, who wrote in the middle of the sixth century, mentions that due to immigration and natural population growth, the Vandal population had increased greatly. Procopius mentions in another place that eighty thousand Vandal men were killed in the war. However, this number is wildly exaggerated and cannot be deduced from the battles he describes. It is more likely that around ten thousand to fifteen thousand were lost, counting dead and captured. To this number we must add losses in the wars against the Moors, as well as those who died of disease. Then we must take into account the increased number of Romans and Germanic elements, as well as natural growth, which must have been great because no major wars were undertaken after 474. The exact numbers cannot be determined, but at the time of the Roman invasion in 533, there were probably somewhat more Vandals than when they invaded North Africa, perhaps one hundred thousand, excluding slaves. However, with the sources as unclear as they are, any estimation of the Vandals' numbers can only be speculation.

As the Vandals were so much outnumbered by the North African Romans, they mainly settled in the Vandal Allotments and Carthage, just as the Ostrogoths chose to settle mainly in north Italy. In these areas they were not a majority but a large minority. Vandals have been found to have settled outside the Vandal Allotments and Carthage in only the cities of Thysdrus (el-Djem), Mactar (Mactaris), Thala, Theveste, Ammaedara, and Hippo Regius. It must be expected that Arian clergy and various officials also lived in the larger cities. This is supported by the statement of Victor of Vita that there were Vandal police and clergy in Tipasa in Mauretania. No evidence of Vandal settlements has been found on the occupied islands, although we know that there was a Vandal garrison in Sardinia, and possibly also small garrisons on the other islands.

THE VANDAL KING

The official title of the king was *Rex Vandalorum et Alanorum* (King of the Vandals and Alans). It was probably created in 418, when the Alans and Silings submitted to the Hasding Vandals, but it does not appear in the sources until the time of Huneric. Geiseric used the title of *rex*—king—certainly by 455. The succession was determined by the so-called testament of Geiseric. As Procopius writes, "Geiseric . . . died at an advanced age, having made a will in which he enjoined many things upon the Vandals and in particular that the royal power among them should always fall to the one who should be first in years among all the male offspring descended from Geiseric himself."

It was a strange succession law, and Geiseric's decision meant that the Vandal kingdom suffered from struggles in the royal family and made it vulnerable to other kingdoms entering the struggle. Of the six kings who ruled the Vandal kingdom in North Africa, three murdered parts of their family to reach or maintain their power. But evidently the ghost of the great Vandal king was still so close in the minds of the Vandals that the law could not be changed.

The succession law ensured that the king would always be from the royal family of the Hasdings. And their common Hasding lineage was indeed one of the strongest bonds binding the Vandal kings together. Geiseric became king because his father and brother had ruled before him. There does not appear to have been doubts among the Vandals that someone from the Hasding family should rule them. In fact, there were never any pretenders to the throne outside the family. Surprisingly, despite ruling for more than a century, the Hasdings, unlike most of the other ruling houses in the barbarian kingdoms in the fifth and sixth centuries, did not make any improbable claims to divine or ancient ancestry. Neither was a claim made to Rome or the ancestral regions north of the Danube. The poet Florentius describes Carthage as the mother city of the Hasdings. Thus the Vandals in many ways saw their history beginning with the occupation of Carthage, just as their calendar did.

We do not know exactly how a new king was made and what ceremonies were demanded. But we do know that there was a time between the death of one king and the creation of a new one, as evidenced by the story of Hilderic, who helped the Catholics during the time after Thrasamund's death but before being made king himself. It may be that the nobles had to be gathered for a formal salutation, but this is speculative. Before Geiseric, the king appears to have been elected by the nobles and possibly the army. We hear almost nothing of the wives of the kings and their actions, apart from Amalafrida, Eudocia, and the unnamed Visigothic princess. But the rebellion of Amalafrida shows that the queens could play an important political role, and they also advised the king when he requested it.

The king was responsible for the foreign policies of the realm. He sent embassies, made treaties, and decided to make war or peace. No doubt he was advised by many counselors, but in the end, the king decided. It appears that the Vandal king ruled as a dictator—he did not have to ask his nobles for permission to do anything—but as the fate of Hilderic shows, he had to act like a Germanic king was supposed to: be warlike and an able warrior. We see the same with the Ostrogothic kings, where the nobles even threatened to rebel at the thought that Athalaric, the boy king, was being brought up as a Roman, instead of being brought up as a Goth in the company of young nobles. Florentius writes that by the time of Thrasamund, annual oaths of loyalty were instituted, but probably only for officials at court.

We don't know much about the trappings of kingship. On coins, as signs of his sovereignty, the king wears a cuirass; a cloak that Procopius tells us was purple, like the one worn by the Roman emperors; and a diadem. His hair was probably worn long at least for the early period of the kingdom, in the traditional manner connected with the Germanic kingship and the royal family. In the time of Huneric, we still hear that the Vandals stuck to their traditional dress, and Roman officials at court were expected to wear the same. We might see a development in the dress of the Vandal kings, moving from the more traditional Germanic appearance of Geiseric to a greater imitation of the Roman emperor under Huneric and particularly Hilderic. On coins this was started by Huneric and continued under Gunthamund, who used the title *Dominus Noster Rex Gunthamundu*—Our Lord, King Gunthamund. The term *Dominus Noster* was copied from the title of the Roman emperor. Basically, many of the Germanic kings, who were unused to the concept of kingship, looked toward the Roman emperor to see what was expected of a king. In general we see a development in the Vandal kings of the concept of *imitatio imperii*—imitating the Roman emperor and his actions—in such areas as supporting the arts, constructing public buildings, and making laws. In his edicts, Huneric says he is doing what God commands, in the same way

Geiseric and the Roman emperors did. Huneric also followed Roman imperial practice when he renamed Hadrumentum Huniricopolis.

THE COURT

The king named the court and his advisers. The noblest of the Vandals were described as table companions of the king. We know of many titles of officials, but little of their tasks. The image is further clouded because our sources may not be using the correct titles. We also know that the king's court in North Africa was considered large.

The highest official was the *praepositus regni*, a kind of prime minister, who ruled according to the king's wishes. It appears that the *praepositus regni* was in charge of the legal system and its enforcement and in many ways had taken over the tasks of the *vicarius Africae*, the chief civil servant in North Africa. In several instances it was the *praepositus regni* who debated with the Catholic bishops during the persecutions. His importance can be seen from his title, *magnificentia*, which belongs to the class of the *illustres*, similar to the highest of Roman officials, but we know almost nothing of his specific duties. He had an office with Roman administrators in which Latin was spoken. Two *praepositus regni* from the time of Géiseric and Huneric are known, with the Germanic names Heldica and Obad.

In general, we have very little information about the Vandal court and rarely hear of it in the sources, unless its members are carrying out royal commands to persecute Catholics. We hear little about the *comites*—followers or companions of the king who at other Germanic courts were very important figures—apart from the fact that such a title existed. We learn, for example, that it was a *comes* who was sent to punish the Catholics of Tipasa for refusing to convert to Arianism. At another time we learn that *comites* were sent to try to convert a number of Catholics who were being exiled on account of their faith. We only have these two references to Vandal *comites*, and so the sources provide us with little knowledge apart from the obvious fact that the companions of the king were sometimes used to execute his orders. No doubt the court was full of young nobles and other men and women who sought to gain favor with the king, as in other Germanic kingdoms. These followers would be used to perform tasks to prove themselves.

One of the major fragments of a fifth or sixth century mosaic found at Bord Djedid in Carthage, depicting a scene from a hunt. The scene shows a Vandal or Alan using a lasso during a hunt. The mosaic is now in the British Museum. (*Author*)

We also know of another type of court official, the *domesticus*. We hear that in one case, *domestici* suggested that Huneric should follow a particular course of action. In another case we learn that bishops and *domestici* assembled to witness the renunciation of Catholicism by Sebastianus (the son-in-law of Count Bonifacius) after his flight to North Africa. From these two descriptions, we may assume that *domestici* were agents and advisers to the king, perhaps similar to the *domestici* of the Roman imperial courts.

The *Latin Anthology* (*Anthologia Latina*), a collection of poetry gathered in Carthage between 523 and 535 and passed on in several manuscripts, refers to a *referendarius* who supervised the construction of a church under Thrasamund, and a senator who held the rank of *primiscriniarius*, but we do not know what lay behind these titles. The royal notaries, *notarii*, wrote the royal edicts and made them public. Most of these were Romans, due to the need for the relevant higher education. At one point a *notarius regis*, royal notary, speaks on behalf of the Arian Patriarch Cyrila.

THE NOBILITY

As in other Germanic kingdoms, the nobles were an important part of Vandal court life and held a great deal of power, particularly in the early period of the kingdom. There existed what we might term an inherited nobility—the old noble families from before the foundation of the kingdom—and the *dienstadel* (as

German scholars term them), a nobility created by the king after the foundation of the kingdom in 439, which consisted of the chiliarchs and the Vandals holding higher positions in the administration. By creating a new class of nobles who owed their status directly to the favor of the king and not to their birth, Geiseric secured his hold over the administration and the army. The *dienstadel* had no possibility of developing an existence and power base outside the environs of the Vandal royal family. For the kingdom, it can only have been a benefit that its higher administrators were chosen for their merits, rather than their birth. Even former slaves, such as Godas, the governor of Sardinia, could attain high positions.

We may see in the uprising of 442 the attempt of the old nobles to suppress the rapidly growing power of the king and the *dienstadel* so as to maintain their position in society. With the decimation of the hereditary nobles in 442, they probably fell into the background, and the new nobility gained more power. If we assume that the thousandships were based on the lesser Vandal subtribes, most—if not all—of the chiliarchs would have belonged to the old nobility before 442. After 442, Geiseric would not have accepted that the central positions in the army were held by an inherited nobility, with its own power and an understanding of that power, so probably most of them were replaced. The nobles who later supported the usurpation of Gelimer were most likely the new nobility of the kingdom.

THE ARIAN CHURCH

A third group in Vandal society was the Arian Church, which may have been created by 435, or at the latest 439. It consisted of bishops, clergy, and administrators. The Arian Church was given the lands of the Catholic Church and so was one of the greatest landowners of the kingdom.

As mentioned earlier, the Hasding Vandals were probably converted to Arianism during their settlement in the region of modern Hungary by missionaries from the Goths of Ulfilas. The Siling Vandals and Alans were probably pagans by the time of the migration to Gaul and Spain and only became Christians after their association with the Hasdings—the Alans possibly not at all. Salvian distinctly describes the Vandals in Spain as heretical (Arian) Christians. We see in the battle of 421 or 422 against the

Romans how highly they regarded their Arian Bible, the Gothic Bible of Ulfilas, which they brought into battle as a form of holy standard. The Vandals are said in some much later sources to have tried to convert Catholics during their time in Gaul and Spain. However, this cannot be proven and is probably incorrect because other, more contemporary sources would have mentioned such a fact. Generally, it appears that the Vandals were not actively trying to spread Arianism before the founding of the kingdom of Africa.

Information about the Arian Church in North Africa is scanty because its writings were destroyed by the Catholics, apart from the so-called *Commentary on the Book of Job*, and just as little remains of the Donatist sources. Thus we see the final and full victory of the Catholic Church, which obliterated all writings it considered heretical. When the Vandals took North Africa, the Catholic bishops and priests were thrown out of their churches and the church property given over to the Arian Church. This appears mainly to have happened in Proconsularis and Carthage; it seems there were few Arian priests outside these regions. Later, under Huneric, all the churches in the realm were given over to the Arians. Widespread destruction of churches is noted, particularly by Victor of Vita, but little damage can be confirmed. The archives of the Catholic bishop of Carthage remained intact through the Vandal period, for example.

The king was the head of the Arian Church. His consent was needed for new bishops to be appointed, and he called for synods or his consent was needed for them. The Arian Church appears in structure to have been similar to the Catholic Church. The bishop in Carthage was named the patriarch and was the highest religious authority in the church after the king, just ahead of the metropolitans. The patriarch was supported by an administration, and notaries are mentioned in the sources. Under the bishops and subject to their punishment were the ordinary classes of lower clergy, such as presbyters and deacons. Monasticism did not exist within the Arian Church.

The Arian Church had a great deal of influence with the king in religious matters but does not appear to have had power in other fields. We know almost nothing of the Arian clergy, but they must have played a great role in local society. They appear in some cases to have systematically supported the persecutions of the Catholics, but we may question whether this was an organized resistance against the Catholics. There were probably many converts between the two forms of Christianity, and in some cases this may have led to local struggles to the death between them.

The Arian Church service was held in the Vandal language, and that was probably an important part of the Vandals' self-identification. Arianism and their language may have been two of the greatest unifiers and definers of the Vandals because they were two of the major differences between them and the subject population. Most of the clergy were of Germanic origin, even the ones with Roman names, such as the cleric Felix mentioned in the *Life of St. Fulgentius*.

Little is known of the lives of the North African sects, which included Donatists, Pelagians, and Manicheans, but they were probably persecuted like the Catholics. Huneric, at least, cruelly punished the Manicheans.

The end of the Arian Church

When Hilderic began to restore the Catholic Church, it was the beginning of the end of the Arian Church. But with its strength in the later years of the Vandal kingdom, the Arian Church still could have survived vibrantly for a long period. The true end of the Arian Church came with the end of the Vandal kingdom.

With the return of the Roman administration, the Catholic Church was also rebuilt. Arians, Donatists, and others were suppressed according to the harsh Roman laws on heretics. If we see Arianism as one of the great definers of being Vandal, as opposed to Roman, Justinian needed to crush Arianism in the lands of the fallen kingdom to avoid any resurgence of the Vandals. In 535, a council was held at Carthage, headed by the new bishop of Carthage, Reparatus, and aimed at putting the Catholic Church back on its feet. To do this, it was implied that the Arians had to be converted or suppressed. Emperor Justinian was honored as the savior of the church after its hundred-year imprisonment—that is, the Vandal occupation. Justinian knew what was expected. He closed the Arian churches—in North Africa as well as the rest of the empire—and confiscated their property, turning it over to the Catholic Church. From Procopius we know that Justinian treated the Arians harshly, which caused unrest in North Africa.

The emperor was probably not the driving force behind the persecution of the Arians but rather the Catholic Church, which needed to stamp out the Arians to regain its position after the war. In fact, Justinian's initial treatment of the Arians was quite humane and conciliatory. Some Arian clergy wanted to convert to Catholicism, and it appears that Arian clergy and bishops were allowed to keep their titles as long as they joined the Catholic Church. However, turning over the church property was delayed, possibly because the emperor did not want ill feelings in large parts of the population from a sudden takeover. The Catholic Church objected to this easy treatment and was particularly mistrustful of the Arian bishop converts, perhaps because it had seen in them their main enemies before the fall of the kingdom. Indeed, the treatment was so lenient that in 535, the Catholic Church complained and demanded a full and immediate restitution of all church properties confiscated by the Arians. The Catholic bishops also asked Pope John II for support against the imperial policy of allowing rebaptized Arian clerics to maintain their offices after their conversion. The pope naturally supported the plea. Justinian listened to the complaints and, in August 535, ordered the handing over of all Arian property to the Nicene church. Arians, even the rebaptized ones, were banned from public office and any imperial administrative post for fear that "heretics may seem to govern the Orthodox."

The persecutions led the Arian priests to strike back as best they could. As noted earlier, on March 23, 536, a rebellion broke out among the Roman troops in North Africa. One of the main causes of the rebellion was that many of the troops were of Germanic origin and therefore Arians. After Justinian proclaimed that no Arians would be baptized or allowed to baptize others, Arian priests approached a number of soldiers, including a group of one thousand Heruli. With Easter coming, the Arian soldiers knew that none of them would be able to participate in the celebrations without renouncing the faith of their forefathers, as Procopius writes. To renounce what had defined them and their forefathers for centuries left them only one option: rebellion.

The Catholic Church in North Africa would continue to show its independence. While Justinian was lauded as a savior after destroying the Vandal kingdom, the three-chapter controversy—a schism in the Catholic Church in the middle of the 540s—would cause the North African Catholic Church to turn against him, and such people as Bishop Victor of Tunnuna saw Justinian as a religious oppressor. It seems that the religious spirit of North Africa had not been suppressed by the Vandal rule.

THE COMMON VANDALS

The fourth and largest group of Vandals consisted of the common-ers. Our sources generally describe the actions of the great and the mighty, so we have little knowledge of the conditions of the common Vandals and must attempt to put together a picture of them through little pieces of information scrounged in other contexts. After the peace of 442, Geiseric created the Vandal Allotments for his warriors. In return for the grants of land, they had to fight in the army. They paid no tax and so had a financially comfortable and privileged life, and probably soon lived like most well-to-do Romans, enjoying the pleasures of North Africa. They did not farm themselves but most likely took over the existing Roman ten-ants on the lands. This meant that they must have had quite a lot of spare time, during which they were probably required to practice for war, both individually and as a unit. We do not know if they lived on their estates or if they were in garrisons around the coun-try when not on campaign. A number of Vandal garrisons, on the islands and in faraway places like Septem Fratres, had to be manned continually. Nor do we know if the warriors had any inde-pendent power, as the army had in some of the other Germanic tribes during the migration period, or if they had to follow their chiliarch in all matters. For that matter, we do not even know if they could influence who became chiliarchs.

THE ADMINISTRATION

Carthage was the capital of the kingdom. Here was the royal cas-tle, no doubt the former dwelling of the proconsul of Africa, the Praetorium, situated along with the royal administration on Byrsa Hill. The Roman provincial partition was kept, although the Vandal Allotments were kept separate from this. No doubt this was also the most practical solution, as they were governed in a dif-ferent fashion. It appears that to a large extent, the Roman admin-istration was also taken over and continued at some level during the Vandal kingdom. In essence, it appears that the Vandal king-dom contained two main groups—the Vandals and the Romans—administered by different laws and governed in different adminis-trative ways.

For the Vandal part of the population, the most important Vandal officials were the chiliarchs, who were in charge of groups of one thousand men—thousandships. The families of the men belonged to the same thousandship to which their husband or father belonged. The chiliarchs administered these groups in war and peace, in legal and fiscal matters. The thousandships were probably made around the time of the invasion of Africa and were based on the former subtribes in the Vandal confederation. The chiliarchs lived from the income of their extensive lands, and were paid through fees on law cases, various other transaction taxes, and possibly also from the royal treasure. Nothing is known of Vandal officials below the level of the chiliarchs.

Outside the Vandal Allotments, the Roman administration was kept more or less in place and was staffed by Romans, who continued to be able to reach high office. These administrators handled the Roman subject population and levied taxes.

LOCAL ADMINISTRATION

The proconsul of Carthage functioned the same under the Vandals, but with less power. We have the names of two proconsuls, Victorianus and Pacideius, which indicate that they were probably Romans. Outside Proconsularis, administrative authority was divided between the provincial, municipal, and episcopal aristocracies. At the provincial level were governors (*iudex provinciae*) with political and legal responsibilities, which appear to have been much reduced after the end of Roman rule. The provincial administration, the curias, and local government continued, as is shown by many inscriptions. However, the struggle of the curias appears also to have continued. This can be traced in the development of the forums in the cities, which lose much of their functions in the fifth century. Archaeologically, the finds show that instead of new public buildings, there was an increase in the construction of private buildings and churches.

We also learn of a curious continuation of ancient Roman offices. At the turn of the sixth century, important Roman families still held offices that had once been connected to the worship of the emperors. Flavius Geminius Catullinus, the proprietor mentioned in the so-called Tablettes Albertini, was *flamen perpetuus* (keeper of the perpetual flame, a priest of the cult of the emperor). Three such officials of the same family lived at Ammaedara in Proconsular Africa. Two, Astius Vindicianus and Astius Mustelus, were *flamines perpetui*, as was Catullinus. A third, Astius Dinamius, was *sacerdotalis provinciae Africae* (priest of the African provinces).

What is quite striking is that this latter office suggests that the provincial council was still meeting at Carthage in the last years of Vandal rule. Some scholars believe that after the Christian emperors of the fourth century had banned emperor worship, the provincial councils had preserved a secularized form of imperial worship and the titles were purely honorary. Others make the connection that because the Vandals were clients of the Roman Empire, and the Hasdings were members of the imperial house of Theodosius due to their marriage alliance, Roman provincials would still venerate statues of the emperors in the fifth and sixth centuries. It is possible, then, that the Vandal kings simply followed Roman tradition by allowing the provincial aristocrats to display their customary loyalty to the Roman state.

The islands were run by a governor, the *praeses*, who ruled in civilian and military matters and reported directly to the king. At least since 484, the islands were ruled as one province by the governor in Sardinia. The use of forests, quarries, and mines were under a number of procurators and appears to have continued as under Roman rule. Instead of the income going to the imperial fisc, it went to the treasure of the Vandal king. The Vandals also maintained the royal post until the Roman invasion in 533.

LAWS

Another dark area in our knowledge of the Vandals is their laws. However, more is known of the development of laws in the other Germanic kingdoms, so we can expand with more or less educated guesses. One of the only statements we have from the sources is from Procopius, who describes the origins of the Vandal tribes. He tells us that the Goths and Vandals shared the same traditional Germanic laws.

Before the Germanic tribes entered the Roman Empire, they had no written codes of law. What we know of early Germanic legal institutions comes mainly from information provided by the Germanic peoples after they settled in the Roman lands, particularly through the later codification of their laws. Their law until then was essentially customary law, meaning the traditions or customs of the people handed down by word of mouth from an almost mythical past. The customs were remembered by the older members of the tribe, who could "speak the law" when required. We know almost nothing of how early Germanic customary law worked in practice, but we can be almost certain that the law was not handed down by a king. Only after contact with the Roman Empire did the tribes form anything more than temporary confederations led by warlords. Later in the middle of the fifth century, the kings became political and judicial leaders, adding to their responsibilities as military and religious leaders.

Before this change in Germanic society, justice lay in the hands of families or kin groups, and it is speculated that there might have been popular courts, attended by the important members of society, and possibly by all freemen in the tribe. Since there existed no "state" to enforce the laws, there existed no territorial law. So for the Germanic tribes, law was personal, and a man was judged by the law of his ancestors, not by the law of wherever he was living at the moment.

By the time of the early sixth century, a number of Germanic kingdoms had been founded on the lands of the fallen Western Empire. As in the Vandal kingdom, the populations of these kingdoms were still by far mainly Roman, and the Germanic peoples constituted only a minority. Accordingly, the kings had to rule in two different fashions—as king of their own people and as magistrates to the Roman population in their kingdom. Paradoxically, the role as Roman magistrate had a much longer foundation in history than that of Germanic kingship, which was still a rather new phenomenon.

Most of the early Germanic kings attempted to codify the traditional customary law of their peoples into written form. This conformed to the expectations of the Roman population, who were used to written law, and was essentially necessary to make their new kingdoms function. Many of the magistrates were still Roman, but they could not administer traditional Germanic law because they had no knowledge of it, and especially if it was unwritten. Furthermore, the Roman emperors had for a long time been the primary source of new laws, so the kings, who naturally looked to the emperor as an example of how to rule, saw the making of written laws as a royal activity.

Legislation in the Germanic kingdoms

The various Germanic kingdoms developed in different ways, mainly according to what part of the empire they settled in. The tribes that settled in the more developed southern parts of the empire met a well-established legal culture, so their legislation shows considerable influence by Roman law and legal practices. The oldest surviving barbarian laws are those of the Visigoths, who settled in Southern Gaul around 418 and later created a kingdom that included Spain. Spain and southern Gaul were old and highly developed parts of the empire, and they presented the Visigothic kings with the task of administering the highly civilized Roman population and the much less civilized Visigoths, few of whom could read and write.

It appears that the Visigothic kings began their first attempts at creating legislation around 458, during the reign of Theodoric II. The *Edictum Theodorici* (Edict of Theodoric) dealt mainly with the resolution of cases that had arisen between Romans and Visigoths. Generally, it was derived from Roman legal sources. It was not a complete code but more a collection of cases, listed as they had arisen, and with little attempt to organize the laws by subject matter. The first true code that has survived from a Germanic kingdom consists of fragments of a code created by Visigothic King Euric II (466–485) around 481. This code was created for the use of Visigoths in their suits against each other and probably also for cases between Visigoths and Romans. Most of the code has been lost, but enough has survived to show a strong Roman influence. In 654, King Recceswinth issued a new Visigothic law that was unified and used for Romans and Visigoths.

The Visigothic legislation is the most Romanized code of early Germanic law and lacks the traditional Germanic legal concepts, such as collective family responsibility (symbolized by the threat of blood feud) and popular participation in the judicial or legislative process. Furthermore, the foundation of the code depends on a strong state, governed by a king who is the giver of the laws, and a judicial system operated by the state instead of the traditional private or family justice.

The Burgundians, who were settled in the Rhône Valley in southeastern Gaul, began their legislative activities around the same time as the Visigoths. They were also settled in a highly Romanized region, and, as with the Visigoths, this involved committing to writing the Burgundian customary law, modified to cope with the increased civilization of the tribes. So at the end of the fifth century, King Gundobad (474–516), and later his son and successor, Sigismund (516–523), issued codes for both the

Burgundian and Roman parts of the population. The Germanic code was issued between 483 and 532, and is known as the *Lex Gundobada*. The laws for the Roman population, the *Lex Romana Burgundionum*, were issued about 517. It is almost certain that Roman jurists were behind the codification.

In the early sixth century, the Franks, who were settled in northeastern Gaul, also created a code, but the details of it are more obscure. There is less Roman influence in the Frankish code, the so-called Salic Law, but it is still evident that it was made by Roman jurists. The Ostrogoths also created a kingdom on Roman land in the late fifth century, and while there is a strong possibility that they followed the legislative acitivity of the other Germanic nations, their laws have not survived the relatively short existence of their kingdom of Italy. Later the Lombards and Anglo-Saxons also created their own codes.

It is most likely that the case of the Vandal kingdom is similar to that of the Ostrogoths. While the Vandal kingdom lasted much longer, the legislative activity and codification probably only—if ever—began around the end of the fifth century or start of the sixth, and so existed only for a brief time, and left no traces. North Africa was highly Romanized, and there is no reason to believe that the development there was any different from the Visigoths in Spain and the Ostrogoths in Italy.

All of the early Germanic law codes are distinct from each other, but all were created under more or less the same circumstances and so had certain common characteristics. The laws changed from coming from the elders or the people to coming from the king. This is seen as reflecting the passing of responsibility for keeping the peace in the new society from the families to the state. All early Germanic laws are judged by a judicial system of royal appointees, although sometimes the system contained representatives of the community. All saw criminal offenses as injuries against a person or his family, and the judicial action to resolve the issue was essentially a suit for civil damages. All except possibly the Visigoths' code relied on the cooperation of the family in order to obtain justice, for the state, as such, merely provided an arbitration court. It was up to the injured party to get the accused before the court. When a case was settled in court, however, a family was not allowed to resort to blood feud to obtain justice.

We can assume that the Vandal kingdom probably issued its own laws, although none have survived. We can also assume that the laws were similar to those of the other Germanic tribes. The king could probably at any time overrule the Roman law. However, it appears that it was part of what we might call the contract between the people, the nobles, and the king that he did not break the Vandal laws. We see this in Huneric's forceful but failed attempt to put his son on the throne against Geiseric's succession law. He tried different stratagems, including attempting to kill those who stood between the throne and Hilderic. Clearly, it must be because he had no other option. At another point, Geiseric explained to a Roman ambassador that he could not force his people to give back prisoners of war. The sources also say that any plunder from war had to be divided by lot among the king and the army—he could not dispose of it as he wanted. Neither could he dispose of private Vandal property. In a poem honoring King Gunthamund, Dracontius mentions a celebrated legal case in which a defendant named Vincomalus secured acquittal from Geiseric. And according to Procopius, Gelimer's explanation for his usurpation was that Hilderic was acting against the "spirit of Geiseric." So the king did not always stand above the law.

Law of the Roman population

The Roman population followed ordinary Roman law, with the addition of various royal edicts. For example, Geiseric issued several laws punishing adultery and pederasty among the Roman population, and he closed the bordellos. The theater and circus were also suppressed to some extent, according to Salvian, as a measure against the voluptuous lifestyle of the Romans. The few surviving fragments of Vandal royal legal enactments from the kingdom of Africa are similar to imperial edicts.

Roman law was needed for, among other things, trade transactions. In 1928, Eugene Albertini discovered thirty-four documents on forty-five cedar wood panels (each about 8.3 by 5.8 inches) in a small pot at the foot of a wall in the Mrata hills some sixty-two miles south of Theveste in modern-day Algeria. These so-called Tablettes Albertini record the selling of objects according to Roman law and are dated May 11, 494.

If disagreements arose between Romans and Vandals, they were probably resolved according to Vandal law. Intermarrying between

Vandals and Romans was probably not allowed—at least we have no examples of it. Smaller cases were decided by the town magistrate (*ordines provinciarum*), and greater cases by the governor of the province in the name of the king. Most of the laws we know of are against the Catholics and the Romans in general. The will of the king is the legal basis for these laws.

The system of punishment was based on a mixture of Roman and Germanic traditions. The death penalty existed and could be carried out by hanging, beheading, burning, drowning, being drawn apart by horses, or being thrown to wild animals in the circus. Corporal punishment included beatings and whippings—both used for higher classes, clergy, and even Vandals. The hair could be pulled out or cut off, which was particularly hard punishment for the long-haired Vandals because of its degrading nature. Other punishments included blinding, cutting off nose, ears, hands, and feet, and cutting out the tongue. Torture was used if needed to make prisoners confess. Punishment could also be in the form of exile to the African desert, Corsica, Sardinia, or Sicily. Property could be confiscated, and people could be sentenced to manual labor in the fields. Incarceration without food and honor punishments, such as being ridden through the city on a donkey, were also practiced. We hear nothing of the traditional *wergeld* of the Germanic tribes, but fines of various types were commonly used. *Wergeld* was a monetary value placed on people and property. If a person was injured or killed, or the property stolen or damaged, the guilty party would have to pay *wergeld* as restitution to the victim's family or to the owner of the property. The concept of *wergeld* was an important part of early Frankish legislation.

It appears that the Vandals created a form of police force in some regions. We learn from an inscription found at Marcimeni in the Numidian borderlands (Ain Beida in modern-day Algeria) that a unit of *vigiles* (watchmen) was created under King Thrasamund. They appear to have been in charge of border security and the prisons. We also know of others engaged in law enforcement termed *servi, executores, custodies,* and *tortores* (slaves dealing with executions, executioners, prison guards, and torturers). We also find *iudices* (judges) and *notarii* (secretaries) in the same system. We hear also of *occulti nuntii*—a form of secret police.

ECONOMY

It appears that there was no difference between state property and royal property. In the oldest times of Vandal history, the income of the king was based on gifts, war booty, and the income from fines and fees in the law courts. Income rose greatly upon the creation of the kingdom, particularly through income tax, trade, income from the extensive royal lands, and tribute from the islands. The royal lands were mainly the former imperial lands but were enlarged by confiscations from the Roman nobility, the Catholic Church, and others. Bishop Victor of Tunnuna states that the unfortunate Bonifacius, who lost the Vandal royal treasure to Belisarius, acted as Gelimer's agent in the confiscation of property. Income was also accrued through such former state industries as coloring, weaving, and mining (such as at the ore mines in Sardinia). Most imperial farms and industries appear to have continued under the management of Roman subjects, but with the proceeds going to the Vandal king. The Vandals appear to have changed nothing about the industries.

State gifts could also be regarded as income. And fees for crimes or fines—for example, when a Catholic see had to be reoccupied—appear to have been so high that they would also have meant a significant income for the king.

The income of the kingdom went to the Vandal royal treasure. The royal treasure was the personal fortune of the king, and he decided how it would be spent. It consisted of minted gold, silver, and copper; jewelry; table service; golden chairs; and wagons, artful weapons, and similar valuable items. Much of the booty—probably mainly artistic objects and jewelry—from the sack of Rome in 455 was still in the royal treasure when the Vandal kingdom fell. For a Germanic people, the royal treasure was just as important as the state. If it was lost, the king could not perform his ritual functions of gift-giving or pay the allied troops and the other costs of the kingdom. This also explains why Gelimer so quickly sought to secure the royal treasure, and why it appears that he brought large parts of it with him on his campaigns.

TAXATION

The Vandals probably kept the Roman system of financial administration fairly intact, including leaving management of the royal lands to the Romans. The Vandal lands were not taxed, but the

Roman population was taxed on a regular basis. The details of Vandal taxation are unknown to us, but we hear from Procopius that the tax registers were destroyed by Geiseric. This, however, might only refer to the Vandal Allotments, or parts of the registers. We hear that Geiseric, Huneric, and Gunthamund taxed the Romans heavily. Under Gunthamund, there were complaints among the people about the oppressive taxes. After the Roman return, however, Procopius mentions that the provincials were shocked by the return to the tax levels of the Roman Empire. Procopius even states that many wished to have the Vandals back because the taxes were lower under them.

It is hard to say how oppressive taxes really were. Just as they do now, people complained about the tax levels, but they were not necessarily unreasonable. No doubt the tax level during the reign of the Vandal king was lower than under the Romans because the kingdom did not have the same costs. There is no reason to believe that more than about 30 percent of gross household income went to the king in taxes. Of course, the population probably did not notice the decline in infrastructure, security, and other public services that the tax paid for under the Romans. The local administrators and decurions (members of the town council) were in charge of collecting the tax in the region and were liable with their own fortune to deliver these to the king. We know nothing of the Vandal toll system, but it was probably no different from the Roman system that existed before the invasion.

The Vandals had taken over one of the richest provinces of the Roman Empire, but they were spared many of the costs of the Roman state. Because of the concept of the Vandal Allotments—giving lands for hereditary military service—they did not face the massive costs of the Roman Empire for military forces. It has been estimated that more than 50 percent of the taxes of the Western Empire in the fifth century went to pay for the army. The Byzantines would later use a system similar to the Vandals' to lower the costs of the army. The major costs for the king were mainly supplies for the army, paying the Moorish auxiliary troops, the royal administration, the *cursus publicus* (royal post), the fleet, gifts, and bribes for foreign officials. Fulgentius also refers to cash gifts to Vandal garrison troops, possibly for those stationed far from their own lands. It seems likely that units garrisoned in outlying towns were paid directly from the king, rather than from their own lands or the estates of their commanders.

TRADE

No doubt the Vandal invasion of North Africa decreased the prosperity of the provinces. They were devastated during the invasions, and the Moorish raids further decreased their prosperity and security, which was needed for trade. The provinces whose tax income we know lost seven-eighths of their revenue because of the Vandal invasion, and it took them years to recover. The Vandals' piratical expeditions probably also kept traders away from Carthage, although after the peace of 474, trade resumed to some extent, or at least we hear of Roman merchants. The trade from Vandal North Africa consisted mainly of grain, olive oil, wild animals for the circus games, pottery, horses, and marble. In recent years, analysis of African amphorae has revealed that around half of them were lined internally with pitch. Pitch would spoil olive oil but was commonly used for wine and fish-sauce amphorae, so it appears that the amount of exported olive oil should be reassessed and the importance of the export of wine and fish sauce was more significant to the trade of the kingdom than formerly believed. In return the Vandals bought gold, fine fabrics such as silk, and other luxury items.

Much of the question of the degree of trade turns on pottery evidence, in particular the diffusion of African red slip ware and African amphorae outside North Africa, which continued during the Vandal period. These vessels were Vandal in the sense that they were produced in the Vandal kingdom. It is clear from the wide distribution of the finds of fifth century North African red slip ware pottery in Italy and southern Gaul that trade continued between these regions at this time. The discovery of coins of North African origin in the coastal regions of Italy and in the Vandal islands corresponds to a large extent to the trade patterns that finds of African fine wares trace. Concentrations of Vandal coins have also been found in southeastern Spain, but less than expected along the southern Gallic coast.

Economic life in the countryside appears not to have been disturbed much by the Vandal overlords. We get a glimpse of late fifth century conditions through the Albertini tablets. They describe the economic activities of a group of tenant families and their land-

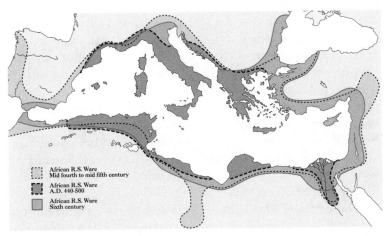

Distribution of African Red Slip Ware.

lords in the period. The majority of the documents record land sales, or, more precisely, the sale of the right to farm small blocks of marginal land on the edges of a large estate called the Fundus Tuletianos, owned by one Flavius Geminius Catullinus and managed on his behalf by three of his kinsmen or freedmen. These parcels of land were exchanged according to the *lex manciana*, a first century Roman law by which tenants could undertake to farm uncultivated marginal land. We can deduce from this that there were still attempts in the late fifth century to develop marginal lands in North Africa, despite the Vandal presence. The Bir Trouch *ostraka*—pot shards used for writing on—found in the Wadi Mitta at the eastern end of the Aures Mountains in Algeria also describe marginal land on the edge of the Vandal kingdom, and they are formally dated by the regnal year of King Gunthamund.

How did the economy of the kingdom develop?

A natural question regarding the Vandal economy is, how did it develop? It appears that there was a negative development, although it was more gradual than might be expected. As the sources indicate, trade declined during periods of war with the Roman Empire. That the Vandals did not radically disrupt existing trade is shown by the great amount of African amphorae and African red slip ware found in the Mediterranean region before, during, and after the Vandal kingdom. While a decline in North African exports appears in the fifth century, overall trade appears to have been quite strong. Several modern archaeologists say that the patterns of the region's economy generally are difficult to match with the political upheavals of the period. But it must be expected that particularly later in the Vandal period, after 455, when the kingdom no longer supplied grain, olive oil, fish sauce, or wine to Rome, the impact must have been massive, as no other similar markets could be found. The impact might have been lessened by increased trade with the Visigoths, Ostrogoths, and Franks, but this would be nowhere near the former level. There is also archaeological evidence which shows a massive increase in African red slip ware in the East in the fourth and early fifth centuries. But after the Vandal invasion, this decreases dramatically, as shown mainly by finds from Athens, and it only increases again after the Roman defeat of the Vandals.

The decreased export of African red slip ware in the middle of the fifth century was serious for the pottery trade, as other Roman pottery factories took over that share of the market. The proportion of African fine wares among the imports of Italy as a whole dropped to around 10 to 20 percent. To compare, in the second half of the fourth century, 90 percent of the ceramics in Rome came from the factories in North Africa. Only around the middle of the sixth century did African red slip ware increase its share of the market and begin to account for some 30 percent of the imported fine wares. The other Roman sources of pottery had the rest of the market. Although the most detailed studies of the red slip trade patterns are from Athens, the same appears to be seen elsewhere.

Coinage

There was no mint in North Africa when the Vandals invaded, so they had to create a new mint at Carthage to produce the coins of the kingdom. It appears that the supply of Roman coins already existing in the Vandal kingdom was so great that in the first decades after the invasion, they were the main—indeed, almost the only—currency. Fiscally, the gold solidus was by far the most important form of currency, and it remained so until the fall of the kingdom. It appears that the Vandals did not produce gold coins during their occupation of North Africa. But if they did, it is likely to have been closely imitative of contemporary or near-contemporary Roman designs. The reason for this lack of Vandal gold coins

A Vandal silver coin which imitates a Roman coin in the name of Honorius. Coins of this type may be connected to the sack of Rome in 455, when great amounts of bullion were captured by the Vandals. (*Courtesy, Coin Museum*)

was probably simply that there were enough Roman gold coins available, and more were steadily brought in by trade and raids.

The Vandal coins were never of great importance compared with the Roman. Patterns of local distribution of Vandal coins within North Africa show that Gunthamund's named issues did not circulate far from the capital, and Vandal copper coins are rarely found outside the main Vandal settlements in Proconsularis, northern Byzacena, and eastern Numidia.

But the curious Vandal monetary system is important to the development of the later Roman coinage. The Vandal coinage had a complex internal structure that was novel and experimental. It is believed that this might be the result of North Africa not having a regular mint since the early fourth century, and so there were no trained personel or traditions of maintaining a coinage system. So they had to start from scratch when creating the new system.

Their silver coins, or at least those struck with the name of the reigning king, commenced with Gunthamund in 487–488, and continued with Thrasamund, Hilderic, and Gelimer. There exists a type of silver coin, which imitates Roman coins, in the name of Emperor Honorius (395–423) and with a reverse design of the goddess Roma seated and the legend VRBS ROMA. It has not been possible to date the coins exactly, but most of them have been traced to a hoard deposited around 480. Scholars believe that they belong to the reign of Geiseric or Huneric, and may be connected to the occupation of Carthage in 439 or the sack of Rome in 455, when great amounts of bullion came into the hands of the Vandals. The Vandal silver coinage of Gunthamund consisted of coins bearing the marks DN (for denarii) and/or XXV as their reverse designs. They weighed 0.07 ounces, 0.035 ounces, or 0.018 ounces. Their values appear to have been 100, 50, and 25 denarii.

Alongside these silver coins there were issued two main series of copper coins, neither of which bore the name of the reigning king. One of these series consisted of four denominations and generally showed a standing female personification as its obverse design—possibly Africa or Carthage—and the marks NXLII, NXXI, NXII, and NIIII as its reverse designs (presumably, the "N" stood for *nummi*, or coins). The first denomination, the reverse mark of which denoted a coin of 42 (XLII) units, weighed about 0.39 ounces. The other three coins, of 21, 12, and 4 nummi, respectively, were of approximately proportional weight. The smallest denomination had what appears to be a royal bust holding a palm branch rather than a standing personification as its obverse design. The reason for the difference is that the former was probably more appropriate for striking a small coin.

The other series of copper coins consisted of three denominations and showed a standing male figure in military dress and the inscription KARTHAGO as its obverse design, and a horse's head (an ancient Punic motif) surmounting the mark of value (XLII, XXI, XII) as its reverse design. Their values were probably 42, 21, 12, and 4 nummi respectively. The reasoning behind the choice of such apparently inconvenient denominations as 42 and 21 nummi, and the relationship between the gold, silver, and copper coins, are both matters of some interest and significance.

The customary division of the gold solidus into 24 *siliquae*, the *siliqua* being at once a weight and an expression of value, meant that the subsidiary coinage—whether copper or silver—should, ideally at least, bear some exact and relatively simple relationship—whether multiple or fractional—to that division. Even ideally this cannot have been easy. For instance, were the *solidus* to be valued at 12,000 nummi, which it appears the Vandals followed, then the *siliqua* would have been worth one twenty-fourth of that, or 500 nummi. But one-sixth of 500 is 83 1/3, one-twelfth is 41 2/3, and one twenty-fourth is 20 5/6. It is with the last two figures that the reasoning behind the choice of denominations of 42 and 21 nummi becomes apparent: they represent 41 2/3 and 20 5/6 rounded up to the next whole number.

Given an original evaluation of the solidus at 12,000 nummi and therefore a *siliqua* of 500 nummi, the coin of 42 representing the nearest possible to one-twelfth of the latter, and its half of 21 nummi representing the nearest possible to one twenty-fourth, the question arises as to how the silver coinage, with its values expressed in terms of denarii, fit into this scheme. The price or equivalence of the silver pound in terms of gold during the later fourth, fifth, and sixth centuries seems—according to most documentary sources—to have fluctuated inflexibly between 4 and more commonly 5 solidi, giving a gold-to-silver ratio of 1:18 and 1:14.4 respectively. It appears that the Vandals followed a much older imperial standard of 1:12—the silver pound, in other words, equaled 6 solidi. Later, under Hilderic, a gold-silver ratio of 1:14.4, which was at that time prevalent in the empire, was introduced, possibly because of his closer connections to the Roman Empire. A monetary system consisting of only copper coinage of 42 and 21 nummi and silver coinage of 100 denarii (500 nummi), 50 denarii (250 nummi), and 25 denarii (125 nummi), would nevertheless have possessed one inherent and serious drawback: because the copper coinage involved the fractions of a division—the *siliqua*—rounded upward, and the silver coinage the division itself and its exact fractions, the former would not have multiplied out satisfactorily into the latter. This drawback appears to have been neutralized by providing additional and smaller copper denominations that singly and ideally formed exact fractions of the unit of 12,000 nummi, and in combination were also capable of forming fractions of its division rounded downward. A mean and hence exact relation between the copper and silver coinages might be obtained. It was this function that the copper pieces of 12 and 4 nummi were evidently intended to perform. This somewhat curious system established by Gunthamund was partly taken over by the Ostrogothic kingdom in 490–491 and was an important source of inspiration for the Roman monetary reform of 498. With the later changes made by Hilderic, the two systems moved even closer.

CULTURE IN THE KINGDOM

When the Vandals entered North Africa, they had probably not been affected much by their migrations through Europe. No doubt they gained many impressions and perhaps a taste for Roman luxury, particularly during their settlement in Spain, but they had not developed their own culture further than during their settlement north of the Danube. Their later settlement together as a group in Proconsularis, their Arianism, and their status as conquerors kept them away from the Roman population and gave them a natural distance. However, it appears that they soon warmed to the pleasures and luxuries of Roman civilization, as expected by Salvian in *On the Government of God.*

The wealth of the Roman nobles caused the Vandals to emulate the Roman way of life. Procopius describes the Vandals as living in luxurious villas, dressed in silk, and wearing gold jewelry. They visited the baths daily and enjoyed the pleasures of the theater, music, the circus, and hunting:

> For of all the nations which we know that of the Vandals is the most luxurious. . . . For the Vandals, since the time when they gained possession of Libya, used to indulge in baths, all of them, every day, and enjoyed a table abounding in all things, the sweetest and best that the earth and sea produce. And they wore gold very generally, and clothed themselves in the Medic garments, which now they call "seric," [silk] and passed their time, thus dressed, in theatres and hippodromes and in other pleasureable pursuits, and above all else in hunting. And they had dancers and mimes and all other things to hear and see which are of a musical nature or otherwise merit attention among men. And the most of them dwelt in parks, which were well supplied with water and trees; and they had great numbers of banquets, and all manner of sexual pleasures were in great vogue among them.

The view that the Vandals succumbed to luxury is probably just a cliché. Although they no longer lived on their horses and in their wagons, they simply took over the way of life of the Roman upper classes, which they had experienced on their long journey through the empire. It is perhaps not so surprising that the chastity that Salvian lauds them for was replaced with the vices of the Romans.

After the initial invasion, The Romans continued their pleasures as usual. There were still horse races in the Roman circuses during the Vandal kingdom. Carthage was still an imposing city under the Vandals. Close to the city, Missua (Sidi Daoud) housed the shipyards for the feared Vandal fleet. The great aqueduct from Mount Zaghouan to Carthage continued to function. Stagnum, a harbor possibly identical with the Bay of Utica, is recorded by Procopius as having had facilities sufficient for five hundred ships. Circling Carthage were many thriving suburbs, such as Tunis, which later became the capital of Tunisia. We do, however, hear from Victor of Vita that the Vandals destroyed the theater and the Odeon in Carthage. This is confirmed by archaeologists. In other parts of the city, the forum and several bath complexes were abandoned or turned to private housing during the Vandal period. We even find burials in former public buildings.

Vandal language

Vandalic was a dialect of Gothic, and it was difficult for a Roman to distinguish between them. The use of the Vandal language continued until the end of the kingdom. Possibly this was strengthened by the differences in religion. To be Arian meant to speak Germanic. Perhaps speaking Germanic was to show yourself to be a Vandal or supporting the Vandals. Little more can be said about the language since, apart from the most traditional proper names, we know of only a few words in Vandal, some of which might actually be Gothic. In an epigram from the *Latin Anthology*, a poet complains of the barbarous sound of the foreign language heard in North Africa, which disturbs his work: "Amongst the Gothic 'cheers' [*eils*] and 'eat and drink' [*scapia matzia ia drincan*], no one ventures to write decent poetry." The only other example is a two-word religious formula, the acclamation "Domine Miserere" (Lord have mercy), which in Vandal was "Froia arme." We know these words from an anti-Arian tract written sometime between 430 and 450 in Hippo Regius.

Geiseric could speak some measure of Latin at the end of his reign, and the kings following him were fully able to speak and write Latin. The entire administration also spoke Latin because of the nature of the administered population, the Roman laws, and the trade. No doubt the Vandal upper classes soon spoke Latin and possibly Greek. We also know that Romans and Vandals went to the same schools in Carthage. We may assume that life for the common Vandals would involve interaction with the Roman-speaking population to such an extent that they probably could speak some Latin as well. However, we have no texts of Vandal writers, and they had no national historian, like some of the other Germanic nations. There exists a bowl of silver, possibly given as a gift to the Ostrogothic court in Italy, inscribed *Geilamir Rex Vandalorum et Alanorum* (Gelimer—King of Vandals and Alans). It is an important point that the Vandal king had such an item inscribed in Latin rather than in his native Vandal language.

We know of no Vandal poets or other writers, but there is little reason to doubt that the Vandals celebrated the deeds of their heroes and myths in songs like the other Germanic tribes. The song that Procopius says Gelimer made to lament his ill fortune might be an invention, but it shows that it was not unusual for a Vandal to sing and play instruments.

Poetry

It appears that the Vandal kings and nobles soon became patrons of the arts, thus following a centuries-old Roman tradition. While Geiseric and Huneric do not appear to have been interested in the arts, a particularly active literary life existed at the courts of Thrasamund and Hilderic. Thrasamund is even recorded as having a reputation as a thoughtful man of letters. Procopius describes him as a sensitive ruler, and his fascination with theological issues led to the disputes with Bishop Fulgentius of Ruspe, which marked a turning point in the religious history of the kingdom.

Many of the writings of that period by such Romans as Luxorius, Flavius Felix, and Florentinus have survived. Their works are mainly laudations of the rulers, epigrams, and verses on mythological matters. They speak of the Vandal kings and nobles, their palaces, their fountains, their public works, their statues, their mosaics, and their characters in various ways. The medicinal herbal garden of Hoageis is even mentioned, and he received a consolatory poem in the common Roman style on the death of his little daughter. The Roman Dracontius also composed two poems on the occasion of weddings. Luxorius celebrates a lucky charioteer, and mocks a gambler and a dwarf pantomimist who plays Helen of Troy. The poetry is not of high quality, but it reflects the standard of the times well.

It has been popular to see the Roman poets of Vandal North Africa as a small group struggling to maintain the traditions of Latin literature. But reality may be somewhat different. While the poets were clearly inspired by the Roman past and wrote in the tradition of their predecessors, it can be argued that the North African poetry is representative of the same evolutionary phase as Latin poetry in other parts of the Roman world. Here Germanic and Roman cultures intermingled, and the Latin literary tradition found new life and changed modes of expression in late antiquity. The poets were a closely integrated part of society in late antiquity North Africa, and they simply expressed the kind of cultural adjustments found in other former Roman regions, as they assimilated and were assimilated by the Germanic tribes that had settled there. The poets also offer a look at Vandal North Africa and the relationship between them and their Vandal patrons, as well as a picture of the values and attitudes of the society.

The poems give no impression that the Roman way of life was deteriorating or that the Romans were oppressed or threatened by their Vandal masters. Of course, such laments would not find their way into the poetry during the Vandal reign, but it must be expected to have appeared after the Roman reconquest, if such had been the opinion of the poets. Even the polemic writings of Fulgentius of Ruspe, or the *Life of St. Fulgentius*, which attacks Thrasamund, acknowledge the king's philosophical and theological interests. Instead, the poems seem to reflect the life of the well-to-do Vandal upper class. The poets simply continued to play their traditional role in celebrating formal occasions by writing verses. In so doing, they worked within the traditional literary genres, but they adapted tradition to their own circumstances and the interests of their patrons and society around them. While there was probably a toning down of the pace of Roman cultural life of North Africa under the Vandals, it certainly continued and adapted to the changes in society.

The poet Blossius Aemilius Dracontius was one of the foremost in late Latin verse, and his work is the most substantial to have survived from the Vandal period. He is the poet of whom we know the most, mainly from his own works but also from annotations in the surviving manuscripts. Dracontius was *vir clarissimus* and legal advocate to Pacideius, proconsul of Carthage, and flourished during the reigns of Gunthamund and Thrasamund (some say also during the reign of Huneric). Gunthamund imprisoned Dracontius for lauding another man—probably the Roman emperor—as his master, instead of the Vandal royal house.

Dracontius wrote many pleading poems while in prison in an attempt to gain his freedom, including *Satisfactio ad Gunthamundum regem Guandalorum* (Amends to Gunthamund, king of Vandals). In it he praised the king's gentleness, asked for forgiveness, and promised to sing only of him as his rightful lord. His masterpiece, *De laudibus Dei*, was also written during his imprisonment. These poems, composed during the reigns of Gunthamund and Thrasamund (who released him), marked a high point of poetic verse in the North Africa of late antiquity. His verse encapsulates many of the great number of topics that fascinated people in late antiquity. Kings were not the only patrons of the arts. We find, for example, Luxorius writing poems for Vandal nobles such as Fridamal and Hoageis.

We know of many other poets of the Vandal kingdom, some through the *Latin Anthology*, including Avitus, Bonosus, Calbulus, Cato, Coronatus, Lindinus, Modestinus, Octavianus, Ponnanus, Regianus, Tuccianus, and Vicentius. The anthology preserves the work of ten or so poets of the Vandal kingdom, notably Luxorius and, if he belongs to this period, Reposianus. Cato, who is known from the time of Huneric, lauds the king's fountains. Luxorius, Flavius Felix, and Florentius praise Thrasamund for his education and good looks. We know Florentius was a Catholic, and to judge from his references to Carthage as a place of learning, he was probably associated with learned circles there. Flavius Felix was, like Dracontius, a *vir clarissimus*. Another poet, Martianus Capella, wrote the *Aegritudo Perdicae*. This little epic tells the unhappy story of Perdiccas, a young man who falls in love with his mother and wastes away as a consequence. All the poets of the Vandal kingdom may have been Catholic, and it is a good indication of how lenient the Vandal kings were in religious matters that this was accepted.

So while the standards and quality of poetry were declining, the number of poets and writers shows that there was still a vibrant cultural life in Vandal North Africa.

Grammar and rhetoric

Roman North Africa had for centuries been a place of learning, and cities such as Carthage, Cirta, Theveste, and even small towns, contained a number of schools. Because of this long tradition, North Africa was the home of celebrated grammarians, rhetoricians, legal advocates, and theologians.

There is no doubt that the Vandal invasion disturbed city life and the traditions of learning, but it did not permanently damage them. North African authors are even prominent among the grammarians of late antiquity whose works survive. The extant *Commentum Artis Donati* (Commentary on the works of Donatus) of the fifth-century grammarian Pompeius is believed to derive from transcripts of his oral teaching. In the late fifth or sixth century, Priscian moved from Caesarea in Mauretania to Constantinople, where he taught and presumably composed his *Institutiones Grammaticae* (Grammatical Institutions) and various other works. When the Romans returned, the schools still existed, and in 534, right after the reconquest, Emperor Justinian provided for the public appointment of two grammarians and two rhetoricians. Some of the poets of the *Latin Anthology* may also have been grammarians, as we know Corippus was.

The Vandals were soon attracted to the lifestyle of the Roman nobles and to the concept of classical education. At least initially, Geiseric did not speak Latin and had to use interpreters. However, later kings such as Thrasamund and Hilderic probably had a classical Roman education. The grammarian Felicianus claimed that under Gunthamund, the sciences, which had fled Africa, returned to Carthage. Dracontius mentions in one of his poems that his teacher Felicianus taught Romans and Vandals in the same classroom. We have already mentioned the break around the reign of Hilderic when the Germanic cultural elements in society were being thrust into the background. We may assume that it is an exaggeration when the grammarian Fabius Planciades Fulgentius (who wrote a number of books during the reign of Gunthamund), possibly reflecting on the imprisonment of Dracontius, states that the barbarians so hated any literary activities that they would torture anyone who could write their name on their own.

Late Roman Africa produced a great number of medical writers, and this tradition continued under the Vandals. The works of Caelius Aurelianus and later Cassius Felix, who both wrote under the Vandal kings, are examples of this. The work of Cassius Felix, *De Medicina* (On Medicine), which is still extant, was written in 447 as a working medical text on the diseases of the body and their cures. Cassius was probably born at Cirta, although his work was most likely composed at Carthage.

Vandal art and architecture

The Vandals did not develop a national art. The only objects we can identify as Vandal, or rather Germanic, are mainly small items such as fibulas in a style similar to Gothic items. We do not know if Roman artisans simply copied Vandal jewelry or if it was made by Vandals. We hear little of construction or architecture. Thrasamund is known to have reconstructed a place called Alianae, where he liked to reside. Here he also constructed baths by the name *Thermae Trasamundiacae* (Baths of Thrasamund), a royal palace, and an Arian church. The Basilica in Ammaedara was constructed between the fourteenth year of Thrasamund's reign and the fourth year of Hilderic's reign, and several other churches were built. According to verses, the nephew of Gelimer, Gibamund, constructed baths in Tunes outside Carthage. Other verses mention the construction of a royal castle at Grasse, the living place of the noble Fridamal, which was richly decorated with marble. The architects and builders were, of course, Roman.

THE ARMY

All Vandal males old enough to carry weapons were warriors, and individual prowess in battle was a central trait to their culture. The Vandal warrior was, like the Visigothic and Ostrogothic warrior, a *millenarius*—a member of a thousandship, to which he belonged in war and peace. In this way, Vandal society was based on military service, and all matters of life were integrated with your position in the thousandship. The chiliarch was master of his thousandship, whether leading his warriors in a battle or judging legal cases in peacetime.

Despite the military foundations of their society, the Vandals were not an aggressive people, notwithstanding their reputation. They attempted no major campaigns after 439, apart from trying to take Sicily in 490–491, and mainly fought against the Moors who threatened their kingdom. After losing Sicily to the Ostrogoths in 491, they made no attempt to retake the island. Their piratical raids were never meant to be more than plundering expeditions. Neither does it appear that they were the aggressive party in the migrations through Europe, but rather were forced into the migrations by stronger tribes or the forces of the Roman Empire. Their military history until the founding of the Vandal kingdom was of one long flight from more-powerful enemies.

While we are influenced by the pro-Roman and pro-Gothic sources, there is no reason to believe that the Vandals were militarily powerful before the amalgation of the Hasdings, Silings, and Alans in Spain in 418.

It is, on the other hand, surprising that Salvian, in *On the Government of God*, describes the Vandals after they took Spain as the most cowardly of Germanic nations. But this is most likely because his aim was to show that the decadent Romans were defeated by the lowest of the low, as there are no other examples of cowardice in the Vandals' history—quite the contrary. Procopius and Malchus did describe the Vandals as weak lovers of luxury, but compared to, for example, the Ostrogoths, who many times surrendered or deserted to the Romans, the Vandals fought bitterly for their country. Even after the fall of the kingdom, the remaining Vandals fought on under their new masters, Stotzas and later Gontharis. Most likely they were neither more nor less cowardly than all the other Germanic tribes.

However, they were not always respected adversaries, and their recorded victories came late in their history. They were defeated by the Langobards on the shores of the Baltic Sea and by King Geberich in Moravia, defeated by the Romans on the Danube and by the Franks on the Rhine—not a glorious record. In Spain, the Silings and Alans were reduced to a remnant by the Visigoths. They were defeated again at Corsica, Agrigentum, and in Campania by the Romans, although these defeats were probably fairly minor. They also lost against the Ostrogoths in Sicily in 490–491. The Moors defeated them at least twice, and later they were defeated at Ad Decimum and Tricamarum by the Romans. Against this line of defeats are the victories in Spain over the Romans and Sueves, the victories over Bonifacius, and the great victory over Basiliscus in 468. It appears that they could win battles only under Geiseric. But this may be because we have all our information on the Vandals from non-Vandal sources, as they must have won a number of battles over the Moors.

After the death of Geiseric, we see a clear strategy of nonaggression by the Vandals, probably a natural development due to the small size of their tribes compared to the huge population they had to control. They had simply conquered as much—or perhaps much more—than they could effectively control with their forces, and so were unable to attempt an aggressive foreign policy. The essential brittleness of the kingdom lay in their army, which could not sustain many defeats. That said, they still fought bitterly in several battles before surrendering to the Romans.

The Vandals are unusual among the barbarian nations of the west in that they developed a fleet. However, this initiative appears not to have affected the army; like the other Germanic kingdoms of the period, they never attempted to change or counter the weaknesses of their army, despite being hard pressed by the Moors. The Vandals fought as their forefathers fought in the time of Emperor Aurelian. Their army was based on their light cavalry, and despite their failures against the Moors in rough terrain, they did not develop their tactical flexibility. They never developed an infantry arm, and instead relied on the Moors to supply them with light infantry and, in general, much-needed manpower.

The army that confronted the invasion of Belisarius had never faced anything but Moorish tribesmen. No doubt the skills of the individual warrior were continually honed, but we would not expect Gelimer's dangerous, complicated plan of trying to destroy the army of Belisarius at Decimum in 533. It risked having the three parts of the Vandal army be defeated separately—which in fact happened. After the battle, Gelimer showed great skill in retreating, uniting his forces, and quickly moving against Carthage with what allied Moors he could find. At Carthage, he blocked the roads and cut the aqueduct, while trying to rally support among the population. He even tried to persuade the Huns in the Roman army to support him. By these measures, Gelimer forced Belisarius to leave the security of Carthage and engage him in open battle, which favored the Vandals. The energy, confidence, and military abilities shown were most surprising in an army and a general that had faced nothing apart from Moorish tribesmen in their lifetime. While the following battle of Tricamarum was a much simpler affair of two battle lines facing each other, the Vandals only broke after the third Roman charge and the death of Tzazon. Despite the result of the battles, the Vandals fought furiously, and the campaign of 533 could easily have ended in a Roman defeat.

The Vandals' nonaggressive approach probably also meant that they had never developed a logistical system, as all their campaigns took place inside the kingdom, where supplies were more easy to procure. On their raiding expeditions, they would probably bring food, fish, and eat what provisions they captured.

Officers

The king was the commander in chief of the army. The Roman subject population was not allowed to serve in the military, but the fleet crews may have consisted of Romans, and this might have been their right exclusively. The king could delegate the command of the army, as Hilderic did, but clearly this was not always wise, as martial ability was expected of the king. Hilderic may indeed have been the first king who did not lead the army in person. Gelimer and his warlike brothers—we learn that Ammatas was a great warrior—were the kinds of military leaders expected of the Hasding family.

The army was partitioned as the people were, in thousandship units, commanded by chiliarchs. Smaller subgroups are not known from the sources, but they must have existed. Larger groups consisting of several thousandships were commanded by generals who were appointed by the king and were mainly, or exclusively, from the royal family.

With regards to discipline, it appears to have been good, but the defeat at Ad Decimum may be put down to the lax assembly of Ammatas's troops or their lack of proper reconnaisance. We do not hear of Vandal deserters, and they fought bravely in their battles—even to the last man, as at the battle of Membresa in 536.

Fortifications

Despite their initial successes in North Africa, the Vandals never learned the art of siegecraft, and it appears that Roman garrisons could generally feel safe behind their walls. If the Vandals could not take the walls by storm—which, no matter the outcome, was very wasteful of troops—they had to starve out the garrison. We might also assume that the cavalry army of the Vandals meant that the troops were not experienced in an infantry role, as Procopius relates. Unfortunately for the Vandals, their supply system during the migrations mainly consisted of living off the land, whereas most of the Roman fortresses were well stocked with provisions. Accordingly, only treachery, lack of Roman supplies, or some stratagem would allow them to take a fortress or city quickly, unless they managed to surprise it by their swift movements.

The Vandals, like the Ostrogoths later, understood their own lack of ability in this field, so Geiseric ordered the walls of the cities in the kingdom razed. There is no doubt that the strategy of razing the city defenses was sound and well thought through. The

Vandals simply did not have enough troops to garrison all the cities and fortresses, and their main strength lay in their formidable light cavalry. Intact fortresses would only tempt Roman uprisings or the Moors. We may assume that most of the fortresses of the Roman border were also destroyed and abandoned. Nor do we know of any Vandal fortresses on the islands. Only Carthage, Hippo Regius, Septem, and Caesarea were still fortified and held a Vandal garrison. Sardinia also had a small Vandal garrison. From these places, the army could move either on expedition via the fleet or to an endangered part of the kingdom. Tripolitania also initially held a garrison, but it was later withdrawn, which may reflect a severe manpower shortage around the time of Gunthamund and Thrasamund that was not solved by later kings. There is no evidence of troops stationed in other places. However, one inscription describes a troop of *vigiles* created by King Thrasamund who were responsible for local security and the prisons. They might also have supported the army in some role, perhaps similar to the *limitanei* of the Roman Empire.

Tactics and weapons

In the words of Procopius:

> The Vandals were horsemen who fought with swords and lances, and they had little knowledge of the use of javelins and bows. Nor were they accustomed to dismounting and fighting as infantry. It was therefore best to fight them from a fortified city or camp to which it would be possible to retreat.

Unfortunately, the sources mention almost nothing else of their tactics. The Vandals had been mounted at least since the time of the wars with Emperor Aurelian in the late third century and were so until the end of the Vandal kingdom. No doubt the imperial stables of North Africa, with their excellent horses, were captured during the Vandal invasion and kept in use. A royal stable is mentioned by the anonymous Ravenna Geographer in the late seventh century. Apart from the mountainous regions, North Africa was perfect for cavalry operations. The ready supply of good horses supported the Vandal army until the end.

The Vandals were not accustomed to fighting on foot and even brought their horses on their overseas raids, as Sidonius

Sarmatian warrior with lance. Marble stele of Triphon found in Tanais, the Bosporan city at the mouth of the Don. The rider is dressed in the manner of the Alan tribes, some of which joined the Vandals during their migration across Europe. (*Hermitage Museum, St. Petersburg*)

Apollinaris writes. They used mainly lances and swords as offensive weapons, rarely bows or javelins. They were not used to using missile weapons, and fighting at a distance did not figure as a tactical option. The cavalry occasionally used the lasso as a weapon, as seen in the mosaic discovered at Bord Djedid in Carthage. They do not appear to have used shields and body armor at all. Their weapons were probably supplied by the Roman military workshops in North Africa. According to Sidonius Apollinaris, they used images of snakes made from colorful wool as standards. No doubt the Vandals' serious deficiencies—the limited use of cavalry in difficult terrain and especially the lack of armor—caused their downfall when they faced the Moors and Roman armies. The Vandals did build fortified camps, but these appear to have been more like stockades for keeping wild animals out or like enclosures for their horses, rather than being defensible works.

The Alan forces

Surprisingly, we know somewhat more of the Alans through the historians Arrian and Ammianus Marcellinus, which allows us to speculate about their tactical role in the Vandal army. Early sources mention that the Alans were like the Sarmatians and used heavy cavalry, with both the rider and horse protected by mail. Their main weapon was the lance, supplemented by a long cavalry sword, and the lancers operated in a compact mass. Thus it would appear that a Vandal force of light cavalry supplemented by Alan heavy cavalry would be nearly unstoppable. However, we have no sources speaking of heavy cavalry or tactics that might indicate the presence of heavy cavalry in the army of the Vandal kingdom. Arrian, in his *Contra Alanos* (Against the Alans) from the middle of the second century, explains that the Alans used feigned retreats to draw the enemy along. They would then turn around and attack the enemy, which was disorganized by the pursuit. This was a common tactic on the steppe that the Huns also used. They would retreat, wheel suddenly, and attack the enemy in the flank. But this is a tactic best used for light cavalry, and it supports the notion that the Alans mainly used light cavalry.

Ammianus Marcellinus tells us that the military customs of the Alans closely resembled those of the Huns, which he describes thus:

> They enter battle drawn up in wedge-shaped masses, while their medley of voices makes a savage noise. And they are lightly equipped for swift motion and unexpected action, they purposely divide suddenly into scattered bands and attack, rushing in disorder here and there, dealing terrific slaughter and because of their extraordinary rapidity of movement . . . they fight from a distance with missiles . . . they gallop over the intervening spaces and fight hand to hand with swords.

Most likely the same description could be used of the Vandal light cavalry. The Alans' fighting prowess as horsemen and their effective use of the lance and bow are generally treated as commonplace. But the sources speak of no horse archers in the Vandal campaigns, and this tactic may simply have gone out of use.

An unbalanced army

The inability of the Vandals to develop a more balanced army meant they were vulnerable to the more sophisticated and flexible form of warfare conducted by the Romans. We may wonder how the Vandals managed to conquer North Africa after 429, but at the time they were battle-hardened through the migration years, as well as being faced by only a few troops. The horse archers of the Romans in the invasion of 533 were superior to the Vandal way of fighting, and this explains their great victories, such as when Gibamund's detachment of two thousandships is destroyed by the Huns with no Roman losses. They could not catch the swift Huns, had no option of engaging at a distance, and their lack of armor on men and horses made them vulnerable to arrows. Against the many types of troops and varied tactical options available to the Roman commanders, the Vandals could only rely on the first shock of the charge and flanking maneuvers. In a similar way, the one-sided Vandal army could not get at the Moors when they retreated to less-favorable terrain. Thrasamund lost a battle against the Moors because the horses disliked the smell of camels, and without the ability to fight at a distance, the Vandals could not engage the Moors effectively.

The Moors in the Vandal army

Perhaps to offset some of their tactical deficiencies, allied Moors were a part of the Vandal army until the end of the kingdom. The Moors supplied a contingent of troops that we first hear of in 455 but that probably existed after 439, when the Moorish tribes submitted to the Vandals. It appears that on raids, the Moors were sent out to gather slaves and booty while the Vandals kept together as a unit and defended the fleet. In 458, Sidonius Apollinaris says, Geiseric no longer used Vandals for war but only Moors. While this must be incorrect, the Moors were needed because the Vandal warriors were not so numerous and forces had to be kept in North Africa. Moors may have been on the ships when the Roman fleet was attacked and burned in 468, as the use of javelins is described. Other advantages in using the Moors was that the Vandals could not absorb great losses, and the Moorish light infantry was an excellent remedy to the Vandal army's tactical deficiencies. The allied contingent probably also functioned as a group of hostages, guaranteeing the loyalty of the Moors.

THE VANDAL NAVY

The Vandal fleet was the second component of Vandal military power. The main tasks of the Vandal navy appear to have been pirating, moving troops, and maintaining naval superiority in the

Western and Central Mediterranean. We may also assume that it was responsible for preserving official communications with the islands. Unfortunately, we know very little of it. It appears that the first instance of the Vandals' using ships was during their time in Spain. Their raids on the Balearic Islands and Mauretania in 425 were certainly conducted in Roman ships, probably merchant and fishing ships, crewed and steered by Roman sailors—paid or forced. We do not know if the Vandals ever learned the skills of sailing from the Romans. A fleet of unknown size supported the Vandal invasion of North Africa, which might explain the quickness of the fall of the ports, which during other barbarian invasions almost always were capable of a succesful defense because they could be supplied and reinforced from the sea. Possidius tells us in the *Life of St. Augustine* that the Vandals used ships when blockading Hippo Regius. When the Vandals besieged Carthage for the first time, the Vandal fleet also helped the blockade. Already by 437, we hear of piratical expeditions of the Vandals, and from then on they were conducted every year of Geiseric's reign. Thus they became masters of the Western Mediterranean. The fleet appears to have been used less after Geiseric, and we hear of no raids but only a few tussles with Roman merchants. The fleet continued to be a powerful factor, however, and the Ostrogoths and Romans were reluctant to face it.

Composition of the fleet

The fleet appears to have consisted of small, fast warships and transports. When Tzazon sailed to Sardinia to suppress the rebellion of Godas, he brought five thousandships on 120 ships. That means each ship could carry around forty soldiers, plus supplies and sailors. But if horses were also taken, some ships would have had to carry more soldiers to make room for the horses. The Vandal warships were probably similar to the Roman dromons, which the shipyards of Carthage likely had experience building. The dromon was a light galley with two tiers of oars. Each tier had twenty-five benches, with two rowers on each bench. It was fast and capable of ramming. The ship was commanded by a captain and had two steersmen and a couple of officers. The Roman crew served as rowers, and there would also have been a contingent of Vandal marines armed with javelins, which they could use from the upper deck, and long pikes, which could be used either for combat or for pushing away boarding enemy ships. The small warships

Reconstruction drawing
of a dromon, probably
similar to the Vandal
warships.

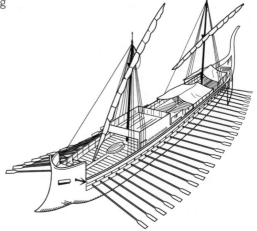

would have been well-suited for the quick hit-and-run raids that the Vandals practiced. A Vandal naval force would probably consist of a combination of dromons and transports.

Victor of Vita mentions that during the reign of Huneric, some of the Catholic bishops were exiled to Corsica to chop trees for the royal shipyards. The forests of North Africa were too sparse to supply enough wood for shipbuilding, so the main source of timber was probably the islands, particularly Corsica and Sardinia.

The crews

Roman seamen from North Africa were most likely the mainstay of the fleet, and the Vandals functioned as marines and perhaps officers. We can make a rough estimate of the number of sailors in Gelimer's fleet. With 120 ships and 55 seamen per ship (a standard crew for a Roman dromon), the fleet would have had 6,600 sailors—certainly a large number and perhaps one-fourth or one-third the size of the Vandal army at the time. Surprisingly, we hear almost nothing of the navy during the invasion of Belisarius, nor do we hear of the capture of the navy or any surrender of the seamen. We may therefore assume that because the sources would have mentioned such a great event as the surrender of a large force of Vandal marines, the crewmen must have been Roman.

Development of the fleet

The fleet during the time of Geiseric was probably greater than that during the invasion of Belisarius. When the expedition to

Rome was undertaken in 455, not all the fleet was used, and still there was room for a great part of the Vandal army and for the booty and thousands of slaves on the return journey. If Tzazon needed 120 ships for his Sardinian expedition, and if Geiseric brought some eight thousand to ten thousand Vandals to Rome and was able to carry booty and perhaps five thousand slaves back, we are looking at at least three hundred ships—truly a great force. In 456, Ricimer defeated part of the fleet consisting of sixty ships, and that appears to have been a small part of the total. We must not discount the possibility that civilian transports were hired according to the needs of the military, and so the standing force might have consisted of only 150 or 200 warships. When Gelimer sent 120 ships to Sardinia, this was probably the entire Vandal fleet, as no mention is made of the fleet when the Romans land. Furthermore, when Gelimer recalls Tzazon, he sends a merchant ship with the letter, possibly because no warship was available. So it appears the fleet became smaller in the time between Geiseric and Gelimer.

The Vandal fleet never won a sea battle, apart from the defeat of the great expedition of 468, where the battle was won mainly by fireships and not by open battle. However, large-scale sea battles were not commonplace, and the pirating actions of the Vandal navy were enough to make it feared on the Mediterranean waters. Indeed it might be said that the Vandal navy was what kept the kingdom safe for its existence. If no fleet had existed, the kingdom probably would have been destroyed by the Romans or Ostrogoths many years earlier. Remarkably, despite the great number of sources from the Vandal kingdom, almost nothing is mentioned about the importance of the fleet.

Roman Emperors in the Fifth and Sixth Centuries

Roman Empire

THEODOSIAN DYNASTY

Reign	Emperor	Notes
379–395	Theodosius I	Made co-emperor for the East by Gratian; died January 17, 395.
383–408 (*East*)	Arcadius	Made co-emperor with his father Theodosius I; sole emperor for the East from January 395.
393–423 (*West*)	Honorius	Made Augustus for the West by his father Theodosius I, January 23, 393; died August 15, 423.
407–411 (*West*)	*Constantine III*	Usurper; proclaimed emperor in Britain; defeated by Constantius III.
409–411 (*West*)	*Constans II*	Usurper; made emperor by his father Constantine III; killed in battle.
409; 414–415 (*West*)	*Priscus Attalus*	Usurper; twice proclaimed emperor by Visigoths under Alaric and twice deposed by Honorius.
409–411 (*West*)	*Maximus*	Usurper; proclaimed emperor in Spain; executed by Honorius.
411–413 (*West*)	*Jovinus*	Usurper; proclaimed emperor after Constantine III's death, executed by Honorius.
412–413 (*West*)	*Sebastianus*	Usurper; appointed co-emperor by Jovinus, executed by Honorius.
408–450 (*East*)	Theodosius II	Son of Arcadius.

421–421 (*West*)	Constantius III	Son-in-law of Theodosius I; made co-emperor by Honorius.
423–425 (*West*)	Joannes	Proclaimed Western emperor, later defeated and executed by Theodosius II in favor of Valentinian III.
425–455 (*West*)	Valentinian III	Son of Constantius III; made emperor by Theodosius II; assassinated. March 16, 455.
450–457 (*East*)	Marcian	Born in 396. A soldier and politician, he became emperor after being wed by Pulcheria, sister of Theodosius II, following the latter's death. Died of gangrene, January 457.

Western Roman Empire

Reign	*Emperor*	*Notes*
455–455	Petronius Maximus	Proclaimed himself emperor March 17, 455, after Valentinian III's death; murdered May 31, 455.
455–456	Avitus	Proclaimed emperor in Gaul July 9, 455; deposed by Ricimer, October 17, 456.
457–461	Majorian	Made emperor by Ricimer April 1, 457; deposed and executed by Ricimer, August 2, 461.
461–465	Libius Severus	Made emperor by Ricimer November 19, 461; died August 15, 465.
467–472	Anthemius	Made emperor by Ricimer, April 12, 467; deposed and executed by Ricimer, July 11, 472.
472–472	Olybrius	Made emperor by Ricimer, July 472; died November 2, 472.
473–474	Glycerius	Made emperor by Gundobad, March 3, 473;

		deposed by Julius Nepos, June 474.
474–480	Julius Nepos	Made emperor by Eastern emperor Leo I, June 474; deposed in Italy by Orestes in 475; continued to be recognized as lawful emperor in Gaul and Dalmatia until his murder in April 480.
475–476	Romulus Augustus	Son of Orestes; also known as Romulus Augustulus. Reigned October 31, 475 to September 4, 476; deposed by Odoacer; fate unknown.

East Roman Empire

HOUSE OF LEO (457–518)

Reign	Emperor	Notes
457–474	Leo the Thracian	A common soldier made emperor by Aspar, February 7, 457. Died of dysentery, January 18, 474.
474	Leo II	Grandson of Leo I. Succeeded upon the death of Leo I, January 18, 474. Died of an unknown disease, November 17; possibly poisoned.
474–491	Zeno	Son-in-law of Leo I. He succeeded upon the death of Leo II, November 17, 474. Deposed by Basiliscus, brother-in-law of Leo; fled to his native country and only regained the throne in August 476; died April 9, 491.
475–476	Basiliscus	General and brother-in-law of Leo I, he seized power from Zeno, January 9, 474, but was again deposed by him in August 476.

| 491–518 | Anastasius I | Son-in-law of Leo I, he was made emperor by Empress-dowager Ariadne, April 11, 491. Died July 9, 518. |

HOUSE OF JUSTINIAN (518–602)

Reign	Emperor	Notes
518–527	Justin I	Commander of the Imperial bodyguard under Anastasius I, he was elected by the army and people upon the death of Anastasius I, July 518. He died August 1, 527.
527–565	Justinian I	Nephew of Justin I. Succeeded upon Justin I's death. Died November 14, 565.
565–578	Justin II	Nephew of Justinian I, he seized the throne on the death of Justinian I with support of the army and senate. Became insane, hence in 573–574 under the regency of his wife Sophia, and in 574–578 under the regency of Tiberius II Constantine. Died October 5, 578.
578–582	Tiberius II Constantine	Commander of the Imperial Guard and adoptive son of Justin II. Succeeded on Justin II's death. Died August 14, 582.
582–602	Maurice	Married the daughter of Tiberius II and succeeded him upon his death. Named his son Theodosius as co-emperor in 600. Deposed by Phocas and executed on November 22, 602, at Chalcedon.

Chronology

2nd century BC: Hasding and Siling Vandals leave their homelands in Denmark and Norway

2nd century BC: Battles between Vandals, Langobards, and Goths in the region of North Germany

ca. 100 BC: Vandal tribes in Silesia

2nd century AD: Vandals in Eastern Hungary and Slovakia

271: Emperor Aurelian defeats the Hasding Vandals in Pannonia

278: Emperor Probus defeats a group of Siling Vandals at the Lech River

ca. 331–337: Battle between Goths and Vandals; Vandals are defeated and their king Visimar is killed

378: Battle of Adrianopolis, Goths are victorious and kill Emperor Valens

395: Division of the Roman Empire under Emperors Honorius and Arcadius

395–408: Ascendancy of Stilicho

397: Revolt of Gildo in North Africa

400: The Hasding Vandals leave their homelands north of the Danube and enter the Western Roman Empire; they are joined by the Siling Vandals, Sueves, and the Alans, as well as semibarbarian peasants from Pannonia

401: Stilicho stops the Vandals' plundering migration through the province of Raetia; they are settled as federates in the provinces of Vindelica and Noricum

401: Alaric the Visigoth invades Italy

402: Stilicho's victories over Alaric near Pollentia and Verona

405: Radagaisus the Goth invades Italy with a great army, and the Vandals begin to move toward the Rhine, possibly joined by more Siling Vandals

406: Battle with the Franks, in which Vandal King Godegisel falls; the Vandals are saved by the timely arrival of Alan forces

406–407: Vandals, Alans, and Sueves cross the frozen Upper Rhine

406–410: Roman garrison leaves Britain

408: Stilicho murdered and Alaric I invades Italy again

409: September 28 or October 13, Vandals, Alans, and Sueves enter Spain

410: Rome is sacked by the Visigoths under Alaric, who dies shortly after

411: Vandals, Alans, and Sueves make peace with Western Roman Empire and are settled in Spain as federates

411: Donatism is condemned at the Synod of Carthage

412: Visigoths settled in Gaul

416: Fredibal, probably the king of the Siling Vandals, is captured by the Visigoths during a raid

418: After the defeat of the Siling Vandals and the Alans by the Visigoths, the Alans and Silings merge with the Hasding Vandals

418: Visigothic kingdom of Tolosa is founded

419: Vandals defeat Suevian King Hermanric in battle

421 or 422: Vandals defeat Roman army in Baetica

425–455: Emperor Valentinian III reigns; his mother, Galla Placidia, rules in his stead until 437

425: Vandals raid Mauretania and the Balearic Islands by ship

427 Aetius becomes *magister militum* in Gaul

429: In May, Vandals cross over to North Africa after defeating Suevian King Hermigarius, who is killed in the flight

430: On August 28, St. Augustine dies during the Vandal siege of Hippo Regius

430–454: Ascendancy of Aetius in the West

435: Peace is made with the Western Roman Empire, and the Vandals are made federates

439: On October 19, Carthage is captured by the Vandals in a surprise attack

439: Arianism becomes the official religion of the Vandal kingdom; Catholics are persecuted

441: Roman attempt to retake North Africa fails because of the invasion of Attila the Hun

442: Peace with the Western Roman Empire; the kingdom of the Vandals in North Africa is now the first independent Germanic kingdom on Roman soil; Huneric given as hostage to the Western Roman Empire

447: Second invasion by Attila

451: Attila is defeated at the Battle of the Catalaunian Fields and retreats from Gaul

451: Council of Chalcedon

452: Attila invades northern Italy but retreats after devastating large areas

453: Attila the Hun dies

454: Battle of Nedao; Germanic tribes defeat remnants of the Hunnish tribes

454: On September 21, Aetius is murdered

455: On March 16, Valentinian III is murdered

455: Rome is sacked by Geiseric; the Vandal kingdom is at its greatest geographical limit

456–472: Ascendancy of Ricimer in the West

462: The imperial hostages Eudoxia and her youngest daughter, Placidia, are given back to the Eastern Roman Empire, on the strong and repeated request of East Roman Emperor Leo

468: Great East Roman expedition is defeated in naval battle off the coast of North Africa

470: Possible second Roman campaign against the Vandal kingdom

470: Peace with the Western Roman Empire

471: In April, Olybrius, the Vandal candidate, is made West Roman emperor by Ricimer, but dies in October or November 472

472: Peace with Eastern Roman Empire; Queen Eudocia leaves the Vandal kingdom to live in Jerusalem

474: New "eternal" peace treaty with the Eastern Roman Empire

476: Western Roman Empire falls; Odoacer becomes King of Italy; peace is made with the Vandals, and Sicily is given to Odoacer in return for an annual tribute

481–511: Clovis establishes the Frankish kingdom

482–484: Huneric persecutes Catholics severely

484–496: Gunthamund becomes king; Catholics are treated more leniently

489: Ostrogoths invade Italy

491: Ostrogoths take Sicily

493: The Ostrogothic kingdom of Italy is founded and lasts until 553

500: Thrasamund marries Amalafrida, sister of the Ostogothic king, Theodoric the Great

507: Battle of Vouillé between Visigoths and Franks; Visigoths are defeated and their king, Alaric II, is killed

525: Catholic synod is held in Carthage

526: On August 30, Theodoric the Great dies

528 or 529: Moorish defeat of Vandal army

530: On June 15, Gelimer deposes Hilderic

532: In spring, Romans make Treaty of Eternal Peace with Persians

533: Revolt of Pudentius in Tripolitania and Godas in Sardinia; Roman troops sent to support the revolts

533: In late August or early September, Belisarius lands in Africa

533: On September 13, at the Battle of Ad Decimum, Belisarius defeats Vandal King Gelimer

533: On September 15, Romans take Carthage

533: On December 15, at the Battle of Tricamarum, Belisarius defeats Gelimer; end of the Vandal kingdom

534: Eastern Roman Empire begins restoring North Africa; Catholic Church is restored

534: In spring, King Gelimer is captured and brought to Constantinople

535: In April, Ostrogothic Queen Amalasuntha is assassinated; the Gothic War begins

535: Moors raid Roman North Africa

535: On December 31, the Romans take Sicily

536: In summer or autumn, mutiny of Roman soldiers led by Stotzas, supported by remaining Vandals, begins in North Africa

536: In autumn, at the Battle of Membresa, Belisarius defeats Stotzas

536: On December 9, at the Battle of Gadiaufala, Stotzas defeats Roman loyalists, and the mutiny in North Africa is rekindled

536: In winter, Germanus, nephew of Justinian, lands in Africa and rallies loyalist Roman troops

536: In winter or early 537, at the Battle of Scalae Veteres, the loyalists are victorious; Stotzas flees to Mauretania

537–539: Moorish raids

543–544: Moorish raids

545: Stotzas returns; he is killed at the Battle of Sicca Venerea, and the mutiny ends; the Moors are subdued

546: New mutiny in North Africa; last Vandals defeated

551: Justinian invades Spain in support of Visigothic pretender Athanagild; Romans take southern Spain

552: Battles of Taginae and Mons Lactarius; Ostrogothic kingdom destroyed

555: Capitulation of the last Ostrogoths in Italy

565: On November 13 or 14, Justinian dies

647: Arabs invade Roman North Africa from Egypt

650: North Africa is Islamisized

ca. 670: Arabs make their capital in North Africa at Qayrawān

695: Carthage captured by Arabs, but retaken by Byzantines

698: Arabs capture Carthage and destroy the city

APPENDIX

Genealogy of the Vandal Kings

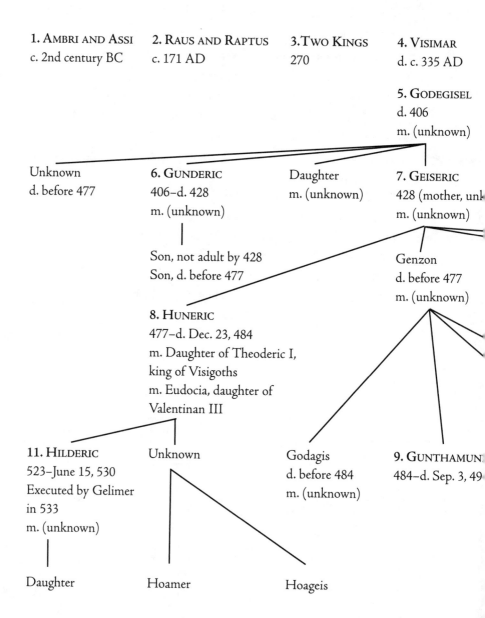

1. AMBRI AND ASSI
c. 2nd century BC

2. RAUS AND RAPTUS
c. 171 AD

3. TWO KINGS
270

4. VISIMAR
d. c. 335 AD

5. GODEGISEL
d. 406
m. (unknown)

Unknown
d. before 477

6. GUNDERIC
406–d. 428
m. (unknown)

Daughter
m. (unknown)

7. GEISERIC
428 (mother, unk
m. (unknown)

Son, not adult by 428
Son, d. before 477

Genzon
d. before 477
m. (unknown)

8. HUNERIC
477–d. Dec. 23, 484
m. Daughter of Theoderic I,
king of Visigoths
m. Eudocia, daughter of
Valentinan III

11. HILDERIC
523–June 15, 530
Executed by Gelimer
in 533
m. (unknown)

Unknown

Godagis
d. before 484
m. (unknown)

9. GUNTHAMUN
484–d. Sep. 3, 49

Daughter

Hoamer

Hoageis

on-Vandal concubine)–d. Jan.25, 477

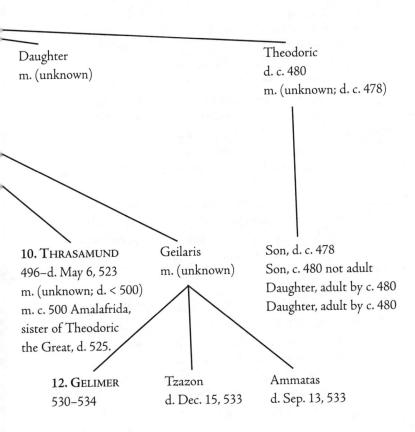

Daughter
m. (unknown)

Theodoric
d. c. 480
m. (unknown; d. c. 478)

10. Thrasamund
496–d. May 6, 523
m. (unknown; d. < 500)
m. c. 500 Amalafrida,
sister of Theodoric
the Great, d. 525.

Geilaris
m. (unknown)

Son, d. c. 478
Son, c. 480 not adult
Daughter, adult by c. 480
Daughter, adult by c. 480

12. Gelimer
530–534

Tzazon
d. Dec. 15, 533

Ammatas
d. Sep. 13, 533

The Sources

The most important modern study of the Vandal state is Christian Courtois's *Les Vandals et l'Afrique*, published in 1955. Courtois was influenced by Julien's *Histoire de L'Afrique du Nord*, a revised edition of which he edited, as well as the historical survey of Stephane Gsell, the regional studies of J. Carcopino, and E. F. Gauthier's analyses of Berber language and society. Courtois, who taught at the University of Algiers, was also influenced by the focus on French North Africa's geography rather than on the Vandal kingdom and the history of the Vandals. Essentially, Courtois made a regional history, combined with accounts of the Vandal prehistory by the earlier works of Gauthier and Ludwig Schmidt. Despite its age, Schmidt's work *Geschichte der Wandalen* (1901, reprinted in 1942), is one of the most important monographs on the Vandals, and he manages to treat all the facets of early Vandal history as well as the later history of the African kingdom. His use of the ancient sources is very good, although he has little modern literature to build upon. Schmidt's work was the main basis for much modern German work on the Vandals.

The thoroughness of Courtois's work appears to have kept later historians from challenging him. Accordingly, there has been little development in the study of the historical sources of the period, despite rapid development within archaeology of the region. Since 1955, only three monographs have appeared on the Vandals: Hans-Joachim Diesner's *Das Vandalenreich* (1968), which brought little new to light; Helmut Castritius's *Die Vandalen* (2007); and *The Vandals* (2010), by Andy Merrills and Richard Miles, the first attempt at a history of the Vandals in English. The last two may be symbolic of a trend over the last decade, which has seen a resurgence in studies of the Vandals and Vandal North Africa. A number of important articles have appeared in *Antiquities Africaines*—the French journal of Classical Africa—and in the proceedings of the Sardinian conferences on Roman Africa, published as *Africa Romana*. But only in the recent works by Castritius and Merrills and Miles do we see concentrated attention to the migration of the Vandals and the Vandal kingdom, also incorporating the archaeological sources. Hanno Helbling treats the Vandals and the historical tradition in his *Goten und Wandalen* (1954). The Alans, who joined the Vandals, are well-treated in Bernard Bachrach's *History of the Alans* (1973).

The great work done on reappraising the Moorish kingdoms appears not to have had much effect on the understanding of the Vandal kingdom. Because of its relatively short existence, scholars believe it was just an element in the decline of Roman North Africa. Where they differ is in whether they believe it speeded up the process. While the Romans imposed their culture on the peoples of North Africa, the contrary appears to be true of the Vandals, who, despite being the conquerors, adopted Roman culture rather than imposing their own on the conquered. Most often modern historians present the Vandals as a small elite minority, trying desperately to hold onto their cultural identity in the face of the enormous influence of Roman culture. This idea is supported by a number of historical sources, such as Procopius. Numerous articles have looked at how quickly the integration of Vandals and Romans took place and whether it happened freely. This image of integration is more detailed than that of the Vandals as the ultimate barbarians—rude, primitive, and destroying everything before them—but reality appears to have been much more complex. The past three decades of studies of the Moorish tribes and their identity have shown us that Roman culture did not crush everything before it, and so this image of the Vandals as being culturally conquered may not be true.

Vandal North Africa, despite being a Germanic kingdom of great importance, has often been left out of the general studies of Germanic Europe in the early medieval period. The ideological and political formation of Vandal kingship has, however, been closely studied in recent years, and that study has contributed to the understanding of kingship in the other Germanic kingdoms. The patterns of economic exchange and urban occupation in North Africa in the fifth and sixth centuries have also received much attention in recent years. Overall interest in the period and subject has increased greatly, and more and more work is being published. There is no doubt that understanding fifth and sixth century North Africa and the interaction between Vandals, Romans, and Moors is essential to understanding the period of late antiquity.

ANCIENT SOURCES

The Gothic and Frankish kingdoms have received great attention from scholars in modern times, whereas less has been done on the Vandal kingdom. That was often said to be due to the shortage of sources about fifth and sixth century North Africa. But the development of late antiquity archaeology in North Africa in the past three or four decades and the great number of surviving *ostraka* from the region with texts pertaining to everyday life have helped change the situation. Also, while the Vandals never received the attention of a national historian, a number of historical, hagiographic, and epistolary sources exist from fifth and sixth century North Africa. Particularly the *History of the Vandal Persecution*, by Victor of Vita, and recent studies of it have helped us understand the second half of the fifth century. Further studies on Procopius, Corippus, Victor of Tunnuna, and the *Laterculus regum Vandalorum* (List of Vandal kings) will no doubt shed more light on the Vandal kingdom.

A great number of religious texts or texts related to the administration of the Catholic Church have also survived. The *Notitia Provinciarum et Civitatum Africae* (List of the Provinces and Cities of Africa) gives a list of the bishops attending Huneric's Council of 484, and has been the basis of prosopographical and analytical studies of the fifth-century church. The conciliar decrees from the same period provide a view of the North African church in operation. The writings of Fulgentius of Ruspe, and Ferrandus's *Life of St. Fulgentius* also present information about the church and the Arian persecutions. An Arian text known as the *Commentary on the Book of Job* has recently been identified as a possible product of early sixth century North Africa. It shows the high intellectual development of the Arian Church and provides a counterweight to the great number of anti-Arian sources. Other religious sources, such as the *Passio Beatissimorum Martyrum* (Passion of the most Blessed Martyrs), the sermons of the exiled Bishop of Carthage, Quodvultdeus, and the extant theological writings of the Orthodox Cerialis are also of great interest.

The *Liber Genealogus* (Book of Genealogy), a world chronicle of the fifth century, discusses the persecutions of the Vandal period. The enormous work of St. Augustine and the religious works of fifth and sixth century North Africa easily compare with those of Germanic Europe in the same period. One of the major problems in the study of the period is that it is so dominated by religious sources that rarely provide an accurate reflection of the beliefs and interests of the wider population. An example of this is seen in fourth and early fifth century North Africa, where the works of the Catholics, particularly St. Augustine, create the impression that the inhabitants of North Africa cared little for anything but difficult religious arguments. The aim of the Catholic sources is, of course, to condemn the Arians and spread the Catholic faith. But while doing so, they also describe many valuable historical and cultural details, even though they are biased.

Important epistolary sources have also survived. Bishop Theodoret of Cyrrhus communicated with Carthaginian exiles during the early part of the Vandal period, and his letters show that North African affairs were important to the rest of the Mediterranean world. We also have Fulgentius, who, in his letters, sought to reassure the African Christians during his period of exile, and the letters of his biographer, Ferrandus, are of considerable interest. Other surviving fragments hint at widespread epistolary activity.

There are also important sources of the literary productions of the Vandal kingdom. In the late fifth century, we have Martianus Capella, who wrote his *De Nuptiis Philologiae et Mercurii* (The Marriage of Philology and Mercury). In the early sixth century, we have the *Commentum Artis Donati* by the grammarian Pompeius, who tried to provide linguistic instruction for his contemporaries. Both of these works were written for a society in which grammarians and the Roman cultural ideals were still important, and thus they attest to the thriving intellectual community in the Vandal kingdom.

That the literary community continued to thrive can be seen from the verses collected in the *Latin Anthology* around 530, and in the works of the poet Dracontius. These literary sources easily rival comparable collections from Europe. Even the purely literary pieces tell us much about the level of education, taste, and cultural affiliations in the Vandal kingdom. As writers, Dracontius and the other poets of the time were perhaps not up to the level of the Gallic poets Ausonius and Sidonius Apollinaris, but they tell us a great deal of the society that produced them.

Perhaps the most important written sources are the epigraphic ones. The volume of material declines in the fifth and sixth centuries, but it is the epigraphic studies, as much as the archaeology and textual sources, that have developed our understanding of the Moorish kingdoms. Epigraphy has also been important in understanding Christian life in the more rural areas of North Africa, and particularly of the survival of saints' cults, for which North Africa is so famous. The epigraphic sources have also been important for developing prosopographical studies of Vandal North Africa, and in reconstructing the continuation of the administration. With regards to the fifth century, it has been noted that North Africa is second only to Gaul in the volume of epigraphical sources.

Roman senator Cassiodorus's works are translated in several editions and provide detailed insight into the workings of Ostrogothic Italy at its zenith. It is useful because it reveals the foreign relations between the Ostrogoths and the Vandals, and because the two kingdoms to some extent faced the same challenges. Jordanes's *History of the Goths*, written in Latin in the middle of the sixth century, is fundamental to Gothic history but must be used with great care because of the author's preference for the Ostrogoths and his lack of ability as a historian. Gregory of Tours, who wrote the *History of the Franks* in the late sixth century, offers excellent insight into the workings of the Frankish kingdoms and mentions a little of the Vandals. Isidorus of Seville's *History of the Goths, Vandals, and Sueves*, written in the early seventh century, is also of some interest but does not provide much valuable information.

For the final campaigns against the Romans, our sources are much better. The military and diplomatic history of the reign of Justinian and his war against the Vandals up to 552 is told in great detail by Procopius in a generally accurate and well-informed account of contemporary history. The gaps in the history of Procopius regarding events in North Africa are filled by a Latin epic by Flavius Corippus, which describes in detail the exploits of John, the unfortunate *magister militum* in Africa from 546 to 548.

The *Notitia Dignitatum* is interesting for military matters despite the difficulties of determining the exact period described. The

Strategikon, written by Maurice in the late sixth century, is an invaluable source of information on the art of war of the period.

Imperial legislation is found in the *Codex Theodosianus* and *Codex Justinianus*, which are both greatly interesting if one remembers that there could be quite a difference between legislating and actual behavior in late antiquity.

ARCHAEOLOGICAL SOURCES

While the study of the historical sources is only now beginning to move since the work of Courtois in 1955, the image of North Africa in the fifth and sixth centuries has developed greatly within the sphere of archaeology. Late antiquity has gained more focus and is interpreted on a much higher level. Particularly the study of the famous African red slip ware found throughout the Mediterranean region, even up to the eighth century, has created more-accurate typologies. This has in turn given us a greater insight into the continued production before, during, and after the Vandal era.

The great UNESCO excavations at Carthage have given us a much clearer image of this great city, as well as of the changing patterns of urban life during late antiquity in the smaller cities and towns of North Africa. The excavations have shown us the destruction mentioned in the historical sources of the Odeon and the theater. Many Vandal burials inside buildings, and the disappearance of the forum as a focus for civic life in the other cities of the region, appear to show the destruction caused by the Vandals and the decline of civic life in the period. However, the Vandals also renovated or constructed public buildings in Carthage. The excavations in Carthage have also revealed what appears to be an important Vandal political focus at the old Roman administrative center on Byrsa Hill—probably the principal Vandal court, which was located in the old proconsular palace—and a large ecclesiastical complex with origins in the fifth century. The merchant harbor of Carthage was also renovated during the Vandal period. While Vandal foreign politics disrupted the grain and olive oil supplies for much of the period, trade was clearly still an important part of the wealth of the Vandal kingdom.

Archaeologists are also finding a number of material objects, such as bronze and silver coins. German scholar Gerd Koenig has made a typology of Vandal material culture that consists of a detailed summary of the objects as well as epitaphs and mosaics commemorating recognizably Germanic individuals. The image created by Koenig also confirms the concentration of Vandals in Africa Proconsularis, as stated by the historical sources. However, only eight graves in North Africa have been confidently identified as Germanic, which is a surprisingly small number. This is also a clear indication of the difficulty in identifying historical enthnicities through material cultures. Differences in dress or ornamentation might just as well reflect social rather than ethnic status.

The last three decades have seen an expansion in the surveying of rural areas, rather than the "prestige" excavations of the major Roman urban sites. These surveys provide a picture on a much grander scale of the development of rural areas from prehistory to the Arab invasion and beyond. Both the Kasserine Survey in Byzacena and the Segermes Survey in Africa Proconsularis suggest that the Vandal era was more a period of gradual change than of sudden decline of prosperity. Another group of sources are the *Albertini Tablets* and a number of *ostraka* and comparable tablets that have been found elsewhere in Vandal North Africa, also showing a continuation of Roman society rather than a break.

The Moorish kingdoms have been less examined archaeologically, possibly also because of the lack of historical records. Only a handful of sites, mainly of prestige value, such as the famous funeral monuments near Tiaret in western Algeria, have been excavated.

To summarize, the archaeological study of North Africa in late antiquity has developed greatly in the past half century. A more-detailed image of Vandal North Africa has been created through new surveying methods and the increasing attention on late antiquity in the regions outside Europe.

GENERAL LITERATURE ON THE PERIOD

A great place to get an overview of fifth and sixth century Europe is *The Later Roman Empire*, by A. H. M. Jones, which covers the period very well and looks into several aspects of ancient society such as trade, the church, education, culture, and the army. The main focus is, of course, on the Roman Empire, but it also gives a general perspective of the fifth century. For a general treatment of the period, see Averil Cameron, *The Mediterranean World in Late Antiquity AD 395–600*; R. Browning, *Justinian and Theodora*; and J.

Barker, *Justinian and the Later Roman Empire*. For the history of mainly Western Europe, see Roger Collins, *Early Medieval Europe 300–1000*. Peter Heathers's *The Fall of the Roman Empire: A New History of Rome and the Barbarians* is excellent for understanding the conditions of the Roman Empire in the fifth century and the Vandals' place in its downfall. My own *The Gothic War* gives an overview of the fall of the Vandal kingdom in the context of Justinian's war against the Ostrogoths, as seen through Roman eyes.

There are many books on the church and religious matters. Peter Brown's works, including especially *The Cult of the Saints*, are useful, as is a collection of articles in *Society and the Holy in Late Antiquity*. For settlement patterns, trade, and archaeological evidence in general, see K. Greene, *The Archaeology of the Roman Economy*, and M. Hendy, *Studies in the Byzantine Monetary Economy ca. AD 300–1450*, which contains a great deal of important material about the fiscal and economic working of the late Roman state and also gives an idea of the economy of the Vandal kingdom. Hendy also has an invaluable detailed analysis of the Vandal coinage system.

Roman Military Equipment: From the Punic Wars to the Fall of Rome, by M. C. Bishop and J. C. N. Coulston, is the best general treatment of the arms and armor of late antiquity. *Byzantium and Its Army 284–1081*, by W. Treadgold, is very good for its examination of the organization and size of the late Roman army and its explanation of the costs of maintaining the army in the days of Justinian.

Selected Bibliography

There are a great number of ancient sources and modern studies on the Vandals and Romans, and I have therefore only thought it relevant to select some of the most important ones. For a complete bibliography, I refer readers to www.oeaw.ac.at/gema/vandbibl/vb1.htm. The website is run by the University of Vienna's project on the Historical Ethnography of the Vandals.

SELECTED ANCIENT SOURCES

I have not cited editions of the standard classical works in the bibliography. Most are found in numerous translations in, for example, the Loeb and Penguin Classics series. All Christian authors are available in *Patrologia Latina* or *Patrologia Graeca* editions, although the form is sometimes outdated.

Agathias. *The Histories.*
Ambrose of Milan. *De fide ad Gratianum Augustum.*
Ammianus Marcellinus.
Anonymous Valesianus.
Anthologia Latina.
Augustine of Hippo, *Confessiones.*
———. *De civitate Dei.*
———. *Epistulae.*
———. *Retractationes.*
———. *Sermones.*
Aurelius Victor. *De Caesaribus.*
Cassiodorus. *Chronica.*
———. *Historia ecclesiastica tripartita.*
———. *Orationes.*
———. *Variae epistolae.*
Claudius Claudianus. *Carmina.*
Codex Justinianus.
Codex Theodosianus.
Cornelius Tacitus. *Germania.*
Cyprian of Carthage. *Epistulae.*

Dexippus. *Chronica.*

―――. *Scythica.*

Diadochus of Photike.

Dracontius. *Satisfactio.*

Ennodius. *Opera.*

―――. *Vita Epifani.*

Eunapius. *Historiarum Fragmenta.*

Evagrius. *Historia ecclesiastica.*

Expositius totius mundi et gentium.

Flavius Corippus. *Iohannis.*

Flavius Renatus Vegetius. *De Re Militaris.*

Fredegar. *Chronicon.*

Fulgentius Ferrandus. *Vita S. Fulgentii.*

Gennadius. *Liber de viris illustribus.*

Gregory of Rome. *Dialogi.*

Gregory of Tours. *Historia Francorum.*

Herodianus.

Hydatius. *Continuatio chronicorum.*

Isidore of Seville. *Historia Gothorum Wandalorum Sueborum.*

Jerome. *Chronicon.*

Joannes Lydus. *De Magistratibus.*

John Chrysostom. *Epistolae.*

John Malalas. *Chronographia.*

Jordanes. *Getica.*

―――. *Romana.*

Laterculus regum Vandalorum et Alanorum.

Lex Romana Visigothorum.

Libanius. *Opera.*

Luxorius.

Malchus. *Fragmenta.*

Marcellinus Comes. *Chronicon.*

Maurice. *Strategikon.*

Menander Protector. *Historia.*

Nestorius. *The book of Heraclides.*

Notitia Dignitatum.

Olympiodorus. *Fragmenta.*

Optatus.

Orientius. *Commonitorium.*
Orosius. *Historia adversus paganos.*
Paulus Diaconus. *Historia Langobardorum.*
Pliny the Elder. *Historia Naturalis.*
Priscus.
Procopius. *The Buildings.*
———. *History of the Wars.*
———. *The Secret History.*
Prosper Tiro. *Epitoma chronicon.*
Prudentius. *Liber peristephanon.*
Quodvultdeus. *Liber promissionum.*
———. *De tempore barbarico.*
Salvian. *De Gubernatione Dei.*
Scriptores Historiae Augustae.
Sextus Julius Frontinus. *Strategemata.*
Sidonius Apollinaris. *Carmina.*
———. *Epistulae.*
Sozomen. *Historia Ecclesiastica.*
Tacitus. *Germania.*
Tertullian. *Apologeticum.*
Victor of Tunnuna. *Chronica.*
Victor of Vita. *Historia persecutionis Africanae provinciae.*
Vigilius of Thapsus. *Contra Varimadum.*
Vita S. Daniella Stylitae.
Zacharias. *The Syriac Chronicle.*
Zosimus. *Historia Nova.*

Modern literature

Abun-Nasr, Jamil M. *A History of the Maghrib.* Cambridge, England: Cambridge University Press, 1971.
Albertini, Eugène. "Documents d' époque vandale découverts en Algérie." In *Comptes rendus de l'Académie des inscriptions et belles lettres* (1928): 301–303.
———. *L'Afrique Romaine.* Algiers, Algeria: Direction de l'Interieur et des Beaux-Arts (Service des Antiquites), 1955.
Alemany, Agustí. *Sources on the Alans: A Critical Compilation.* Leiden, Holland: Brill, 2000.

Alexander, Margaret A., and Mongi Ennaifer. *Corpus des Mosaiques de Tunisie.* Tunis: Institut national d'archéologie et d'arts, 1973–1996.

Amory, Patrick. *People and Identity in Ostrogothic Italy, 489–554.* Cambridge, England: Cambridge University Press, 1997.

Andrzejowski, Jacek. *Nadkole 2: A Cemetery of the Przeworsk Culture in Eastern Poland.* Monumenta Archaeologica Barbarica, vol. 5. Kraków, Poland: Secesja, 1998.

Anke, Bodo. *Studien zur reiternomadischen Kultur des 4. bis 5. Jahrhunderts.* Beiträge zur Ur- und Frühgeschichte Mitteleuropas 8. Weissbach, Germany: Beier & Beran, 1998.

Arce, Javier. *Bárbaros y romanos en Hispania 400–507 A.D.* Madrid: Marcial Pons, 2005.

———. "Dress Control in Late Antiquity: Codex Theodosianus 14.10.1–4." In *Kleidung und Repräsentation in Antike und Mittelalter,* edited by Ansgar Köb and Peter Riedel, Mittelalter Studien 7, 33–44. Munich: Wilhelm Fink, 2005.

———. "Los vándalos en Hispania (409–429)." In *Antiquité Tardive* 10 (2002): 75–85.

Arnheim, Michael T. W. *The Senatorial Aristocracy in the Later Roman Empire.* Oxford: Clarendon, 1972.

Arslan, Ermanno A. *Le Monete di Ostrogoti, Longobardi e Vandali.* Catalogo delle Civiche Raccolte Numismatiche di Milano. Milan: Ripartizione cultura e spettacolo Comune di Milano, 1978.

Bachrach, Bernard S. *A History of the Alans in the West: From Their First Appearance in the Sources of Classical Antiquity through the Middle Ages.* Minneapolis: University of Minnesota Press, 1973.

Bakay, Kornél. "Bestattung eines vornehmen Kriegers vom 5. Jahrhundert in Lengyeltóti (Komitat Somogy, Kreis Marcali)." In *Acta Archaeologica Academiae Scientarum Hungaricae* 30 (1978): 149–172.

Baldwin, Barry. "Peasant Revolt in Africa in the Late Roman Empire." In *Nottingham Mediaeval Studies* 6 (1961): 3–11.

Banniard, Michel. *Europa: Von der Spätantike bis zum frühen Mittelalter.* Munich/Leipzig: Paul List Verlag, 1993.

Baratte, François, and Noël Duval. *Catalogue des mosaïque romaines et paléochrétiennes du musée du Louvre.* Paris: Musée du Louvre, 1978.

Barker, Graeme, David Gilbertson, Barri Jones, and David J. Mattingly, eds. *Farming the Desert*. The UNESCO Libyan Valleys Archaeological Survey 1, 2. Paris: UNESCO Publishing, 1996.

Barker, John W. *Justinian and the Later Roman Empire*. Madison: University of Wisconsin Press, 1966.

Barnish, Sam J. B. "Taxation, Land and Barbarian Settlement in the Western Empire." In *Papers of the British School at Rome* 54 (1986): 170–195.

Barnwell, Paul S. *Emperor, Prefects, and Kings: The Roman West, 395–565*. London: Gerald Duckworth, 1998.

Belda, Francisco Morales. *La Marina Vándala: Los Asdingos en España*. Barcelona: Ariel, 1969.

Bell-Fialkoff, Andrew, ed. *The Role of Migration in the History of the Eurasian Steppe: Sedentary Civilization vs. "Barbarian" and Nomad*. London: St. Martin's, 2000.

Ben Abdallah, Zeïneb. *Catalogue des inscriptions latines païennes du Musée du Bardo*. Rome: Ecole francaise de Rome, 1986.

Ben Abed Ben Khader, Aïcha. "L'Afrique au Ve siècle à l'époque vandale: nouvelles données de l'archéologie." In *Carthage: L'histoire, sa trace, son écho: Catalogue de l'exposition à Paris*, 308–315. Paris: Ministère des affaires étrangères, 1995.

Ben Abed Ben Khader, Aïcha, and Noël Duval. "Carthage: La capitale du royaume vandale et les villes de Tunisie à l'époque vandale." In *Sedes regiae, ann. 400–800*, edited by Gisela Ripoll and Josep M. Gurt, 163–218. Barcelona: Reial Acadèmia de bones lletres, 2000.

Berndt, Guido M. "Architecture and the Vandal Elite in Africa." In *Hortus Artium Medievalium* 13, no. 2 (2007): 291–300.

———. "Die Heiratspolitik der hasdingischen Herrscher-Dynastie: Ein Beitrag zur Geschichte des nordafrikanischen Vandalenreiches." In *Mitteilungen des Vereins für Geschichte an der Universität Paderborn* (now named *Paderborner Historische Mitteilungen*) 15, no. 2 (2002): 145–154.

———. *Konflikt und Anpassung: Studien zu Migration und Ethnogenese der Vandalen*. Historische Studien 489. Husum, Germany: Matthiesen, 2007.

Berndt, Guido M., and Roland Steinacher. "Die Münzprägung im Vandalenzeitlichen Nordafrika: Ein Sonderweg?" In *Altertum und Mittelmeerraum: Die antike Welt diesseits und jenseits der Levante.*

Festschrift für Peter Haider zum 60. Geburtstag, edited by Robert Rollinger and Brigitte Truschnegg. Oriens et Occidens 12, 599–622. Stuttgart, Germany: F. Steiner, 2006.

———. "Minting in Vandal North Africa: Coins of the Vandal Period in the Coin Cabinet of Vienna's Kunsthistorisches Museum." In *Early Medieval Europe* 16, no. 3 (2008): 252–298.

———, eds. *Das Reich der Vandalen und seine (Vor-)Geschichten.* Österreichischen Akademie der Wissenschaften, Denkschriften der phil.-hist. Klasse 366, Forschungen zur Geschichte des Mittelalters 13. Vienna: Verlag der Osterreichischen Akademie der Wissenschaften, 2008.

Berthier, André. *L'Algérie et son passé.* Paris: A. et J. Picard, 1951.

Bertini, Ferrucio. *Autori latini in Africa sotto la dominazione Vandalica.* Genoa, Italy: Tilgher, 1974.

Bishop, Michael C., and Jon C. N. Coulston. *Roman Military Equipment from the Punic Wars to the Fall of Rome.* London: Batsford, 1993.

Blockley, Robert C. *East Roman Foreign Policy: Formation and Conduct from Diocletian to Anastasius.* ARCA Classical and Medieval Texts. Papers and Monographs 30. Leeds, England: Francis Cairns, 1992.

Böhme, Horst Wolfgang. "Archäologische Zeugnisse zur Geschichte der Markomannenkriege (166–180 n. Chr.)." In *Jahrbuch des Römisch-Germanischen Zentralmuseums Mainz* 22 (1975): 153–217.

———. *Germanische Grabfunde des 4. und 5. Jahrhunderts zwischen unterer Elbe und Loire. Studien zur Chronologie und Bevölkerungsgeschichte.* Münchner Beiträge zur Vor- und Frühgeschichte 19. Munich: Beck, 1974.

Bóna, István. *Das Hunnenreich.* Stuttgart, Germany: K. Theiss, 1991.

Bourgeois, Claude. "Les Vandales, le vandalisme et l'Afrique." In *Antiquités Africaines* 16 (1980): 213–228.

Bowlus, Charles R. "Ethnogenesis: The Tyranny of a Concept." In *On Barbarian Identity: Critical Approaches to Ethnicity in the Early Middle Ages*, edited by Andrew Gillett. Studies in the Early Middle Ages 4, 241–256. Turnhout, Belgium: Brepols, 2002.

Brand, C. E. *Roman Military Law.* Austin: University of Texas Press, 1968.

―――."Warum und wann Vandalen Silingen hießen." In *Studien zu Literatur, Sprache und Geschichte in Europa. Wolfgang Haubrichs zum 65. Geburtstag gewidmet*, edited by Albrecht Greule, Hans-Walter Herrmann, Klaus Ridder, and Andreas Schorr, 635–639. St. Ingbert, Germany: Rohrig, 2008.

Chapman, John, and Helena Hamerow. *Migrations and Invasions in Archaeological Explanation*. British Archaelogical Reports. International Series 664. Oxford: Archaeopress, 1997.

Charles-Picard, Gilbert. *La Carthage de Saint Augustin*. Paris: Fayard, 1965.

―――. *Nordafrika und die Römer*. Stuttgart: Kohlhammer, 1962.

Cherry, David. *Frontier and Society in Roman North Africa*. Oxford: Clarendon, 1998.

Chevallier, Raymond. *Roman Roads*. London: Batsford, 1976.

Claude, Dietrich, and Hermann Reichert. "Geiserich." *Reallexikon der Germanischen Altertumskunde*, vol. 10, 567–584. Berlin: Walter De Gruyter, 1998.

Cleland, D. John. "Salvian and the Vandals." In *Studia Patristica* 10 (1970): 270–274.

Clover, Frank M. "Carthage and the Vandals." In *Excavations at Carthage* 7 (1982): 1–22.

―――. "A Game of Bluff: The Fate of Sicily after AD 476." In *Historia* 48 (1999): 235–244.

―――. "Geiseric the Statesman: A Study in Vandal Foreign Policy." PhD diss. University of Michigan, 2006.

―――. *The Late Roman West and the Vandals*. Aldershot, England: Variorum, 1993.

―――. "Timekeeping and Dyarchy in Vandal Africa." In *Antiquité Tardive* 11 (2003): 45–63.

Collins, Roger. *Early Medieval Europe 300–1000*. London: Macmillan, 1991.

―――. *Early Medieval Spain: Unity in Diversity 400–1000*. London: Macmillan, 1983.

Conant, Jonathan P. *Staying Roman: Vandals, Moors, and Byzantines in Late Antique North Africa, 400–700*. PhD diss. University of Michigan, 2004.

Courtois, Christian. *Les Vandales et l'Afrique*. Paris: Arts et métiers graphiques, 1955.

―――. *Victor de Vita son oeuvre. Étude critique.* Algiers: Imprimerie officielle du Gouvernement Général de l'Algérie, 1954.

Csallány, Dezső. "Das Land der Wandalen im Karpatenbecken." In *Actes du VIIIe Congres International des Sciences Préhistoriques et Protohistoriques. Rapports et Corapports* 3, 295–298. Belgrade: L'Union, 1973.

Dahmann, Saïd. *Hippo Regius.* Sites et monuments d'Algérie. Algiers, Algeria: Ministère de l'information et de la culture, 1973.

Demandt, Alexander. *Die Spätantike: Römische Geschichte von Diokletian bis Justinian 284–565 n. Chr.* Handbuch der Altertumswissenschaft 3, no. 6. Munich: C. H. Beck, 2007.

―――. *Vandalismus. Gewalt gegen Kultur.* Berlin: Siedler, 1997.

de Souza, Philip. *Piracy in the Graeco-Roman World.* Cambridge, England: Cambridge University Press, 1999.

Diesner, Hans-Joachim. "Comes, domesticus, minister(ialis) im Vandalenreich." In *Forschungen und Fortschritte* 40 (1966): 174–176.

―――. *Das Vandalenreich Aufstieg und Untergang.* Stuttgart: Kohlhammer, 1966.

―――. "Die Lage der nordafrikanischen Bevölkerung im Zeitpunkt der Vandaleninvasion." In *Historia* 11, no. 1 (1962): 97–111.

―――. *Die Völkerwanderung.* Leipzig, Germany: Bertelsmann Lexikon-Verlag, 1976.

―――. *Der Untergang der römischen Herrschaft in Nordafrika.* Weimar, Germany: H. Bohlaus Nachfolger, 1964.

―――. "Gildos Herrschaft und die Niederlage bei Theveste." In *Klio* 40 (1962): 178–186.

―――. "Grenzen und Grenzverteidigung des Vandalenreiches." In *Studi in honore di Edoardo Volterra* 3 (1971): 481–490.

―――. "Mobilität und Differenzierung des Grundbesitzes im Nordafrikanischen Vandalenreich." In *Acta Antiqua Academiae Scientarum Hungaricae* 15 (1967): 347–358.

―――. "Vandalen." In *Paulys Realencyclopädie der Klass. Altertumswissenschaft,* supplement 10 (1965): 957–992.

―――. "Zum vandalischen Post- und Verkehrswesen." In *Philologus* 112 (1968): 282–287.

―――. "Zur Katholikenverfolgung Hunerichs." In *Theologische Literaturzeitung* 12 (1965): 893–895.

Diesner, Hans-Joachim, Hannelore Barth, and Hans-Dieter Zimmermann, eds. *Afrika und Rom in der Antike*. Wissenschaftliche Beiträge der Martin-Luther-Universität Halle-Wittenberg. Halle, Germany: Martin-Luther-Universitat Halle-Wittenberg, 1968.

Dossey, Leslie D. "Christians and Romans: Aspiration, Assimilation and Conflict in the North African Countryside." PhD diss. Harvard University, 1998.

Drew, Katherine F. *The Laws of the Salian Franks*. Philadelphia: University of Pennsylvania Press, 1991.

Dunbabin, Katherine M. D. *The Mosaics of Roman North Africa*. Studies in Iconography and Patronage. Oxford Monographs on Classical Archaeology. Oxford: Clarendon, 1978.

Edmondson, Jonathan Charles. "Mining in the Later Roman Empire and Beyond: Continuity or Disruption?" In *The Journal of Roman Studies* 79 (1989): 84–102.

Eger, Christoph. "Silbergeschirr und goldene Fibeln. Die vandalische Oberschicht im Spiegel der Schatz- und Grabfunde in Nordafrika." In *Antike Welt* 2 (2004): 71–76.

———. "Vandalische Grabfunde aus Karthago." In *Germania* 79 (2001): 347–390.

Eichler, Fritz. "Die beiden Gräberfunde von Osztrópataka." In Eduard Benninger, *Die germanischen Bodenfunde in der Slowakei*, 148–156. Leipzig, Germany: Kraus, 1937.

Elton, Hugh. *Frontiers of the Roman Empire*. London: Batsford, 1996.

———. *Warfare in Roman Europe, AD 350–425*. Oxford: Clarendon, 1996.

Evans, James A. *The Emperor Justinian and the Byzantine Empire*. Westport, CT: Greenwood, 2005.

Fasoli, Gina. "Le città siciliane tra Vandali, Goti e Bizantini." In *Felix Ravenna* 119/120, 4th series (1980): 95–111.

Ferrill, Arther. *The Fall of the Roman Empire: The Military Explanation*. London: Thames and Hudson, 1986.

Ferris, I. M. *Enemies of Rome: Barbarians Through Roman Eyes*. Stroud, England: Sutton, 2000.

Fiebiger, Otto, and Ludwig Schmidt. *Inschriftensammlung zur Geschichte der Ostgermanen*. Kaiserliche Akademie der Wissenschaften in Wien, Philosophisch-Historische Klasse, Denkschriften 60, no. 3. Vienna: A. Holder, 1917.

Fiebiger, Otto. *Inschriftensammlung zur Geschichte der Ostgermanen.* Akademie der Wissenschaften, Philosophisch-Historische Klasse, Denkschriften 70, no. 3. Abhandlung. Vienna: A. Holder, 1939.

Finley, Moses I. *The Ancient Economy.* London: University of California Press, 1999.

———. *Ancient Sicily.* London: Chatto & Windus, 1979.

Fouracre, Paul, ed. *The New Cambridge Medieval History* 1, c. 500–c. 700. Cambridge, England: Cambridge University Press, 2005.

Freising, Fritz. *Die Bernsteinstraße aus der Sicht der Straßentrassierung.* Archiv für die Geschichte des Straßenwesens 5. Bonn: Kirschbaum Verlag, 1977.

Frend, William H. C. *The Donatist Church. A Movement of Protest in Roman North Africa.* Oxford: Clarendon, 1952.

———. "A New Eyewitness of the Barbarian Impact on Spain, 409–419." In *Antiguedad y Christianismo* 7 (1990): 333–341.

———. *Orthodoxy, Paganism and Dissent in the Early Christian Centuries.* Ashgate, England: Variorum, 2002.

Fulford, Michael G. "Carthage: Overseas Trade and the Political Economy, c. AD 400–700." In *Reading Medieval Studies* 6 (1980): 68–80.

———. "The Long Distance Trade and Communications of Carthage, c. A.D. 400 to c. A.D. 650." In *Excavations at Carthage: The British Mission*, vol. 1, pt. 2, *The Avenue du Président Habib Bourguiba, Salammbo: The Pottery and Other Ceramic Objects from the Site*, edited by Michael G. Fulford and David P. S. Peacock (1984): 225–262.

———. "Pottery and the Economy of Carthage and Its Hinterland." In *Opus* 2 (1983): 5–14.

Gibbon, Edward. *The Decline and Fall of the Roman Empire.* London: Strahan & Cadell, 1777–1788. Reprint, London: Wordsworth Editions, 1999.

Giesecke, Heinz-Eberhard. *Die Ostgermanen und der Arianismus.* Leipzig: Teubner, 1939.

Gillett, Andrew, ed. *On Barbarian Identity: Critical Approaches to Ethnicity in the Early Middle Ages.* Studies in the Early Middle Ages 4. Turnhout, Belgium: Brepols, 2002.

Giunta, Francesco. *Genserico e la Sicilia.* Palermo, Italy: Manfredi, 1958.

Godlowski, Kazimierz. *The Chronology of the Late Roman and Early Migration Period in Central Europe.* Prace archeologiczne 11. Kraków, Poland: Nakadem Uniwersytetu Jagiellonskiego, 1970.

Goetz, Hans-Werner, and Karl-Wilhelm Welwei, eds. *Altes Germanien: Auszüge aus den antiken Quellen über die Germanen und ihre Beziehungen zum römischen Reich. Quellen der Alten Geschichte bis zum Jahre 238 n. Chr.* Ausgewählte Quellen zur deutschen Geschichte des Mittelalters 1a. Darmstadt, Germany: Wissenschaftliche Buchgesellschaft, 1995.

Goffart, Walter. *Barbarian Tides: The Migration Age and the Later Roman Empire.* Philadelphia: University of Pennsylvania Press, 2006.

———. *Barbarians and Romans, AD 418–584: The Techniques of Accommodation.* Princeton, NJ: Princeton University Press, 1980.

———. "Rome, Constantinople, and the Barbarians." In *The American Historical Review* 86, no. 1 (1981): 275–306.

———. *Rome's Fall and After.* London: Hambledon, 1989.

Gordon, Colin Douglas. *The Age of Attila: Fifth-Century Byzantium and the Barbarians.* Ann Arbor: University of Michigan Press, 1966.

Görres, Frank. "Kirche und Staat im Vandalenreich 429–534." In *Deutsche Zeitschrift für Geschichtswissenschaft* 10 (1889): 14–70.

Gourdin, Henri. *Genséric, soleil barbare.* Paris: Alif, 1999.

Greene, Kevin. *The Archaeology of the Roman Economy.* London: Batsford, 1986.

Grempler, Wilhelm. *Der Fund von Sackrau.* Brandenburg/Berlin: Spamer, 1887.

———. *Der II. und III. Fund von Sackrau.* Berlin: Spamer, 1888.

Hachmann, Rolf. "Die Goten und Skandinavien." In *Quellen und Forschungen zur Sprach- und Kulturgeschichte der germanischen Völker,* vol. 34 (158), 145–220. Berlin: Walter De Gruyter, 1970.

Hald, Kristian. "Angels and Vandals." In *Classica et Mediaevalia* 4 (1942): 62–78.

Halsall, Guy. *Warfare and Society in the Barbarian West 450–900.* Warfare and History. London: Routledge, 2003.

Hamann, Stefanie. "Vorgeschichte der Sueben in Spanien." PhD diss. University of Munich, 1971.

Hampel, József. *Der Goldfund von Nagy-Szent-Miklós.* Budapest, Hungary: F. Kilian, 1885.

Harhoiu, Radu. *Die frühe Völkerwanderungszeit in Rumänien.* Bucharest, Romania: Editura Enciclopedica, 1998.

Harries, Jill. *Sidonius Apollinaris and the Fall of Rome AD 407–485.* Oxford: Clarendon, 1994.

Hauck, Karl. "Carmina Antiqua. Abstammungsglaube und Stammesbewusstsein." In *Zeitschrift für Bayerische Landesgeschichte* 27 (1964): 1–33.

Hayes, John W. *Late Roman Pottery.* London: The British School at Rome, 1972.

Heather, Peter J. *The Fall of the Roman Empire: A New History of Rome and the Barbarians.* Oxford: Oxford University Press, 2006.

———. *The Goths.* Oxford: Blackwell, 1996.

Helbling, Hanno. *Goten und Wandalen. Wandlung der historischen Realität.* Zürich: Fretz & Wasmuth, 1954.

Hendy, Michael F. *Studies in the Byzantine Monetary Economy c. 300–1450.* Cambridge, England: Cambridge University Press, 1985.

Hodges, Richard, and William Bowden, eds. *The Sixth Century: Production, Distribution and Demand.* The Transformation of the Roman World 3. Leiden, Holland: Brill, 1998.

Hoffmann, Dietrich. *Das spätrömische Bewegungsheer und die Notitia Dignitatum.* Düsseldorf, Germany: Rheinland-Verlag, 1969/1970.

Horst, Fritz, and Friedrich Schlette, eds. *Frühe Völker in Mitteleuropa.* Berlin: Akademie-Verlag, 1988.

Howe, Tankred. *Vandalen, Barbaren und Arianer bei Victor von Vita.* Studien zur Alten Geschichte 7. Frankfurt am Main: Verlag Antike, 2007.

Hultén, Pontus, ed. *The True Story of the Vandals.* Museum Vandalorum Värnamo. Värnamo, Sweden: Museum Vandalorum, 2001.

Isaac, Benjamin. "The Meaning of the Terms *Limes* and *Limitanei.*" In *Journal of Roman Studies* 78 (1988): 125–147.

Isola, Antonino. *I Christiani dell'Africa Vandalica nei sermones del tempo 429–534.* Milan: Jaco, 1990.

Jacobsen, Torsten Cumberland. *The Gothic War.* Yardley, PA: Westholme, 2009.

James, Edward. *The Franks.* London: Blackwell, 1988.

Janßen, Tido. *Stilicho. Das weströmische Reich vom Tode des Theodosius bis zur Ermordung Stilichos (395–408)*. Marburg, Germany: Tectum Verlag, 2004.

Jaskanis, Jan. *Cecele: Ein Gräberfeld der Wielbark-Kultur in Ostpolen*. Monumenta Archaeologica Barbarica 2. Kraków, Poland: Drukarnia Secesja, 1996.

Jeffreys, Elizabeth, Brian Croke, and Roger Scott, eds. *Studies in John Malalas*. Sydney: Australian Association for Byzantine Studies, 1990.

Jones, Arnold Hugh Martin. *The Later Roman Empire 284–602: A Social, Economic and Administrative Survey*. Norman: University of Oklahoma Press, 1964. Reprint, Baltimore: Johns Hopkins University Press, 1992.

———. "Were the Ancient Heresies National or Social Movements in Disguise?" In *Journal of Theological Studies* 10 (1959): 280–298.

Julien, Charles-André. *Histoire de l'Afrique du Nord: Tunisie—Algérie—Maroc*. Paris: Payot, 1931.

Kaegi, Walter Emil. "Arianism and the Byzantine Army in Africa, 533–546." In *Traditio* 21 (1965): 23–53.

———. *Byzantine Military Unrest, 471–843: An Interpretation*. Amsterdam: Hakkert, 1981.

———. *Byzantium and the Decline of Rome*. Princeton, NJ: Princeton University Press, 1968, repr. 1970.

Kazanski, Michel. "Belgrad- Ostruznica: Siedlungs- und Grabfunde aus der Pannonia Sirmiensis." In *Germanen, Hunnen und Awaren. Schätze der Völkerwanderungszeit, Ausstellungskataloge des Germanischen Nationalmuseums*, edited by Gerhard Bott, 223–233. Nuremberg, Germany: Verlag Germanisches Nationalmuseum, 1987.

Kilian, Lothar. *Zum Ursprung der Germanen*. Bonn: Habelt, 1988.

Kislinger, Ewald. "Zwischen Vandalen, Goten und Byzantinern: Sizilien im 5. und frühen 6. Jahrhundert." In *Byzantina et Slavica Cracoviensia* 2 (1994): 31–51.

Kokowski, Andrzej, and Christian Leiber, eds. *Die Vandalen: Die Könige, die Eliten, die Krieger, die Handwerker*. Ausstellungskatalog Weserrenaissance-Schloß Bevern. Nordstemmen, Germany: Trigena Mediateam, 2003.

Kolnik, Titus. *Römische und germanische Kunst in der Slowakei.* Bratislava, Czechoslovakia: Tatran, 1984.

König, Gerd G. "Wandalische Grabfunde des 5. und 6. Jhs." In *Madrider Mitteilungen* 22 (1981): 299–360.

Kossinna, Gustaf. "Die Wandalen in Nordjütland." In *Mannus* 21 (1929): 233–255.

Kotula, Tadeusz. "Zur Frage des Zerfalls der römischen Ordnung in Nordafrika." In *Klio* 60 (1978): 511–515.

Kulikowski, Michael. *Late Roman Spain and its Cities.* Baltimore: Johns Hopkins University Press, 2004.

L'Afrique Vandale et Byzantine. Part 1. Antiquité Tardive 10. Turnhout, Belgium: Brepols, 2002.

L'Afrique Vandale et Byzantine. Part 2. Antiquité Tardive 11. Turnhout, Belgium: Brepols, 2003.

Lancel, Serge. *Saint Augustin.* Paris: Fayard, 1999.

Leone, Anna, and David Mattingly. "Vandal, Byzantine and Arab Rural Landscapes in North Africa." In *Landscapes of Change: Rural Evolution in Late Antiquity and the Early Middle Ages*, edited by Neil Christie, 135–162. Aldershot, England: Ashgate, 2004.

Lepelley, Claude. "The Survival and Fall of the Classical City in Late Roman Africa." In *The City in Late Antiquity*, edited by John Rich, 50–76. 2nd ed. London: Routledge, 1996.

Letizia, Pani Ermini. "La Sardegna e l'Africa nel periodo Vandalico." In *L'Africa Romana 2. Atti del 2. convegno di studio, Sassari 14–16 dicembre 1984*, edited by Attilio Mastino, 105–122. Sassari, Italy: Edizioni Gallizzi, 1984.

Lewitt, T. *Agricultural Production in the Roman Economy AD 200–400.* Oxford: Tempus Reparatum, 1991.

Lindner, R. "Nomadism, Huns and Horses." In *Past and Present* 92 (1981): 1–19.

Llewellyn, Peter A. B. *Rome in the Dark Ages.* New York: Praeger, 1970.

Lund, Allan A. *Die ersten Germanen: Ethnizität und Ethnogenese.* Heidelberg, Germany: C. Winter, 1988.

Lütkenhaus, Werner. *Constantius III: Studien zu seiner Tätigkeit und Stellung im Westreich 411–421.* Habelts Dissertationsdrucke: Reihe Alte Geschichte 44. Bonn: Habelt, 1998.

Mackensen, Michael. "Centres of African Red Slip Ware Production in Tunisia from the Late 5th to the 7th Century AD." In *La ceramica in Italia: 6.–7. secolo. Atti del convegno in onore di John W. Hayes. Roma 11–13 maggio 1995*, edited by Lucia Saguì, 23–39. Florence, Italy: All'Insegna del Giglio, 1998.

Macmullen, Ramsay. *Soldier and Civilian in the Later Roman Empire*. Cambridge, MA: Harvard University Press, 1963.

M?czy?ska, Magdalena. "Die Endphase der Przeworsk-Kultur." In *Ethnographisch-Archäologische Zeitschrift* 39 (1998): 65–99.

———. *Die Völkerwanderung: Geschichte einer ruhelosen Epoche im 4. und 5. Jahrhundert*. Zürich: Artemis & Winkler, 1993.

Maenchen-Helfen, Otto J. *The World of the Huns: Studies in Their History and Culture*. Berkeley: University of California Press, 1973.

Maloney, John, and Brian Hobley, eds. *Roman Urban Defences in the West*. London: Council for British Archaeology, 1983.

Manton, E. L. *Roman North Africa*. London: Seaby, 1988.

Marec, Erwan. *Hippone la Royale: Antique Hippo Regius*. Algiers, Algeria: Direction de l'interieur et des beaux-arts, Service des antiquités, 1954.

Martens, Jes. "The Vandals: Myths and Facts about a Germanic Tribe of the First Half of the 1st Millenium AD." In *Archaeological Approaches to Cultural Identity*, edited by Stephen Shennan, 57–65. London: Unwin Hyman, 1989.

———. "Wie wohnten die kaiserzeitlichen Fürsten und Völker? Einige Bemerkungen zur polnischen Wielbark-Archäologie aus einer skandinavischen Sicht betrachtet." In *Kultura Wielbarska w mlodszym okresie rzymskim (materialy z konferencji) 2*, edited by Jan Gurba and Andrzej Kokowski, 299–312. Lublin, Poland: Uniwersytet Marii Curie-Sklodowskiej, 1989.

Martindale, J. R. *The Prosopography of the Later Roman Empire*. Vol. 2, AD 395–527. Cambridge, England: Cambridge University Press, 1980.

Mattingly, David J. "Libyans and the 'Limes': Culture and Society in Roman Tripolitania." In *Antiquités Africaines* 23 (1987): 71–94.

———. "Oil for Export? A Comparison of Libyan, Spanish and Tunisian Olive Oil Production in the Roman Empire." In *Journal of Roman Archaeology* 1 (1988): 33–56.

———."Olive Oil Production in Roman Tripolitania: Town and Country in Roman Tripolitania." In *British Archaeological Reports. International Series* 274 (1985): 27–46.

———. *Tripolitania*. London: Batsford, 1995.

———. "War and Peace in Roman North Africa: Observations and Models of State-Tribe Interaction." In *War in the Tribal Zone: Expanding States and Indigenous Warfare*, edited by R. Brian Ferguson and Neil L. Whitehead, 31–60. Santa Fe, NM: School of American Research Press, 1992.

McCormick, Michael. *Origins of the European Economy: Communications and Commerce, AD 300–900*. Cambridge, England: Cambridge University Press, 2001.

Meier, Mischa. *Justinian: Herrschaft, Reich, und Religion*. Munich: Beck, 2004.

Menghin, Wilfried, Tobias Springer, and Egon Wamers, eds. *Germanen, Hunnen und Awaren: Schätze der Völkerwanderungszeit*. Nuremberg, Germany: Verlag Germanisches Nationalmuseum, 1987.

Merrills, Andy H., ed. *Vandals, Romans and Berbers: New Perspectives on Late Antique North Africa*. London: Ashgate, 2004.

Merrills, Andy H., and Richard Miles. *The Vandals*. Oxford: Wiley-Blackwell, 2010.

Modéran, Yves. *Les Maures et l'Afrique romaine. 4e.–7e. siècle*. Bibliothèque des Écoles françaises d'Athènes et de Rome, 314. Rome: Ecole francaise de Rome, 2003.

———. "L'établissement territorial des Vandales en Afrique." In *Antiquité Tardive* 10 (2002): 87–122.

Mommsen, Theodor. "Vandalische Beutestücke in Italien." In *Theodor Mommsen, Gesammelte Schriften* 4, 565–566. Berlin: Weidmann, 1965.

Moorhead, John. *Justinian*. London: Longman, 1994.

———. *Victor of Vita: History of the Vandal Persecution*. Translated Texts for Historians 10. Liverpool, England: Liverpool University Press, 1992.

Musset, Lucien. *The Germanic Invasions: The Making of Europe. AD 400–600*. University Park: Pennsylvania State University Press, 1975.

Neumann, Günter, and Helmut Castritius. "Lugier." In *Reallexikon der Germanischen Altertumskunde*, vol. 19, 30–35. Berlin: Walter De Gruyter, 2001.

Olędzki, Marek. "The Wielbark and Przeworsk Cultures at the Turn of the Early and Late Roman Periods: The Dynamics of Settlement and Cultural Changes in the Light of Chronology." In *Zentrum und Peripherie—Gesellschaftliche Phänomene in der Frühgeschichte*, edited by Herwig Friesinger and Alois Stuppner. *Mitteilungen der Prähistorischen Kommission* 57 (2004): 279–290.

———. "Zu den Trägern der Przeworsk-Kultur aufgrund schriftlicher und archäologischer Quellen." In *Ethnographisch-Archäologische Zeitschrift* 40 (1999): 43–57.

Onesti, Nicoletta Francovich. *I Vandali, Lingua e storia*. Rome: Carocci, 2002.

Pergola, Philippe. "Economia e religione nella Sardegna vandala: nuovi dati da scavi e studi recenti." In *L'Africa Romana 6. Atti del VI convegno di studio. Sassari 16–18 dicembre 1988*, edited by Attilio Mastino, 553–559. Sassari, Italy: Edizioni Gallizzi, 1989.

Pescheck, Christian. "Wandalen in der Wetterau zur Spätlatènezeit." In *Germania* 25 (1941): 162–170.

Petersen, Ernst. "Neue wandalische Grabfunde aus dem 2.–4. Jahrhundert n. Chr." In *Altschlesien* 4 (1934): 139–156.

Pieta, Karol. *Die Púchov-Kultur*. Nitra, Czechoslovakia: Archaologisches Institut der Slowakischen Akademie der Wissenschaften zu Nitra, 1982.

Pischel, Barbara. *Kulturgeschichte und Volkskunst der Wandalen*, vol. 1, *Wanderspuren und Kunststile der Wandalen*. Europäische Hochschulschriften 19. Volkskunde/Ethnologie A, vol. 17. Frankfurt am Main, Germany: Lang, 1980.

Pohl, Walter. *Die Völkerwanderung: Eroberung und Integration*. Stuttgart: Kohlhammer, 2002.

———, ed. *Kingdoms of the Empire: The Integration of Barbarians in Late Antiquity*. The Transformation of the Roman World 1. Leiden, Holland: Brill, 1998.

Pohl, Walter, and Helmut Reimitz, eds. *Strategies of Distinction: The Construction of Ethnic Communities, 300–800*. Leiden, Holland: Brill, 1998.

Pringle, Denys. *The Defence of Byzantine Africa from Justinian to the Arab Conquest: An account of the Military History and Archaeology of the African Provinces in the Sixth and Seventh Centuries.* 2 vols. British Archaeological Reports. International Series 99. Oxford: British Archaeological Records, 1981.

Prohászka, Péter. *Das vandalische Königsgrab von Osztrópataka (Ostrovany, Slovakia).* Edited by Èva Garam and Tivadar Vida. Monumenta Germanorum Archaeologica Hungariae 3. Budapest, Hungary: Magyar Nemzeti Múzeum, 2006.

Quast, Helmut W. *Geiserich: Vandale ohne Vandalismus.* Gernsbach, Germany: Katz, 1987.

Randers-Pehrson, Justine Davis. *Barbarians and Romans: The Birth Struggle of Europe, AD 400–700.* Norman: University of Oklahoma Press, 1983.

Raven, Susan. *Rome in Africa.* 3rd ed. London: Routledge, 1993.

Réau, Louis. *Histoire du Vandalisme: Les monuments détruits de l'art francaise.* Paris: R. Laffont, 1994.

Riché, P. *Education and Culture in the Barbarian West.* Columbia: University of South Carolina Press, 1976.

Rickman, Geoffrey. *The Corn Supply of Ancient Rome.* Oxford: Oxford University Press, 1980.

Rosen, Klaus. *Die Völkerwanderung.* Munich: C. H. Beck, 2002.

Rosenblum, M. *Luxorius: A Latin Poet among the Vandals.* New York: Beagle, 1961.

Ruprechtsberger, E. M. "Byzantinische Befestigungen in Algerien und Tunesien." In *Antike Welt* 20 (1989): 3–21.

Schmidt, Ludwig. *Geschichte der Wandalen.* 2nd ed. Munich: C. H. Beck, 1942.

Schreiber, Hermann. *Die Vandalen: Siegeszug und Untergang eines Germanischen Volkes.* Bern/Munich: Moewig, 1979.

Schwarz, Ernst. "Der Quaden- und Wandalenzug nach Spanien." *Sudeta* 3 (1927): 1–12.

Shaw, Brent D. *Rulers, Nomads, and Christians in Roman North Africa.* Aldershot, England: Variorum, 1995.

Shea, George W. "Justinian's North African Strategy in the Johannis of Corippus." In *Byzantine Studies* 10 (1983): 29–38.

Southern, Pat, and Karen Ramsey Dixon. *The Late Roman Army.* London: Batsford, 1996.

Spielvogel, Jörg. "Arianische Vandalen, katholische Römer: die reichspolitische und kulturelle Dimension des christlichen Glaubenskonfliktes im spätantiken Nordafrika." In *Klio* 87 (2005): 201–222.

Wolfram, Herwig. *Die Germanen.* Munich: Beck, 2000.

———. *Die Goten: Von den Anfängen bis zur Mitte des sechsten Jahrhunderts. Entwurf einer historischen Ethnographie.* Munich: Beck, 2001.

———. *Gotische Studien: Volk und Herrschaft im frühen Mittelalter.* Munich: Beck, 2005.

———. *History of the Goths.* Berkeley: University of California Press, 1988.

Wolfram, Herwig, and Falko Daim, eds. *Die Völker an der mittleren und unteren Donau im fünften und sechsten Jahrhundert.* Österreichische Akademie der Wissenschaften, phil.-hist. Kl. Denkschriften 145, Veröffentlichungen der Kommission für Frühmittelalterforschung 4. Vienna: Verlag der Österreichischen Akademie der Wissenschaften, 1980.

Wroth, Warwick. *Catalogue of the Coins of the Vandals, Ostrogoths and Lombards and of the Empires of Thessalonica, Nicaea and Trebizond in the British Museum.* London: British Museum, 1911. Chicago: Argonaut, 1966.

Index